THE SHIN

Philip Gardiner has spent the last sixteen years reading and researching the history of man, science, religion and philosophy. He believes that much of orthodox history is based upon propaganda in one form or another, and his search for the truth has led him to uncover historical evidence previously unseen for what it is. He is the author of *Proof: Does God Exist? Is there any evidence for the existence of God?* And co-author of *The Serpent Grail*

Gary Osborn has been a writer on mysticism and esoteric traditions for over ten years. He describes himself as an 'initiate into the mysteries'. Best known for his 'Neutral Point Theory', he has written articles covering subjects related to ancient mysteries: esoteric traditions, alchemy, mysticism, ancient shamanism and the nature of human consciousness. He is co-author of *The Serpent Grail*.

By the same authors:
The Serpent Grail

THE
SHINING
ONES

THE WORLD'S MOST POWERFUL
SECRET SOCIETY REVEALED

Philip Gardiner and Gary Osborn

WATKINS PUBLISHING
LONDON

First published in the UK and USA in 2006 by
Watkins Publishing, Sixth Floor, Castle House,
75–76 Wells Street, London W1T 3QH

This edition published in 2010

1 3 5 7 9 10 8 6 4 2

Designed and typeset by Jerry Goldie

Printed and bound by Imago in China

British Library Cataloguing-in-Publication Data Available

Library of Congress Cataloging-in-Publication Data Available

ISBN: 978-1-907486-10-4

www.watkinspublishing.co.uk

Distributed in the USA and Canada by Sterling Publishing Co., Inc.
387 Park Avenue South, New York, NY 10016-8810

For information about custom editions, special sales, premium and
corporate purchases, please contact Sterling Special Sales
Department at 800-805-5489 or specialsales@sterlingpub.com

Contents

Part Three: The Shining Ones Today

DEDICATION

My contribution to this book is dedicated to my parents,
Eric Osborn and June Day, and my daughter Li.

Gary Osborn

To my father and mother – for constant support
and encouragement.

Philip Gardiner

Acknowledgements

My gratitude to editor Peter Bently, publishing manager Penny Stopa and copy editor Lizzie Hutchins.

My thanks to authors Andrew Collins, Michael Hayes, Colin Wilson and Graham Hancock, for their support and of course their inspiring work. My heartfelt thanks to my friends Ken Ward, Dennis Smith, Paul Bultitude, writer on Shamanism Mark Dunn and researcher Claude Courvoisier.

Special mention to my brother Paul Osborn, his wife Yvonne, their children Paul, Natalie and Emma, and special thanks to my wife Jacqui for her unfailing support of me and our children, Ben, Victoria, Cameron, Freya and Angel.

Gary Osborn.

I would like to acknowledge the wisdom of our ancestors and acknowledge without arrogance that they were our equals in every way. I would also like to acknowledge the help of the many researchers and authors out there who have aided and assisted me along the way – there are simply too many of you to name.

Philip Gardiner.

LIST OF PLATES

LIST OF FIGURES

All figures are by Gary Osborn unless stated.

Preface

This is a story that some do not want to be told, but one that must be. Everything you previously held to be true will be challenged in the following pages. As a magician hides the mechanics of his tricks from the audience by means of smoke and mirrors, so the true history of the secret priesthood of the Shining Ones has been hidden behind a tightly woven tapestry of symbols, misinformation and lies. But now it can be revealed.

Much of the symbolism in the world has been created over time by various cults and societies, faiths and creeds, and these symbols can be interpreted on many levels. If we believe the religious element of these secret messages, then that is all we shall see. If, on the other hand, we choose to reject that religious element, then we shall begin to see the hidden meanings within the symbolism. We shall also find that these meanings are the same the world over.

During my research on another book I began to stumble across these peculiar similarities and came to realize that there was a major long-term and worldwide secret society in existence. Its members even gave their name: *the Shining Ones*. From then on, the more I found, the more amazed I became. It was as if a veil had lifted: once I knew how to look, I really began to *see*. I found that the truth had actually been in front of our eyes the whole time. When ancient texts are reread in the light of the new perspectives this book will offer, we abruptly start to see the real story which has been there all along.

While conducting investigations for this book, I met a direct descendant of the Prophet Muhammad who said that Islam had possessed the truth from the very beginning. Muhammad tried to show this truth, but history and its authors had manipulated it and created the Islamic faith of today. It seems that many people know that there is more to history and religion than meets the eye, but few of them have the whole story, and even fewer of them dare say so.

When I met up with Gary Osborn I found he too believed in the workings of an 'underground stream' and was coming up with similar conclusions. Together we have given ourselves the task of uncovering the mysteries that have been veiled from us.

There was an old man, an author now deceased, who said to me, 'You will never get this book published. The inheritors of the Shining legacy control the media and everything in it. Keep them out of the tale and you have a fighting chance, but what you say will not be the truth.' What he meant was that we were not to try and indulge our instincts and show that the inherited beliefs of the Shining Ones were still current among contemporary power brokers. But the fact remains: secret societies such as the Freemasons, the Rosicrucians and even the modern-day Knights Templar still hold beliefs originally set out by the Shining Ones. We cannot hide what is there; we cannot destroy evidence.

Truth is all. Without it, we have nothing.

Philip Gardiner

Introduction

'This is meant to be only an essay. It is a first reconnaissance of a realm well-nigh unexplored and uncharted. From whichever way one enters it, one is caught in the same bewildering circular complexity, as in a labyrinth, for it has no deductive order in the abstract sense, but instead resembles an organism tightly closed in itself, or even better, a monumental "Art of the Fugue".'[1]

So begins the celebrated book *Hamlet's Mill* by Giorgio de Santillana and Hertha von Dechend, first published in 1969. As this remarkable work demonstrated, our distant ancestors felt it necessary to preserve their advanced knowledge by passing on complex information in the form of stories and anecdotes about gods, creatures and humans. Yet the mystery to which the authors of *Hamlet's Mill* could offer no solution was *why* the ancients had encoded this knowledge. This was the task that had been laid before us.

It may be difficult to believe, but strong evidence does suggest that advanced technical knowledge was around long before the conventional dates given to human prehistory[2] and that an unknown culture had encoded traceable 'hints' of this knowledge. The key medium through which this knowledge was delivered and disseminated was the myths and fables passed down orally from generation to generation, largely by simple folk who were unaware of the secrets these stories and 'fairy tales' contained.[3]

During the course of our research we discovered that a large number of the world's major literary works, architecture and works of art, both ancient and modern, also contained hidden clues, small fragments of significant data, pieces of a 'giant jigsaw'. Such fragments of

cleverly-encoded data turn up in various religious texts and more esoteric works, notably in the Hindu scriptures and particularly in the
writings of the alchemical, Hermetic, Kabbalistic, Sufi, masonic,
Rosicrucian, Gnostic, Templar and Theosophical mystery schools.

One of the richest veins associated with this 'underground stream'
of knowledge is art – sculptures, paintings and illustrations down the
ages that contain a profusion of symbols, secret codes and sacred
geometry. We also find this ancient knowledge encoded in the buildings and structures erected not only by our distant ancestors but also
by certain individuals living in our own times.

In his book *At the Edge of History* William Irwin Thompson reflects
on the fact that the wisdom and knowledge encoded in this way show
that the primitive cultures that preserved them were not the beginning
of something but *the end of something else.* Considering the technology we have today and the myths that seem to allude to a previous
technical and scientific era, we could be forgiven for suggesting that
humankind has perhaps come 'full circle' – and that this has happened many times.

The mythical terrain is difficult: the evidential but subtle 'key references' are frequently interwoven with nonsensical schemes and plots
and conveyed via a narrative that is often florid and tiresome, and so
it is sometimes impossible to place what *is* understood into some kind
of logical order. But we believe we are now close to understanding
exactly why our distant ancestors encoded these clues and references –
the keys to the profound knowledge they held in their grasp.

We both discovered that this encoded information was linked to an
ancient system of knowledge developed by a mysterious, primordial,
shamanic-based culture known universally as the Shining Ones. This
peculiar culture seems to have all but vanished, although its influence
is very much alive today.

This ancient knowledge is very different from the present world-
view of the majority of humankind. It is more holistic, imbued with a

profound wisdom and spiritual excellence which are in striking contrast to the 'humble' or 'primitive' beginnings from which we are generally believed to have evolved.

We would emphasize that, like present-day humanity, none of the traditional early civilizations we know of had a complete and thorough understanding of this ancient system of knowledge. It is clear that it belonged to a former time in humankind's long history and had been passed on, often in fragmentary form, and been misinterpreted, misconceptualized and further degraded by new belief systems that were forever springing up. However, we believe that at any one time a number of initiates would have understood it. We also believe that down the centuries such individuals deliberately encoded certain key themes in myth, legend, writings, art and architecture in order to preserve them for those who came after them.

We would propose (a) that this information was symbolically encoded when many of these mythological stories and other works were first being conceptualized, disseminated and cultivated; and (b) that the information was subsequently augmented by further data introduced by those who were initiated into this knowledge. To give just one example, this is evident in the small changes and additions that have been made over the centuries to the phoenix myth *(see Chapter Seven)*.

When individual or maybe even a few such 'clues' are spotted, their broader significance may be easily overlooked, ignored or explained away as something mundane or at best a 'coincidence'. Many lead us on a highly convoluted trail of double and sometimes multiple meanings. However, *when they are looked at in total*, the deeper meaning becomes apparent. Now, with much of this research completed, we can say that we have come much closer to achieving this 'holistic' view, and it is truly breathtaking.

Who Were the Shining Ones?

Who were the preservers of this ancient knowledge? In our view, the Shining Ones were a shamanic priesthood that was known by many names in many different cultures: the Abgal, Abkarlu, Akeru, Akhu, Anak, Anannage, Ancient Masters, Angels, Annedoti, Anunnaki, Apkallu, Devas, Elders, Elohim, Feathered Serpents, Fish Beings, Gibborim, Grigori, Jabaariyn, Jinn, Nagas, Nephilim, Neteru, Nommos, Rephaim, Rishis, Seraphim, Seven Sages, Serpents, Shemsu Hor, Tuatha dé Danaan, Urshu, Watchers – the list goes on and on. Over time, because of their scientific knowledge, spiritual wisdom and supposed extrasensory abilities, they came to be thought of as 'gods', 'sons and daughters of the gods' and 'shepherds of men' by the less developed peoples who lived peacefully beside them. It was said that they civilized humankind, perhaps following a global catastrophe. The majority of mainstream historians do not take seriously either the existence of this mysterious 'godlike' culture or the 'worldwide catastrophe scenario', even though an increasing number of individual researchers have concluded otherwise.

The Shining Ones also embraced a 'rebel' group known in legend as the 'Fallen Ones' ('fallen angels' or 'Watchers') who are recorded as having married and reproduced outside their own kind – their hybrid offspring being known as the 'Nephilim' or 'Egregor' and described as 'giants'. The story goes that the catastrophe that nearly wiped out the human race was a great deluge due to the wrath of 'God' – or rather the wrath of the Elohim or Shining Ones, who somehow initiated it in order to destroy the rebels and their hybrid offspring.

Although fleeting references to the Shining Ones can be found in the Old Testament, there is much more about them in *The Book of Enoch*, an ancient work that was omitted from the Bible (except in Ethiopia, where the book is revered to this day as holy scripture).[4]

The Shining Ones were held in such awe by later generations that they were revered as deities and linked with the heavens. Some writers today have suggested that they were therefore of extraterrestrial origin. However, our own view is that these so-called 'gods' were human and of earthly origin – but were scientifically advanced and able to manipulate those who believed that they held 'divine' powers.

We stated above that the Shining Ones were intrinsically shamanic in origin. Their cosmology contains the same key concepts that we find in the shamanic tradition and it would seem that their power base evolved from the influence that the early shaman had over the tribe. Over millennia this developed into an élite 'brotherhood' or 'priest-hood' well versed in the propaganda skills needed to maintain both religious and political authority.

Our purpose in this present work is to introduce the reader to the many important themes alluded to in the esoteric symbolism of the Shining Ones and to explain their relevance for us now. Their belief system was a working cosmology in which all the religions we know today have their origin. We also found that many, if not all, of the world's unexplained mysteries point to the Shining Ones and their advanced scientific and metaphysical knowledge. In this book we will explore just what these ancient shamans were experiencing and how it relates to us today.

PART ONE

A System of Knowledge

1

The Prehistoric Link

Early Religious Beliefs
and Rituals

'They who long after success in action on Earth worship the
Shining Ones.'

Bhavagad Gita, IV, 12

Uncovering the roots of the Shining Ones' system of knowledge is
not easy. The most complicated factor is simply that their origins
go far back into the mists of time and, as far as we are aware, to a
period even before there was writing. So the task of discovering who
they were is incredibly challenging.

To determine their origins we must first take a trip through the
various mythologies and histories of the ancient world using the new
light of understanding that we now have – the understanding that
there may once have existed a wandering priesthood, possibly the survivors of an advanced civilization now lost, which traversed the globe,
passing on its agricultural, medical and astronomical knowledge and
also the wisdom of an 'enlightenment experience' – as generally experienced by the shaman.

Early Shamanism

Many of our traditions, beliefs and archetypal symbology seem to have developed from early shamanism. The word 'shaman' itself is from Tungusic, the language spoken by the Tungus nomads of Siberia. Some claim that the word is also derived from the Pali *samana* and ultimately from the ancient Sanskrit *sramana*, meaning 'one who knows', or possibly from a Slavonic term denoting the practice of the Samoyeds of Siberia and meaning 'to become excited' and 'ecstatic'.

It is said that the various techniques and means (such as natural hallucinogens) of inducing altered-state or trance experiences – which brought about evolutionary changes in human consciousness – go back almost 50,000 years. The ancient shaman, like the shaman today, filled the role of tribal priest, magician, seer and healer, and was able to deal with 'otherworldly' powers and speak with the 'gods' in much the same way as the avatars and prophets of later religions. He or she was also able to heal using ancient and secret techniques.

There is a saying: 'What doesn't kill you makes you stronger.' This certainly applies to the shaman, who lives at the edge of both society and reality. Few have the stamina to endure the external hardships and personal crises the work entails, or indeed the courage to venture into the 'heavenly' or 'hellish' 'worlds' of the mind – all of which go to make the shaman a *medium* between this world and the higher and lower worlds, or states of consciousness.

It is our theory that the knowledge and traditions that belonged to the Shining Ones' culture were primarily based on information gathered by the earliest shamans via altered states of consciousness. And so, although they were an advanced people, and understood things in a scientific way that went far beyond the shamans' view of the cosmos, they were nonetheless a shamanic-based culture. The 'excited' or 'ecstatic' aspects of shamanic trance states are, we believe, the source of the description 'Shining'.

This new understanding of the Shining Ones throws light on many aspects of human history, including the supposedly 'spontaneous' eruption of similar beliefs and ideas around the globe. The fact that so many of our beliefs today are basically the same, and the extraordinary links between the various buildings and monuments of early man, stand as a testament to this. Before we go any further, though, we should take a brief look at the origin of humankind.

The Origin of Humankind

First, we should bear in mind that not everything we have been led to believe regarding the origin of humankind is true. Once most of us believed – and many of us still believe – in the religious ideas of God the Creator, whether this is from a Christian, Islamic or other main-stream religious viewpoint. In our relatively recent history we have theorized about our origins from a purely rational and logical point of view. Unfortunately, in our rationalist zeal, we have thrown out a lot of useful information, such as the anthropological theory that myths and folktales should be seen as relics of ancient cultures and of actual occurrences and beliefs, and therefore taken seriously.

Second, we should be aware that somewhere back in the mists of time, humans evolved from *something*. This statement is about as accurate as we can get given current data, although many books state our evolutionary progression as fact. However, to say anything other than 'we evolved in some way' is pure hypothesis. There are tools in existence, for example, which have been found to date from around 25 million years ago[1] and yet modern anthropologists inform us that early humans, in one form or another, came from Africa between a mere 1.5 and 2 million years ago. If we also consider the fact that anomalous 'anachronistic artefacts' suggestive of a previous techno-logical era have been found all around the world, then we see that our 'date of origin' simply cannot be defined with any hard and finite accuracy.[2]

Of course we must tread carefully in our assessment of such evidence, as some 'discoveries' have been proven to be false. However, many apparently anachronistic artefacts still remain unexplained and open to debate and therefore we cannot simply ignore them as many have done.

Indeed, even fully authenticated and undisputed archaeological discoveries challenge our assumptions about the technological sophistication of ancient or 'primitive' peoples. Examples include the famous 2,000-year-old Baghdad battery found by German archaeologist Wilhelm König in 1938, or the mechanical device with 30 gears that turned up among the haul from the sunken wreck of a 2,000-year-old Greek ship. It has been suggested that the device, which predates the supposed 'original' mechanical calculator by about 1,500 years, was built to calculate the motions of the sun and moon.

Traditional archaeology and anthropology tell us that approximately 100,000 years ago, humankind, *Homo sapiens*, apparently split into *Homo sapiens sapiens* (modern humans) and *Homo sapiens neanderthalensis* (Neanderthal man) in the Middle East. However, at Bilzingsleben, Germany, archaeologists have found three circular structures made from bone and stone dating from around 400,000 years ago. At Terra Amata in France there are post-holes and stone circles dating from 300,000 years ago. In fact, vast numbers of tools and religious artefacts from 2.5 million years to 125,000 years ago have been discovered in Gona, Ethiopia and Europe.[3] These include bones dusted with red ochre[4] and skulls packed with clay and raised up on posts.

Are we supposed to believe that an apelike ancestor could create such things? What we are seeing here are the ritualistic remnants of ancient humans. Many years later, Neolithic humans were painting themselves with red ochre as a symbolic gesture of rebirth and initiation into the new life of the gods. The red ochre and 'skulls on posts' were elements that would last for thousands of years.

Rites of Red Ochre

Around 46,000 BC, a Neanderthal man was buried in a cave in what is now the south of France. His body had been packed with red ochre clay. This substance has become known as the 'blood of the earth' and it is believed that this style of burial was a symbolic returning of the body to the earth whence it came – a re-entering of the blood-red womb of 'mother Earth', or the shamanic 'world mother'. Blood, and hence also the colour red, was associated with pain and death, as it was linked with those wounded in accidents, fights and battles – mostly males.

Blood and red were also associated with menstruation and child-birth – the newborn is often smeared with blood as it enters the world. Female blood, particularly menstrual blood and the blood shed at birth, was therefore venerated, as it was associated with new life. It was foreign to male experience and was believed to hold mysterious magical powers. In some African cultures a menstruating woman is led around the home of a woman who wishes to become pregnant and asked to touch everything. The onset of menstruation marks the move from child to woman and so it is no surprise to learn that it was cele-brated with mother goddess rituals and, much later, within the 'taking of blood' in the Christian Eucharist. Blood was therefore held in both awe and fear, and this may account to a large degree for the use of red ochre in the rituals of ancient humans.

The colour red was also associated with 'rebirth' when it was later understood that the phenomena of the world were cyclical in nature. For instance, the sun is bathed in red when it 'dies' at night and is 'born again' in the morning. Ancient peoples perceived that the female men-strual cycle, the ocean tides and the waxing and waning of the moon were linked, and all three phenomena have had a profound effect upon both ancient and more recent religious beliefs. When the moon is full, or in the Earth's shadow during a lunar eclipse, its colour will some-times appear a dark blood red. The full moon was believed to coincide with the monthly menses and the new moon with ovulation – the release of a new egg.

The highly sophisticated rituals evidenced by the numerous ancient 'red ochre' burials around the world show a remarkable understanding of the cycles of life and death. They seem to represent the belief that the dead may rise up from the earth and return once again. One well-known ancient idea – the moulding of the first man from clay, as recounted in the Book of Genesis – may have represented a more widespread early belief about the creation of humans by the gods. Perhaps, therefore, stuffing a corpse with red ochre clay was symbolic of giving new life to the body and represented a type of reincarnation or rebirth in the afterlife or 'ancestral home'.

Another example of red ochre burial, dating from almost as far back as the French one, was discovered in Swaziland, in southern Africa. The skeleton of a child buried in around 41,000 BC had been returned to the earth and dusted with ashes and red ochre. Later cults from this area held to the idea of rebirth and reincarnation, so there is no reason to assume this belief was not held earlier as well.

Just how widespread this belief may have become can be seen in the burial of a young Native American child in around 6400 BC at the settlement known as Koster in southern Illinois. The body had been dusted with red ochre, possibly in an attempt to persuade the gods to offer the prematurely dead child new life in the 'land of the ancestors', or paradise. This extrapolation is not implausible, as it is no different from the methods used by anthropologists, and it is also borne out by similar finds.[5]

By 7,500 BC to 6,000 BC in the so-called 'cradle of civilization', the Middle East, there were cults of the female bull as well as sun, serpent and skull worship. As shown by discoveries at the site of Catal Hüyük in Turkey, this skull cult involved packing the skulls of the dead with red ochre clay and placing shells (perhaps symbolic of the sun's shining rays of light and the illumination of awakening) on the eye sockets. In this region, the bull was taken to represent the sun, the skull was symbolic of the human and the serpent was the fertile 'earth goddess' or 'world mother' *(see Chapter Two)* or moon goddess – thus we see a trinity of beliefs developing.

The belief that an individual is smeared with the blood of the 'world mother' at the moment of birth was sometimes reflected in human or animal sacrifice. There is much evidence to support this. For example, the sacrifice of bulls and rams was common within the cult of Mithra, an ancient Persian solar deity who became popular throughout the Roman empire. In this cult, bathing in the blood of the sacrifice was considered to have a redemptive effect. As the Roman saying went: 'By the bull sacrifice and the ram sacrifice, born again for eternity.' There is evidence that Mithraists believed the act of sacrifice would give new life. It is no coincidence that the festival of Mithra took place around 25 December, the time of many midwinter festivals welcoming the 'return to life' of the sun and Earth.

A Wandering Priesthood

At a site dating back to 60,000 BC in Moldova, archaeologists discovered *portable* tents and windbreaks made from mammoth bones. Other sites, equally as old, reveal similar artefacts. Is there any reason why nomadic peoples such as these (some say the Kurgans, the 'mound builders') could not have travelled with an ancient priesthood?

There is no explanation of how the people of Catal Hüyük built up their technical abilities so quickly. Moreover, the *religion* at Catal Hüyük was well developed and elaborate from day one. Could there have been influence from some outside source? Could this source possibly have been a wandering priesthood able to pass on a world's supply of knowledge? Some of the skills expressed in Catal Hüyük were known in other parts of the world, but there is no evidence of migrating peoples. This has always been the problem when cultures are seen to have risen apparently from nowhere but we do not find other groups disappearing or any genetic evidence of alien peoples inwardly migrating.

As the red ochre burials have already shown, evidence of strikingly similar religious beliefs and practices has been discovered in places separated by many thousands of miles. In America, finds from burial mounds in Ohio (which include circles, octagons, crosses and pyramids) and the Mississippi valley have revealed that bracelets were buried with burned skeletons. This was a similar practice to those of the Hindus, and the jewellery itself resembles bangles made in Persia and India. Why would this be? There can come a point where the coincidence of similar beliefs arises too frequently, and we must ask whether this can surely be just another freak occurrence.

To have a common belief system spread over vast areas of the globe, especially when most of it is covered with water, would require an early understanding of the stars for navigation and a possible 'homing instinct' involving the use of lodestone, or magnetite. Of course, the technical ability to create seagoing vessels must also have been available, and the evidence is beginning to prove that ancient sea travel was possible. It is well known that ancient humans developed vessels for river travel thousands of years ago, because it was easier than crossing land (the stones to build Stonehenge were transported by river from south Wales). Boats that are also capable of sea travel have been discovered dating from at least 3,000 BC, and some from as long ago as 40,000 years. In the Middle East, canoes hollowed out from whole tree trunks have been found which date back to around 7,500 BC and there is evidence that around 4,500 BC sailing boats on the Euphrates used the stars to navigate.

In southern Asia, there are engravings and cave paintings of deep-sea creatures which it would have been impossible to know of without having gone out to sea.[6] There are also paintings of dolphins and whales. Plato claimed that in the time of Atlantis (around 9000 BC or 900 BC depending on how it is taken) it was possible to travel from Atlantis to the further islands, a possible reference to America. In Holland, there is evidence of ancient boats capable of carrying large stones, possibly for early stone circles. The biblical Noah myth, the Babylonian *Epic of Gilgamesh* and the ancient myth of Yu, China's Noah, who stopped the floods, also indicate that the idea of seafaring dates back far into prehistory.

From archaeological data, it is possible to state that the basic belief system that spread worldwide with the wandering shamanistic priesthood could have developed as far back as 100,000 years ago. Local minor ethnic alterations became more apparent as time passed and our 'wandering priesthood' took on the various local differences and merged them into first one 'front' religion and then another. What emerged first were the 'surface' religions of the politicians and leaders, which were incorporated into the politics of the relevant culture. But underlying that surface, the basic elements and patterns of an ancient priesthood remained. These elements emerged directly from the original reasons why humans developed their sacred beliefs.

Close examination reveals that all parts of the world share the same fundamental belief system. Over centuries, the life-giving light of the sun merged into the 'God' of the Western world. 'Mother earth' and the 'moon goddess' also superficially merged with other entities, but were always there below the surface. The worship of a female deity is worldwide. Where Christianity has taken root, the Virgin Mary has been substituted. Where Islam is dominant, Fatima, the daughter of Muhammad and mother of three, is esteemed. The stars in the sky became minor deities to lead us through the seasons of life.

One of the most revealing finds was made in 1917 at a known Neanderthal bear-hunter site dated to around 73000 BC at Drachenloch, near Vättis in the Swiss Alps.[7] Inside a cave, an 'altar' was discovered which consisted of a rectangular stone chest with a great stone slab as a lid. Inside the chest *seven* bear skulls had been placed with their muzzles pointing toward the entrance of the cave. Commenting on the significance of this discovery, the author Michael Hayes writes:

> 'So the number seven, above all other numbers, was engrained in the consciousness of the hominid tens of thousands of years before the Egyptians and Sumerians came on the scene. Did the Neanderthals stumble on the [occult significance of the] number seven purely by accident, or were they subconsciously reading what was written in their very genes?'[8]

If we are correct in our interpretation of the symbolic arrangement of these seven skulls, then this is indeed significant, because the deeper meaning of the number seven that is being conveyed here (and discussed in Chapter 3) would require a profound knowledge of the metaphysical principles developed by the shaman from his own internal experiences – but it is said that shamanism only goes back some 50,000 years. Did the Neanderthals themselves possess this metaphysical knowledge? Or was their ritualistic behaviour evidence of some outside influence? As with many of us today, it is possible that the Neanderthals were not really aware of the deeper understanding that lay behind their own rituals.

It is essential to understand the original conceptions that have led to many of our present-day beliefs – many of which now fall very short of the original meaning behind them and also, more often than not, are taken too literally. It is only by revealing the deeper connections which people have overlooked that we can gain some idea of the source of this wisdom.

First, we are looking for concepts of the sun as the giver of life. This universal belief could have sprung up anywhere at any time without outside influence, although when we see that so many other concepts also sprang up all over the globe the mathematical probability of such a universal 'belief explosion' is small. The cyclic pattern and life-giving nature of the sun is the key to the secrets of the ancient Shining Ones. The movements of the sun have inspired tales of where the sun god goes and why he comes back, of battles fought and death overcome. This idea of overcoming death gives us the first hint of how people have used 'sun god' fables and also 'moon goddess' mysteries to hide ideas about how we ourselves could, supposedly, be reincarnated, or given 'new life'. These ideas are closely linked to the process known as *kundalini*: the 'enlightenment experience'.

Kundalini and the Inner Sun

Solar Cults and the Enlightenment Experience

> 'This Mechanism, known as Kundalini, is the real cause of
> all so-called spiritual and psychic phenomena, the biologi-
> cal basis of evolution and development of personality, the
> secret origin of all esoteric and occult doctrines, the master
> Key to the unsolved mystery of creation, the inexhaustible
> source of philosophy, art and science, and the fountainhead
> of all religious faiths, past, present and future.'
>
> Dr Lee Sanella, *The Kundalini Experience*

The universal phenomenon of sun worship is intrinsically linked, in all beliefs, to the illumination effect of the internal 'awakening' or 'enlightenment' experience. This enlightenment process, spoken of by the Buddha, Christ and hundreds of other mythical avatars, is what is known to Hindus and yogic practitioners by the ancient Sanskrit term *kundalini*.

In Hindu esoteric teaching, kundalini refers to the internal processes associated with the system of seven *chakra*s, or energy vortices, which are said to align with the spine and the seven endocrine glands in the body. These processes are associated with the propagation throughout the physical system of the 'life-force' energy, known as *prana*, also a Sanskrit term. Prana is considered to be the 'ground-force energy of consciousness itself.

We are normally unconscious of these internal processes, but we are told that we can become conscious of them through intense meditation, as practised in yoga, resulting in a spiritual or mystical experience known as a 'kundalini awakening'. This is the Hindu term for the rare 'enlightenment experience' achieved by certain individuals throughout history and sought after by many mystics and yoga practitioners.

For ancient humans, the life-giving physical sun also represented the 'inner sun' which is reached at the point of enlightenment and is known as the 'void' or *bindu*, and traditionally located three finger-widths above the head. The 'immortals' – the gods and goddesses (that is, the Shining Ones) of the ancient Egyptians – were depicted with the sun disc above their heads – in the same location as the bindu. Sometimes the solar disc is encircled by a snake, the *uraeus*, which is usually portrayed extending from the brow. As we will see, this symbolism refers to the 'third eye' trance state and to one's awakening to the wisdom of the 'kundalini serpent'.

This early sun/head imagery developed into the halo of radiating light as depicted behind the head of Christ as well as the heads of gods, mystics, saints and avatars in Christian and mystical Hindu iconography.

The Power of Kundalini

According to those who have claimed to have experienced the kundalini awakening, during the first stages of this rare experience one will feel an awesome, powerful vibration begin in the body, an energy which then moves up and down the spine, oscillating back and forth and ascending rapidly in frequency. It is said that often this activity along the spine will end with the consciousness separating from the body and other paranormal effects. Sometimes the experience will become painful, especially in spontaneous awakenings when one is not ready for it and one's mind and body are not balanced properly to receive it. In such cases, it is said the energy will become blocked at a certain point along the spine and one will feel a terrible heat or burning sensation – hence the name 'liquid fire' or 'serpent fire' – which, if not handled properly, could bring insanity or even death.

The dangers one can face during this experience were described by Gopi Krishna, who claimed to have experienced the sudden and 'full-blown' force of this energy, which he believed was 'the evolutionary energy in man'[1] and the bestower of genius. Since his account is an accurate description of what happens during this rare experience, it is worthwhile quoting it in some depth. The experience began one morning during Christmas 1937. Krishna was following his usual daily routine of meditating while facing east and sitting in the lotus position. As he wrote, 'What followed on that fateful morning in my case, changing the whole course of my life and outlook, has happened to few.'[2]

> 'Suddenly, with a roar like that of a waterfall, I felt a stream of liquid light entering my brain through the spinal cord. ...
> The illumination grew brighter and brighter, the roaring louder, I felt a rocking sensation, and then felt myself slipping out of my body, entirely enveloped in a halo of light. It is impossible to describe the experience accurately. I felt the point of consciousness that was myself growing wider, surrounded by waves of light. It grew wider and wider, spreading outward while the body, normally the immediate object of its perception, appeared to have receded into the distance, until I became entirely unconscious of it. It was now all consciousness without any outline, without any idea of a corporeal appendage, without any feeling or sensation coming from the senses, immersed in a sea of light simultaneously conscious and aware of every point, spread out, as it were, in all directions without any barrier or material obstruction. I was no longer myself, or to be more

accurate, no longer as I knew myself to be, a small point of awareness confined in a body but instead was a vast circle of consciousness, in which the body was but a point, bathed in light and in a state of exaltation and happiness impossible to describe.

'What had happened to me? Was I the victim of a hallucination? Or had I, by some strange vagary of fate, succeeded in experiencing the Transcendental? Had I really succeeded where millions of others had failed? Was there, after all, really some truth in the oft-repeated claims of the sages and ascetics of India, made for thousands of years and verified and repeated generation after generation, that it was possible to apprehend reality in this life if one followed certain rules of conduct and practised meditation in a certain way? My thoughts were in a daze. I could hardly believe that I had a vision of divinity. There had been an expansion of my own self, my own consciousness, and the transformation had been brought about by the vital current that had started from below the spine and had found access to my brain through the backbone.

'I recalled that I had read long ago in books of Yoga of a certain vital mechanism called Kundalini, connected with the lower end of the spine, which becomes active by means of certain exercises and when once roused carries the limited human consciousness to transcendental heights, endowing the individual with incredible psychic and mental powers. Had I been lucky to find the key to this wonderful mechanism, which was wrapped up in the legendary mist of ages, about which people talked and whispered without having once seen it in action in themselves or in others?'[3]

A few days after his first initial awakening, Gopi Krishna began to experience the more negative effects of this energy. He suffered terrible burning pains, as if he were *burning from the inside out* – a description that corresponds with what seems to have happened to some victims of spontaneous human combustion.[4]

Just as Gopi Krishna was about to succumb to what he believed to be his imminent death, a 'hidden intelligence' from within communicated to him through his intuition and told him exactly what to do and so he was then able to stabilize and control this formidable energy that had been released within him.

If one's initial experience is successful, like Krishna's, then at the climax one experiences the inner sun – indeed, one actually *becomes* it – as the oscillations and vibrations of energy end with an explosion of bright white light at the centre of the head. This explosive energy seems to radiate outwards throughout all of creation.

For the individual, this ecstatic experience, also known as *nirvana,* is one of 'rebirth': the mind becomes revitalized and flooded with new information and knowledge, and one attains a higher perception of oneself and the cosmos – what Buddhists call *bodhi*, enlightenment, or awakening to the true nature of reality. It is no surprise to learn that the pagan and Christian belief in resurrection and the Eastern belief in reincarnation all have their source in this experience.

Kundalini, the Shaman and Solar Gods

The ancient shaman gathered information and knowledge about the enlightenment experience and anything related to it and sought to conceptualize and communicate the experience by noting the correspondences and parallels it had in the world around him. It was only logical and obvious, then, that the life-giving sun at the centre of our solar system should be seen to correspond with the bright 'inner light' one experiences during the climactic phase of enlightenment. The external sun reflected the internal sun, conveying the information that we do indeed possess an inner sun that sustains us and that our lives are positioned at the centre – in the balance – between both suns. Which came first, the worship of the external or internal sun, is impossible to ascertain.

Man may indeed have worshipped the physical sun. But the shaman and mystic who had experienced kundalini enlightenment understood the real meaning behind such solar worship. It was the *inner sun*, the rare enlightenment experience, that made a person a Shining One – a god.

Evidence for this link between shamanism and the kundalini enlightenment experience is abundant. As the scholar Mircea Eliade notes in *Shamanism*, among the Iglulik Eskimos, who were driven out of some unknown homeland, a sequence of initiations concludes with the *angakoq*, meaning 'lightning' or 'illumination'. This *angakoq*, writes Eliade, consists of 'a mysterious light which the shaman suddenly feels in his body, inside his head, within his brain, an inexplicable searchlight, a luminous fire which enables him to see with both eyes, both literally and metaphorically speaking, for he can now, even with closed eyes, see through darkness and perceive things and coming events which are hidden from others'.[5]

In truth, all are connected by this internal experience through which one reaches the divine – it requires no 'middle man' such as the Church. Hence the reason the Church, which came to power via the exploitation of these ancient shamanic-pagan concepts and principles, at times felt so threatened as to want to stamp out any 'heretics' who carried on these ancient spiritual traditions – people who had the eyes to see through the scam.

Ultimately, we can see then that all solar worship has its origin in shamanism and that the shamanic and pagan solar god through which one could control a people via their religious focus on this god was really based on the Shining Ones – those shamans who had had this enlightenment experience and had developed their cosmology around it. The archetypal shaman who came to embody the experience later became the pagan 'sun god' – and ultimately the 'sun/son of god' of the Christians.

This link between solar worship and the enlightenment experience further reduces the mathematical probability of worldwide sun cults erupting independently.

Now we have identified what the sky god or sun god really refers to, we need to establish whether there are any symbols or titles centred on this deity. 'Father' and 'light' are the two most basic, and many different names stem from these titles.

The next deity to identify correctly is one that gives us an understanding of the process or technique by which one is able to initiate the enlightenment experience. This deity is the wife or consort of the sun god: the moon goddess, the mother of us all.

The Archetypal Goddess

She is worshipped as the 'earth goddess' or 'world mother' who mates with the sky god and maintains the cycle of life and death. She is also the goddess of the moon, mainly because the cycles of the moon were once believed to coincide with the female menstrual cycles. She is the archetypal priestess, the initiator of wisdom. She was worshipped in ancient Sumeria as Ninkharsag, in Egypt as Isis, in India as Kali, and was identified with Matronit, or Shekinah, and the Gnostic Sophia, to give just a few of her many manifestations.

The mysterious power of the female which led to the early goddess cults was based on her association with fertility and her birth-giving role. As all humans are born into this world through the female, it was naturally believed that the female was closer to the *source* of existence itself and therefore closer to the mysteries of life, sex and death. As mentioned earlier, menstrual blood came to symbolize this power, as it too was believed to flow from the original source of creation.

We are told that the Sumerian mother goddess Ninkharsag created humans out of clay, bringing them to life by infusing them with her 'blood' (it has been claimed that the name 'Adam' actually translates as 'bloody clay').[6] Some, like author Zecharia Sitchin, have interpreted this to mean that the Sumerian deities were an extraterrestrial race who created us through genetic manipulation to be their slaves and dogsbodies. However, theorists like Sitchin have overlooked the widespread beliefs and rituals associated with menstrual blood stretching back tens of thousands of years. For instance, the Egyptian pharaohs believed they would become 'immortal' by ingesting the 'blood of Isis' – their version of Ninkharsag – which they called *sa*. This was obviously menstrual blood. The hieroglyph for *sa* 'was the same as the sign of the vulva, a yonic loop like the one on the Egyptian *ankh* [cross of life].'[7] 'The Greeks believed the wisdom of man or god was centred in his blood, which came from his mother.'[8] 'Chinese sages called menstrual blood the essence of mother earth, the yin principle giving life to all things.'[9]

Menstrual blood was believed to be so powerful that even the Church felt threatened by it. 'From the eighth to eleventh centuries, the Christian churches refused communion to menstruating women',[10] even though the eucharistic 'red wine' given to people to sip during the Catholic Mass was based on the partaking of menstrual blood – the blood of the original Sumerian serpent or 'snake goddess' Ninkharsag.

As our investigations have revealed,[11] the red wine of the Eucharist not only symbolizes menstrual blood but also the powerful blood of the Shining Ones, who, like the female, were believed to be closer to the source through their own 'internal' experiences, and the blood of the snake, which was used in shamanic healing. Our initial theory was that the ancients would mix snake venom with snake blood in a ceremonial bowl to produce a powerful healing elixir now proven by modern science to enhance T-cell replication and thus boost the immune system. We believe that this was the basis of the legendary 'elixir of life' and that the ceremonial bowl, based on the human skull, came to be called the 'Grail'. The reason for this, as we understand it, is that the centre of the head is where illumination and enlightenment take place.

The association these Shining Ones had with the serpent or snake is the symbolic clue, and it was possibly they who first acquired the knowledge of the venom-and-blood elixir.

How did they attain the wisdom of the serpent? *They acquired it through the power of woman.* The story of Adam and Eve and the serpent is one allegory that points to the source of these early shamanic beliefs and the experiences and knowledge that developed alongside them. It was believed that 'serpent knowledge' and 'serpent wisdom' – the processes associated with kundalini, which is often represented in Hindu art as a snake – is found within or via a woman.

So the 'world mother' was originally based on the female shaman, or shamaness. She is the consort of the shaman and assists him in his 'otherworldly' travels via the trance state. She is also the pagan 'Threefold Goddess' associated with the phases of the moon and the three Marys associated with Jesus.

The shaman, having observed that all of us enter the world by being born through the female, believed that during trance he was re-entering the womb of the world mother to get back to that spiritual source whence he came. The world mother was represented by his female consort, with her body representing the world and her ovum its centre. The shaman believed that through her body he also entered the 'underworld', which was believed to be located inside or under the Earth. So he believed he was penetrating the female via his mind to find the answers to all the mysteries of life and death that she had come to represent.

This interaction between the shaman and the shamaness

symbolized the union or fusion between the male-related 'conscious self' and the female-related 'subconscious'. This is the simple truth: the female was believed to represent what we today would call the 'subconscious' – the shaman's 'underworld' – and it was this belief that really constituted her power.

In terms of the kundalini awakening experience, the archetypal goddess or world mother, in personifying the subconscious, actually represented the rising energy of the kundalini. It was believed that it was she who carried the subject's conscious self inward, through the different layers of the subconscious, by going upward through the spine to the brain and to the centre of all intelligence and creation.

This fusion in the mind also had its correspondence in the physical realm – the sexual intercourse that creates a child. The early shaman understood that in order to recreate the 'child within' and then with childlike eyes to 'see' internally into the 'other worlds' and perhaps ultimately experience the inner sun of enlightenment, the male 'conscious self' must first enter and penetrate the female 'subconscious', just as the phallus enters the vagina and the sperm penetrates the egg. More importantly, the shaman understood that one must always be 'consciously aware' and 'attentively awake' during this internal fusion process.

We should emphasize again that this alchemical fusion of opposites really takes place within the shaman's own consciousness, and so it is his own subconscious that he enters 'consciously' and merges with. He is able to achieve this 'awakened fusion' through the shamanic trance state, known technically today as the 'hypnagogic state'.

The Union of Opposites in the Hypnagogic Trance State

As we make the transition from the waking state into sleep, we pass through a kind of veil or 'twilight zone' – the 'hypnagogic state'. As we move back from sleep into wakefulness we pass through the same veil, this time known as the 'hypnopompic state'. Both terms indicate the same state in consciousness. They are also both referred to as the 'transliminal' state, from the Latin for 'crossing the boundary' or 'threshold'. What we are talking about here is a classic cycle consisting of two main phases with a third phase that is crossed twice as one enters and leaves each of the main phases.

The ancients also observed that the waking-sleeping cycle was like all other cycles in that it contained three distinct phases – positive (wakefulness), negative (sleep) and neutral (transliminal) phase. For

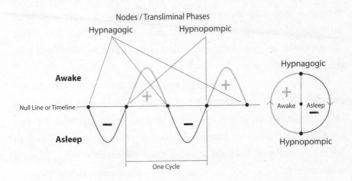

Figure 1: The Waking-Sleeping Cycle

Like any cycle, and like a travelling sine wave, the 'transliminal phase' occurs twice in the cycle – where positive, or peak, crosses into negative, or dip, and vice versa. In the waking-sleeping cycle these 'zero nodes' where the opposites (as in the two halves of a cycle) are briefly united, are the hypnagogic and hypnopompic states. Both are really the same state and, as regards conscious-ness cycles, this is the psychic 'gateway' that leads into the centre, as marked by the dot at the centre of the circle (cycle) on the right. This resembles the ancient Egyptian sun symbol (see fig. 25) and conveys the same understanding.

example, these phases have their correspondence in the three phases of the moon associated with the Threefold Goddess – waxing (positive), waning (negative) and the full moon or new moon (neutral).

The ancients also realized that the 'slower' waking-sleeping cycle was the one that could be used to access the inner sun, the 'Eternal Now', through psychic means. The positive half of the cycle (wakefulness) was related to the active male, the conscious self – everyday external physical reality. The negative half of the cycle (sleep) was related to the receptive female, the subconscious – internal mental reality, the realm of imagination, memories and dreams. The third phase (transliminal) was neutral. It briefly presented itself twice in the cycle, when the positive (waking) half of the cycle crossed into the negative (sleeping) half (hypnagogic) and vice versa (hypnopompic).

Everyone knows that we do not recall exactly the point where we fall asleep or wake up. This 'neutral point' in the cycle is where the opposites meet and are briefly unified – neutralized as separate phenomena. Therefore, for the ancient shaman, this formed a correspondence with the sexual union of male and female which produces that 'creative spark'.

By observing all cyclical phenomena and noting the two neutral points in every cycle, perhaps the ancient shamans realized that indeed our own consciousness is 'cycling' – that is, oscillating many times a second – and that we become *briefly unconscious* as our 'point of focus' or 'train of thought' crosses these two points internally. Of course we do not notice such transient moments of unconsciousness, as the oscillations are extremely rapid. But if we were to take a recording of these oscillations and slow them right down, we would perhaps notice that our consciousness is flickering between three states – just like the moon going through its three phases.

In terms of psychology, if the everyday objective consciousness is the waking half of the cycle and the subjective subconscious the sleeping half, then these 'voids' or 'blips' which appear at the end-beginning

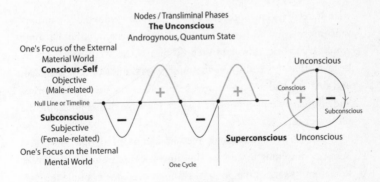

Figure 2: Consciousness: A Cyclical Process

This diagram applies the four psychoanalytical states (conscious, subconscious, unconscious and superconscious) to the cycle. Our consciousness is also a wave-like cycle, and in every instant we fluctuate momentarily between conscious and subconscious, with the unconscious 'zero node' crossed twice every cycle. If we become conscious at these points, as in the hypnagogic state, then everything collapses into the centre or superconscious. (Compare with the slower 'waking-sleeping cycle' illustrated in fig. 1.)

point of each cycle and also at the halfway point where each opposite crosses into the other would represent the 'unconscious' and also the 'collective unconscious' of Carl Jung.

The ancient shaman realized that if he were simply *to remain conscious and aware* at the point of going to sleep he would enter a different state of consciousness altogether, where another reality would present itself in vision and sound, becoming ever clearer the more he sustained awareness in this 'crossover' state. The hypnagogic trance state was therefore seen as a 'gateway' or 'portal' to the 'underworld' and 'other worlds' – the vast internal worlds of the mind.

In these 'other worlds' or 'other-dimensional realms', the shaman encountered all kinds of creatures, even human-animal hybrids, as we see depicted in the typical animal and bird-headed deities of the ancient Egyptians. He also 'met' and interacted with dead people, friends, relatives and ancestors who would sometimes pass on important information which he could use to his benefit, although some would try to trick him and even do him harm. We can see why he believed that this realm was the underworld, the world of the dead, and that one had to access it first before accessing the 'higher worlds' and, ultimately, enlightenment – which for some shamans became the ultimate goal.

To obtain enlightenment, the shaman realized one must first become conscious *of* and *at* this unconscious point in the cycle. Remaining awake at the point of going to sleep, for example through practising meditation, seemed a simple enough task to try to master. In time this practice led to the discipline of what in Indian tradition is called yoga, a system of strenuous spiritual and physical exercises that developed largely from intuition but also from the knowledge obtained through the trance state and the kundalini enlightenment experience. Yoga is of course associated with kundalini and has enlightenment as its ultimate goal. The term *yoga* is Sanskrit and means literally 'yoking together' – meaning to unite or 'yoke' the opposites within oneself as one would first tame and then 'yoke' two wild horses together.

We can see then that to obtain this ascent to enlightenment, one must first balance or still the mind through meditation and enter the

Figure 3: The
Masonic Level or
Plumb Line

'midpoint' of the trance state. And this midpoint is achieved through the successful synchronization of opposites, both those related to our own duality and to the duality of all things we experience, for everything is vibrating and oscillating, swinging like a pendulum between one extreme and the other.

This neutralization of opposites came to be symbolized by the neutral, genderless hermaphrodite or androgynous being, as depicted in alchemical art. This is the 'child within', born through the fusion of opposites; it is the soul, which is non-dual and genderless.

We can see now why the ultimate god is always portrayed as androgynous – sexless or neutral. In masonic symbolism, the third, centred state is symbolized by the 'plumb rule' or 'plumb level' featuring a weighted cord – the pendulum at rest in the centre.

Eclipse: The Fusion of Sun and Moon

As we have seen, by observing the phenomena of the world around him, the ancient shaman was able to note the correspondences between these phenomena and his own fusion in consciousness. In alchemical symbology, the sun (day) and the moon (night) that cycle across the sky correspond to the male and female opposites, and of course also reflect the male-related conscious and the female-related

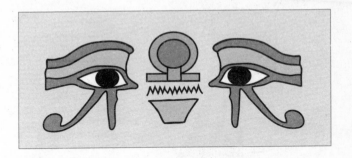

Figure 4: The Two Eyes of Horus
This drawing is based on ancient Egyptian depictions. On the left is the Eye of Ra, associated with the male-related sun (conscious self) and connected to the left brain. On the right is the Eye of Thoth, associated with the female-related moon (subconscious) and connected to the right brain. Note the sun disc in the centre enclosed within the *shen* ring (see fig. 27). This symbolizes the central thalamus – the 'inner sun' and the real 'third eye' – and in terms of the triad this represents the neutral point or 'third force' (see fig. 6).

subconscious opposites, as well as the left and right hemispheres of the brain. This is why in ancient Egypt the sun and the moon were believed to be the two eyes of the solar god represented by Horus, the Shining One, each associated with a side of his brain. These two sides were brought together in the eclipse.

Eclipses were particularly important – at these times the two great bodies in the sky came together and were believed to 'mate' to fertilize the Earth with new abundant life. This symbolism of course extends to this synchronization of opposites in the individual and the moment of fusion which one must try and capture to initiate one's own rebirth.

Many ancient buildings and writings show that eclipses were eagerly predicted all over the world, perhaps because such times were originally deemed 'sacred' by the early shamans precisely because they reflected the midpoint that they sought to capture. The void or 'black hole'-like image of the solar eclipse was seen as the 'gateway' or 'portal'

Figure 5: The Goddess Hathor-Isis
The goddess with the sun disc above her head, between two cow horns, symbolizing the fusion of opposites, as seen in the solar eclipse. The two horns have been interpreted as the sun's corona during the solar eclipse, as well as the waxing (left-facing crescent) and waning (right-facing crescent) moons. A drawing based on a later ancient Egyptian depiction.
By this time Hathor and Isis were seen as aspects of one great goddess, the 'divine mother' of Horus.

between this world and others. It is possible, then, that initiates would go into trance at the moment of an eclipse in order to facilitate their entrance into the other worlds and perhaps even reach the point of enlightenment and become Shining Ones.

Other important times utilized for this purpose were the spring and autumn equinoxes – the two neutral points in the annual solar cycle – which are known as the 'in-between times' by modern pagans, especially Wiccans, and have become associated with ceremonial magic.

The sun disc or full-moon disc depicted on the heads of some Egyptian deities is sometimes held between two cow's horns. This is often seen with images of Hathor, the goddess of rebirth. The cow's horns are said to be the two crescents of the moon, associated respectively with the waxing and waning phases of the lunar cycle. Here the female-related moon is again associated with the 'subjective subconscious' and the male-related sun with the 'objective conscious'. It has also been remarked that the horns could represent the crescent light of the solar corona during an eclipse. It is our understanding that the sun held by the two crescents of the moon above the head really illustrates the fusion of the two opposites – sun and moon, male and female, conscious and subconscious – as we also find in the eclipse.

This symbolism reveals that the Shining Ones were able to achieve a 'neutral point eclipse' in consciousness, and to us this is one of the original meanings behind the solar-lunar headwear worn by these deities.

The name 'Hathor' is the Greek version of the Egyptian *Hwt Hor*, meaning literally 'Mansion of Horus'. She is the womb of Horus, the place from which Horus, the great Shining One, emerges and rises to the heavens. This would mean that Hathor is also the archetypal goddess who represents the energy of the kundalini that rises up the spine, carrying the consciousness of the individual upwards through the spinal cord and into the brain to the point of enlightenment.

Interestingly, in yogic practice kundalini is often visualized as a snake coiled at the base of the spine, and Hathor could be represented as a snake.

On the subject of yoga, the Sanskrit term *hatha*, as in hatha yoga, has the esoteric meaning of sun (*ha*) and moon (*tha*), indicating once more the union of opposite (male sun and female moon). Through yoga and meditation, one 'yokes' the sun and moon together in one's consciousness.

One who is going though the kundalini is both 'alive' and 'dead' at the same time within a neutral *quantum state* just like the 'alive/dead' cat that features in an analogy devised by physicist Erwin Schrödinger to describe the Uncertainty Principle of quantum theory. It would seem that the ancients understood this in their own way, and so we could say that in order to access the inner sun, one's consciousness should first be in a 'state of eclipse' – awake and asleep, as in the hypnagogic state, and therefore 'alive' and 'dead' at the same time. It is significant that Jesus was said to be crucified – thereby becoming an enlightened Shining One – at midday during what is widely understood to have been a solar eclipse.

It was believed that life and death themselves also constituted a cycle – hence the widespread belief in reincarnation. Being conscious in the hypnagogic state meant that one could also be conscious at the transition point in the life-death cycle.

In any case, it was realized that one could enter into the 'underworld' as if 'born' into it, while returning from it was like a 'rebirth' or 'resurrection', because during the journey the shaman had attained new insight which granted him a deeper perception of the nature of reality. (Similar outcomes are reported today for those who have undergone the near-death experience.)

However, in having retrieved this wisdom by entering and fusing with the feminine, as he believed, the male shaman became ever more confident in his power, and inevitably the goddess or moon cult gave way to the male-related cult of the solar deity. In consequence the female was robbed of her power. The Sabbath or seventh day (that the Wiccans refer to as the 'heart-rest of the moon'), originally Monday ('moon day'),[12] was later taken over by the Jews, who turned it into their day of rest (Saturday) and rejected the maternal lunar religions in favour of the worship of their paternal 'sun god'. Christians took this further, even moving the day of rest to Sunday. Sunday was the day dedicated to popular solar gods like Mithras – and the day on which Jesus was 'resurrected', returning from the underworld as an enlightened Shining One. The cults of some of the many goddesses linked with the moon – including Aphrodite, Astarte, Badb, Brigit, Demeter, Persephone, Hecate, Inanna, Isis, Ishtar, and the Gnostic Sophia, or Wisdom – carried on, kept alive in secret by their devotees while they were subtly battling the growing influence of the solar and male-oriented gods such as Mithras and the Judaeo-Christian God.

Soon the male-oriented Christian Church would change the ritual menstrual blood to Christ's blood. This is ironic when we consider that the Christian Christ was based on the archetypal shaman who is 'resurrected' through the goddess. The bread that came to represent 'the body of Christ' and the red wine that represented his blood being brought together in the chalice or Grail also symbolized the fusion of opposites that one must attain within the mind in order to reach enlightenment. The bread represented the material domain and the male-related conscious. The red wine represented the domain of the mind and the female-related subconscious. This symbolism is now clear and brushes all other interpretations aside.

Other Heavenly Bodies

Like the sun, the stars (which are of course distant suns) were also important to the ancient Shining One shaman. The stars are the great Shining Ones of the heavens. They inform us of times, seasons and longer-term cycles. They guide us around our world and we can

31

predict much from their movements. They are the many eyes of the unreachable gods looking down upon us. It was believed that a person could indeed become a star through the enlightenment experience and at death take his place in the heavens.

The different constellations were used as tools to convey the mythical stories of the Shining Ones and to display their knowledge – and as we know, knowledge is power. It is no wonder that the Shining Ones came to be seen as gods.

Another way they revealed their knowledge was through numbers. Now that we have an idea of the consciousness processes utilized by early shamans and the Shining Ones priesthood, we can look at the symbolic use of numbers with new perception.

3

Three and Seven

The 'Law of Three' and 'Law of Seven' in Shamanic Cosmology

'One should ever make one's own self radiant by the light of the three jewels.'

Sacred Book of the Jains

There is no faith or belief system on Earth that does not in some way respect, revere or attach mystical significance to numbers. Some would have us believe that God's existence can be proven via mathematics, and maybe that is part of what the ancients intended with their weaving of patterns and the strange symbolic passages in the pages of obscure and ancient scriptures.

As many will know, the most significant numbers in pagan, occult and religious lore are the numbers 3 and the 7. It is said that one who understands both the 'Law of Three' and the 'Law of Seven' is an initiate into 'the mysteries' – hence our interest in the seven bear skulls that were left by Neanderthals in the Drachenloch cave. Perhaps this was just a coincidence, but the correspondences associated with these two numbers actually reveal the internal processes associated with the shamanic trance state and the enlightenment experience.

The Three Worlds

The shamans of Central Asia believed in 'three worlds' or 'three cosmic zones' positioned on an axis or spindle known as the 'world tree' – the *axis mundi*, 'axis of the world', which is fastened in place by the 'world mountain'. The three cosmic zones are:

- *The sky plane* (heaven)
- *The middle plane* (the Earth on which we live)
- *The lower plane* (the 'underworld', later known by pagans and Christians as Hades or Hell).

It is said that if the shaman, while in trance, reaches the 'trunk' of the world tree and/or the centre of the world mountain and climbs it, he will reach the higher planes and a powerful mystical experience will result.

Many people are confused as to why there is both a mountain and a tree and why they are referred to as if they are one and the same thing. We would agree that a tree or pillar is not a mountain, so why is this?

First of all, we discovered that again, this 'climbing of the trunk of a tree' is a metaphor which reflects an internal process associated with the spinal column and skull of the shaman himself, an experience described in many accounts.

And the mountain? In his books, author Colin Wilson mentions what he describes as the 'ladder of selves':

'This ladder seems to have one peculiarity. Unlike the ordinary ladder, its sides slope inward so the rungs become shorter. Everyone who has been through some personal crisis knows that in order to develop a new level of being, we need to make an effort of compression – we even use the phrase 'pulling ourselves together' to express what we do when we have to achieve a higher level of organization.'[1]

These words are interesting. But what are Wilson and the shamans really describing? They are trying to convey a simple understanding of the triad (a simple equilateral triangle, represented by the three-sided form of the 'mountain') and its seven levels (the tree) *(see figs. 6 and 8)*. Ultimately, of course, although Wilson does not go so far as to say so, they are also referring to the kundalini enlightenment experience.

Of course there are many other reasons why trees and mountains have become important to humankind – not least among them is their navigational and time-monitoring uses. One thing that was important to our ancestors was knowing where and when they were.[2]

Gurdjieff's Law of Three and the World Mountain

The metaphysical principles locked up within the symbol of the triad were adopted by the Sufi mystic Gurdjieff and have now become familiar to us via his own system, in which he referred to its hidden principle as the 'Law of Three'.

The esoteric meaning of the triad is really quite simple to understand and we have already seen what it applies to. It was understood long ago that the *one* energy of consciousness was really 'neutral' but was divided into *two* equal forces: the positive and negative polarities which are reflected in the world around us in a multitude of ways.

More importantly, it was also believed that it was *we* – our own consciousness – who divided this energy in two. This division was necessary in that the reality around us was actually being created from it. In other words, the 'interference patterns' being created from the interactions of these two opposite energies are what creates 'form'.

This understanding, and the desire of certain individuals to *reverse* this process so that they could escape the repeating patterns and cycles of a reality which they considered illusory, is illustrated in the *sacred triad*.

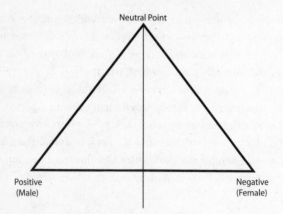

Figure 6: The Triad

In this diagram, the two opposites are divided by a 'neutral' centre line. Imagine that the line is a string holding a pendulum and that it is swinging (oscillating) between opposites – like the cycle diagrams (figs. 1 and 2). The centre point, crossed twice in the cycle, would represent the point where we become momentarily unconscious in the cycles. This is the point that the shaman aimed to capture via the hypnagogic trance state, which could also result in a fusion in consciousness. Both opposites unite in an inward and ascending spiral path to the apex, or centre – the path to enlightenment associated with the kundalini awakening. This simple triad diagram relates closely to the shamanic 'world mountain' (see fig. 8).

In terms of opposites, the two base points of the triad or triangle are *positive* (masculine) and *negative* (feminine). The apex is *neutral*. Gurdjieff called this neutral point the 'Third Force' – the point of fusion where both the positive and negative opposites are cancelled out and become *pure energy* again.

As Gurdjieff tells us, 'In reality all the Three Forces are equally active and appear as active, passive, and neutralising, only at their meeting points, that is to say, *only in relation to one another at a given moment*.'[3] Elsewhere he states: 'All that exists exists as a result of the converging action on the same point, at the same time of Three Forces: Active, Passive and Neutralising.'[4]

And so in the triad shown above, with the neutral centre line that divides the opposites but where both opposites can be brought together and united, we also see the world mountain – the shaman's 'tree' or 'pillar', which was also symbolized by the obelisks, columns, pillars and totem poles of many ancient cultures *(see Chapter Six)*. Remember Gopi Krishna's account of the liquid energy rising up the spine and entering his brain?

As if adhering to this original shamanic cosmology, we find that almost every nation and culture has a mythical sacred mountain whose summit is the 'abode of the gods'. The Greek Mount Olympus and the Norse Asgard come immediately to mind. In Greek myth, it is said that the original mountain was Atlas, the mountain or volcano that once stood at the centre of Atlantis. This is all purely symbolic. In India there is the spiritual Mount Meru, and in more ancient myths, such as those of Egypt, this mountain also represents the Earth itself and is known as the 'sacred mound' or 'primordial mound' – relating again to the first act of creation.

The same simple image and the understanding behind it, especially in regard to the shamanic concepts just outlined, is present in the building of the Step Pyramid of Saqqara and the Great Pyramid of Giza in Egypt, also in the ziggurats of ancient Sumer and Babylonia, the pyramids of Central America, the Buddhist stupas and pagodas of India and the Far East, and the 'sacred mounds' of Europe – all of which usually have seven levels to them. These seven levels or steps are associated with the 'Law of Seven'. It is obvious that the kundalini enlightenment experience, centring on the spine and the seven chakras, is what these pyramid and ziggurat structures are really all about.

We can also see that Colin Wilson's 'ladder' is the shaman's world pillar or tree, and indeed the shaman often describes it as a 'sky ladder', 'rope ladder', 'vine' or even a 'spiral staircase'. With the mountain image, we can see how all this refers to taking an inward and upward or ascending spiral path to the apex, or indeed to the centre. Not only does this make sense in regard to the kundalini energy phenomenon, but it also refers to the trance state which triggers this experience.

As already outlined, to ascend to the sky plane (the unconscious) one must achieve union between the objective Earth plane (conscious self) and the subjective lower plane (subconscious). This fusion gives the individual more energy to become sentient of the unconscious, therefore becoming *superconscious* as all three worlds, all three states of consciousness, become one.

The ascending levels (the rungs of the ladder or steps of the ziggurat or pyramid world mountain) are associated with different frequencies of energy. Everything converges at a pinpoint – the apex of the world mountain or world pillar, the point of enlightenment as experienced in the centre of the head. The shaman believed this was the centre of the Earth as well as the centre of all creation.

The seven-stepped spiral staircase and the ladder also both feature to this day in masonic symbolism, which should not really surprise us as this so-called 'secret knowledge' is really based on shamanic principles as gathered by the ancient Shining Ones. As we will discover, it is this kundalini experience which is at the heart of all the knowledge preserved by the various secret societies and mystery schools.

The Shamanic Underworld

The underworld – where it was believed we go when we die and from which we are then 'reborn' into the world – was believed to be underneath or inside the Earth. In the shamanic rite of passage associated with the kundalini awakening, the shaman believed that he was entering the Earth and climbing the *axis mundi* or Earth's axis, ascending the frequencies associated with his own spine. The interior of the Earth, the underworld, represented the womb of the goddess or world mother, who represented the Earth itself.

In some cases, the underworld was the ovum or egg of the goddess, the central point of enlightenment which was pierced – impregnated – by the mind of the shaman to initiate his own rebirth. We could also say this was the 'proto-atom' of the Universe before the Big Bang. All these terms are metaphors for the 'source-centre' of creation – *the void from which one could be reborn.*

Furthermore, the underworld, called the *Duat* or *Tuat* by the ancient Egyptians, was also believed to be *inside* us – or it could be reached by *going inside ourselves* – which is what we have been saying all along.

Lakes or rivers were associated with the underworld because still water, like a mirror, reflected the landscape – especially the trees, their branches being reflected as roots. In this way the outspread roots (the underworld or 'lower world') would reflect the outspread branches (the heavenly world). There is evidence that the ancient Celts would uproot a tree and plant it upside down in a lake as an offering to the ancestral heroes and gods they believed resided in the underworld.

Similarly, the dark night sky with the stars and their constellations was both the heavenly world *and* a reflection of the different worlds or sub-domains which existed within us and inside the Earth – the underworld.

The Source Centre and the Shamanic Underworld

Overleaf is our own simple illustration based on the shamanic concepts associated with the underworld:

Compare this with the world mountain with its seven ascending levels *(fig. 8)*. The only difference is that the seven levels in the sphere are like the electron orbits or shells we find in an atom, layered on top of one another like onion skins. As regards the beliefs of the shaman, these seven levels are the sub-domains of the underworld through which one 'ascends in frequency' to reach the centre of the sphere.

This picture of the sphere of consciousness and its three cosmic

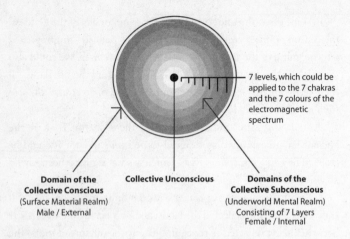

7 levels, which could be
applied to the 7 chakras
and the 7 colours of the
electromagnetic
spectrum

**Domain of the
Collective Conscious**
(Surface Material Realm)
Male / External

Collective Unconscious

**Domains of the
Collective Subconscious**
(Underworld Mental Realm)
Consisting of 7 Layers
Female / Internal

Figure 7: The Sphere of Consciousness
Based on the matrix of the earthly sphere and the 'three cosmic worlds' or
'zones'.

zones or realms is not that far removed from how the ancient shamans
would have imagined it. Their own illustrations were very similar, as
revealed by the widely distributed prehistoric rock markings known as
'cupmarks' (see fig. 9).

Cupmarks resemble the ancient Egyptian sun symbol, a simple
circle with a dot in the centre *(fig. 25)*, and the later circular *mandalas*.
The ancient Chinese had a similar symbol in the form of the *pi*, a jade
disc with a hole in the middle, which symbolized the void or creative
principle and was associated with heaven.

Australian Aboriginal shamans sometimes sit around a ground
painting of a concentric-ringed circle. The emphasis is obviously on
the centre of this circle or sphere. Again, this circle corresponds with
the concentric-ringed cupmarks which have been found everywhere
around the world in one form or another. This circle or sphere represents the *vortex* – which is really modelled on the vortex within one's
psyche – and these shamans also wear this circle on their heads in the

form of a headdress. The one who sits in the middle of the circle wears a tower on his head – like a phallic pillar – indicating the vortex and the Hindu descriptions of the bindu point above the head, which is said to be accessed via the shamanic trance state and the enlightenment experience. Through the trance state he aims to penetrate through to the centre of the sphere, like the phallus penetrating the vagina or the sperm piercing the egg so as to fertilize the world mother and perhaps produce a new pattern in his mundane reality, along with his own rebirth.

The ancient shaman imagined his consciousness to be a circle or sphere, like the Earth on which he lived,[5] which he envisaged as concentrated more at the centre. The three cosmic planes around the *axis*

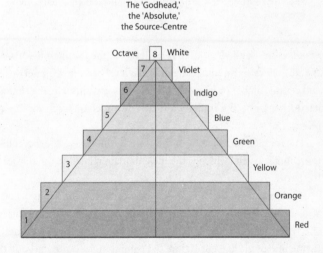

Figure 8: The Triad as the Shamanic 'World Mountain'

Ziggurats and stepped pyramids usually have seven levels. The eighth level – the octave (the Void, or Infinity) – is rarely included in these structures. Perhaps this is why the capstone of the Great Pyramid is missing.

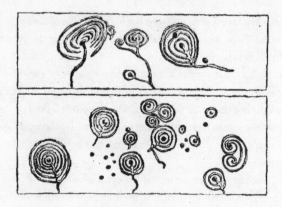

Figure 9: Cup-and-Ring Marks
These prehistoric markings from Scotland have up to seven concentric rings (the cupmark at bottom left). The 'serpents' penetrating the centre of these vortex spheres resemble sperm seeding and fertilizing the nucleus of an egg. An analogy can be made with the fusion of opposites or the quantum fusion of binary values.

mundi corresponded with the three levels of the Earth/consciousness sphere – surface (middle plane or Earth level); interior (underworld) and centre (higher or heavenly plane). This explains why the shaman has to penetrate the underworld first in order to reach the higher plane.

The middle 'Earth plane' of the cosmic zones would be the 'collective conscious self', which is the male domain related to the *surface* of the Earth.

As already discussed, the underworld or 'lower world' was believed to be inside or under the Earth. We have added seven levels (concentric rings) to this internal realm. These seven levels are a common theme in esoteric and occult lore . The point in the centre, beyond the seventh level, the place where all seven levels become 'one', would be considered the *eighth* level (octave) in some esoteric systems.

The heavenly blue 'sky plane' would equate with the 'collective unconscious' – seen in the dark sky at night. This is also the source-centre, which has its place *at the centre of the sphere.*

To summarize:

Surface of the Earth: The middle plane, the conscious self

Interior of the Earth: The lower plane or underworld, the subconscious

Centre of the Earth: The higher plane, the unconscious, but when the initiate becomes conscious of it, the *superconscious.*

Reaching the centre, as in the enlightenment experience, is rare, and it is usually the underlying *matrix of information* – the seven levels of the collective subconscious – that the shaman is able to access via the trance state.

The ancient shaman learned he could enter the underworld at will by *feigning death* so that he was able to come back again. This feigning of death is achieved through the reintegration of the divided person-ality or mind (ego), which is said to also happen at the point of dying – as in the *bardö* experience described in the *Tibetan Book of the Dead.* The word *bardö* means 'gap' or 'between two', i.e. an 'in-between' state, not only between 'life and death' or 'this world and the next' but also between opposites, as in male and female, conscious and subcon-scious, and so on. We can see how the deeper meaning behind *bardö* also applies to the crucial point in all cycles, waves and periodic systems. This cannot be stressed enough, as these correspondences with the three phases of the cycle grant us the answers to most myster-ies relating to human consciousness.

This threefold world belief, as illustrated in the world tree and the world mountain, and the concentric sphere of up to seven levels, as seen in cupmarks, labyrinths, mandalas and other similar designs, are indications of the original cosmology of the Shining Ones and reflect an understanding of the processes we have already outlined. They are the historical beginnings of many of the major beliefs we have today – beliefs whose origin has been kept secret down the years by numerous secret societies and mystery schools.

Snakes and Ladders: The Chakra System and the Endocrine Glands

The Hindu chakra system, which we introduced earlier, has become a bit of a cliché in New Age literature, with every self-acclaimed psychic, mystic and 'urban guru' jumping on the bandwagon, despite the fact that many of them have not experienced the enlightenment associated with it. What is not well known is that it is this system which underlies all allegorical myths, legends and related symbolism. This indicates its importance in regard to the experiences we have so far outlined. However, although the chakra system explains the experiences of shamans, yogis and mystics, and has even been 'seen' psychically by many people, it remains outside scientific study, mostly because it cannot be 'physically' detected or measured.

Let us explain more about the chakra system. *Chakra* itself is the Sanskrit for 'wheel' and the seven chakras are often described as invisible swirling energy vortices, potent energy centres that exist at the 'etheric' or 'non-physical' level. We have seen how the shamanic world tree is also the shaman's own spinal column. The notches, rungs or steps are the seven chakras that align the spine. We have also seen how the world mountain symbolizes the ascent up the spine of rapidly increasing wave frequencies associated, according to mystics, with each of the chakras.

The chakras are located at the base of the spine, the navel, spleen, heart, throat, between the eyes and at the top of the head. They are intimately related to the seven endocrine glands that are aligned with the cerebro-spinal axis, which itself is considered one's centre of gravity and is formed by the brain and the spinal cord. These glands are the gonads, lyden, adrenal, thymus, thyroid, pituitary and pineal. Just as each chakra corresponds to the nearest physical organ in the body, so it also corresponds with one of the seven endocrine glands.

The seven chakras are considered to be the metaphysical counterparts of the physical glands in the body and are said to 'knot' the spiritual aspects of man to the physical vehicle. Because they exist at the etheric level, we cannot physically see or feel them, but they can be seen internally via the trance state.

The illustration overleaf is a traditional depiction of the physio-chakra system and shows the chakras surrounded by lotus petals. It has been said that the different numbers of petals assigned to each chakra are associated with the energy vibration or oscillating frequency of that chakra.

The energy of the spinning chakra vortices is seen by shamans, mystics and psychics as swirls of colour – each chakra producing one of the colours of the spectrum. This is the source of the rainbow-coloured 'aura' which these intuitives see enveloping the body like a sphere or egg. Many psychics assert that there are seven main layers to the aura, each progressive layer being less dense than the one before it and each associated with a different chakra level.

Evidence for the reality of the aura and of the chakras themselves exists in the many well-documented accounts of people who have been able to see them through being able to enter the transliminal hypnagogic state at will. It should be said that such people also include a fair number of doctors and physicists.

To see this energy usually takes many years of meditation and training. It is not something that can be tried in a laboratory or tested at home. Drugs may be used to induce this sight, but only after much training. Seeing these energy points helps the healing process and measures our spiritual progression – it is basically the secret of the alchemical process. (In China, acupuncture techniques may have something to do with being able to see these energies. Also, the witch's

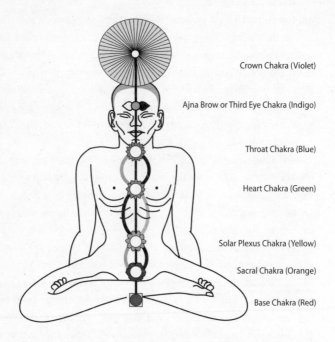

Crown Chakra (Violet)

Ajna Brow or Third Eye Chakra (Indigo)

Throat Chakra (Blue)

Heart Chakra (Green)

Solar Plexus Chakra (Yellow)

Sacral Chakra (Orange)

Base Chakra (Red)

Figure 10: A Diagram of the Chakra System

This diagram, based on Hindu representations, shows the position of the seven chakras or energy vortices. Note the Pingala and Ida nadis, or meridians, crossing at the centre of each of the seven chakras, which are aligned along the central sushumna channel. The channel culminates in the seventh, or Crown, chakra, above the head – its centre is the bindu, the 'point of enlightenment', or 'inner sun'. Compare this with the sun disc above the heads of the ancient Egyptian deities in figs. 5 and 39.

'broomstick', made from a branch of a *tree* and upon which she flies, is an obvious reference to the spinal column and the chakra system and its connection with altered states of consciousness through which one can 'fly' 'astrally' as in the out of body experience.)

It is said that the quality of our thoughts and actions depends on which chakra level our minds are working at any moment. The higher

levels are associated with our more intelligent, creative and construc-
tive modes of thought and action. Here we are more conscious of that
source-centre within us. Not surprisingly, our most basic instincts are
related to the lower chakra levels, which we drop to when we are more
unconscious of that source. Also, each chakra has a positive and negative polarity, and so for our energy to move upward to another level, it
has to be gathered together and centred within the chakra we are
moving from. A simple analogy would be a seven-storey building and
everyone on a particular floor walking to and entering an elevator at
the centre of the building to go to the next floor, where they separate
again.

According to many esoteric systems, prior to the actual moment of
enlightenment an individual will experience both opposites and all the
chakras coming closer together, as if converging and becoming one at
the apex. This apex is the bindu – the centre of the seventh chakra.
This chakra is known as the *Sahasrara* or 'crown chakra' and visualized
as a thousand-petalled lotus. It has been described as a mini-vortex
which grows taller and brighter like a flame when a person is in a
joyous state.

The cartoon light bulb that appears above the head of a person who
has a sudden flash of insight stems from an esoteric understanding of
this centre – as do the conical hats worn by witches and wizards. The
conical hat represents the whirling vortex of energy, which contracts
down to a 'point of singularity' during illumination or enlightenment.
The conical 'dunce's cap' has negative connotations now, but originally
it was worn in the belief that bringing attention to that centre above
the head might grant the wearer more brain power.[6]

The halo of light portrayed around the heads of saints and avatars
indicates the fused energy at this centre, which, according to the
Hindu scriptures, brings superconscious enlightenment to the individual. The flames that rise from the heads of the spiritually cleansed
apostles in Chapter Two of Acts may be a reference to this effect. After

all, the crown of the head – known as the *Bregma* by the Hindus and *Kether* by the Kabbalists, and considered in all cultures to be the vehicle for the soul – would be the place to symbolize the fire and light of God. It is the crown or corona of the inner sun, just as the real sun has its own flaming corona. Now we know why monks shave the crowns of their heads – the bald patch known as the tonsure.

It is worth noting too that Native American chiefs wore a headdress of many feathers and the edges of their leather costumes were also adorned with feathers. These are symbolic of the radiating light associated with the aura. One could say that the tribal chief was considered a Shining One.

The seventh chakra enlightenment level is associated with the pineal and pituitary glands in the brain. These can activate the sixth or 'third eye' chakra (behind the brow) during meditation, which can then lead to the seventh, and this is why these particular chakra centres and the related endocrine glands in the head were considered important to the ancients. We believe that the significance of these glands was understood by an advanced ancient society who passed on their knowledge to future generations of initiates in encoded form. This would explain why many sacred temples and other structures around the world are *repositories* of this ancient wisdom, translated into the language of sacred geometry and symbolism for the instruction of spiritual heirs.

The Shining Ones: Subatomic Scientists?

Looking back at the concentric sphere of consciousness utilized by the shaman to enter into the centre, there is compelling evidence that the ancient Shining Ones understood that the seven levels are also expressed – 'as above so below' – in the tiny building blocks of matter we know as atoms and subatomic particles. We may be accused of grafting our own contemporary science on the minds of our ancestors, but it would be no surprise to find that our shamanic ancestors were *intuitively* correct if not actually 'instructed' in this knowledge.

Explained simply, an atom is an energy vortex consisting of a nucleus with up to seven energy layers, or orbits, surrounding it. The 'electron' – an elementary particle – will orbit the nucleus at these seven different levels. The level, or shell, in which the electron is orbiting will depend on the amount of 'light-energy' the electron is absorbing or emitting every instant. The electron needs to gain energy in order to reach the outer orbits of the atom so as finally to escape it. More often than not, the escaping electron will be captured by another atom – another miniature vortex.

As regards the sphere of one's own consciousness, this picture of the atom is *inverted* in that to escape the cycles or vortices of reality, an individual's energy needs to *reach inwards* towards the source-centre of its own 'sphere' by ascending the different frequency levels – much

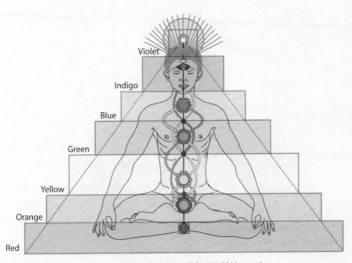

Figure 11: The Chakras and the World Mountain
The chakra system as it relates to the seven ascending steps of the shamanic 'world mountain' (see fig. 8).

like climbing the ancient primordial mound or sacred mount towards the central apex. Again, these levels are associated with the seven chakras or energy levels that align the human spine.[7]

The Red and White Channels

And what about the snakes or serpents?

Serpents symbolize the serpentine waves of energy we see in a sine wave, but also the nerve channels through which opposite energies are said to flow up and down the body, in, out and around the chakras, in a spiral fashion – hence the symbol of the spiral staircase adopted by Freemasonry.

In the chakra system, there are three meridians or nerve channels, called *nadis*. The *pingala nadi* is visualized as red and represents the red-hot solar 'fire element' of the masculine principle. The *ida nadi* is

Figure 12: Caduceus
In this ancient symbol, the two snakes equate to the Pingala (male) and Ida (female) nerve channels of the chakra system, while the central staff is the neutral sushumna (see also fig. 13).

white and represents the cool lunar 'water element' related to the feminine principle. These interweave around the central *sushumna*, the black cerebrospinal channel. The zero-point centres of the chakras are aligned with the sushumna and are the points at which the red and white channels cross.

Red and white symbolism, sometimes joined by black, keeps cropping up in myth, legend and sacred lore the world over. For example, there are the red and white dragons of Chinese myth and philosophy – dragons being the Far Eastern equivalent of the serpent. There are also the intertwined male and female serpents that cross each other at

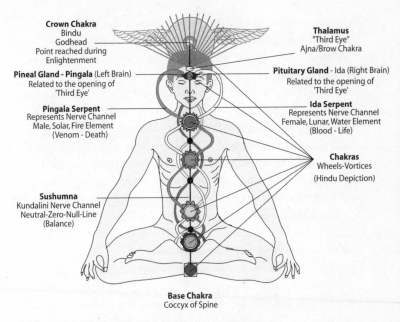

Figure 13: The Caduceus and the Chakra System.
The chakra system as it relates to the ancient caduceus symbol. See also figs. 10 and 12.

specific *neutral* 'power points' around the caduceus staff – a kind of ancient standing-wave diagram.[8] All this symbolism derives first and foremost from the triad and the chakra system.

We can now see how closely the shamanic experience of capturing the crucial crossover point in all standing-wave cycles is related to the chakra system. This transliminal point would be found at the centre of each of the seven chakra vortices that align the spine.

The sushumna nerve channel which runs along the centre of the spinal cord is the 'zero-null line' – a *superconductive* channel on which the red and white energies unite and cross each other. The zero-null line and the crossing points on it – the chakra centres or 'zero nodes'

– are what we find in a standing wave *(see figs. 1 and 2)*. These points are where the opposite energies are *neutralized*, cancelled out.

Our understanding of this process is that every second of our lives the two energies are racing up and down the body via the two opposite nerve channels – that is, spiralling up and down and around the spine – but we are unconscious of this process. In other words, the life-force energy is oscillating back and forth, constantly separating, fusing together and separating again as it goes in, out and around the chakra 'wheels' or vortices. The point where the two energies fuse together briefly, at any one of the seven nodes (chakra centres) along the spinal axis, is the moment when we become momentarily unconscious.

Our minds are constantly 'flickering' on and off and we are unconscious *many times a second*. However, instead of one value for 'on', as we would find in ordinary computer binary-code language, the 'on' point in consciousness has two values, both of which can be measured – a 'positive charge' (conscious self) and 'negative charge' (subconscious). The real 'off' point is where and when we become totally unconscious. This midpoint in the cycle is *neutral* – seen to have 'no charge' – but it is the brief phase in the sequence where we tap into the life-force energy of the source. Really, therefore, it is *infinite* and *immeasurable*.

To the shaman this point is the gateway in and out of reality, and also the gateway to 'God'. Accessing it is just a case of becoming conscious of it *and at that point*. A Siberian shaman described his own trance-state experience. He saw a hole in the earth that grew larger and larger, and descended through it with his spirit ally, arriving at a river with two streams flowing in opposite directions.

The 'hole' in this description would be the portal in consciousness created by the superimposition of the two opposites. In other words it is the node point which the shaman's mind zooms in on, reducing into it, which is why it grows larger and surrounds him, like the 'black tunnel' often described in the near-death experience.

The 'river' is the sushumna null-line in the centre and the 'two streams' flowing in different directions are clearly the two opposite energies that oscillate up and down the spine in a standing-wave fashion.

The Siberian shaman's descriptions of opposite-flowing 'rivers', 'streams' and a 'hole in the earth' are just his own way of communicating what he has perceived internally. We can see that it is really a microscopic experiential description of the physiological chakra system at the subtle etheric level of his own physical body.

So the chakra system agrees intimately with everything we have seen so far – and especially in terms of 'wave phenomena'. This is where the Shining Ones became advanced in their knowledge.

Because conscious attention within the hypnogogic state would often trigger the enlightenment experience, it was realized that it constituted an 'awakening' at one of the node points in the cycles of the physiological life-force distribution process associated with the chakras. It was observed that it also altered one's consciousness in some way, in that afterwards, when one came out of trance, one would be more creative and also more intelligent and intuitive – intellectually and spiritually 'reborn', if you will.

All of us have our own predominant level of consciousness which we will keep to and work from. However, it was discovered that depending on how intense the awakening experience was, the two opposing energies would fuse together and carry the level of consciousness to the next chakra level – that is, a level closer to the source of intelligence itself. This explained the changes in the consciousness of the individual concerned and also accounted for the paranormal experiences and psychic abilities involved.

Further, it was realized that if this awakening was sustained and intense enough, then the two energies would ascend through all the higher levels and possibly reach the top level, the source-centre, where all nodes and chakra levels become fused together, collapsing into one point, the 'point of infinity' or Eternal Now, where one becomes superconscious.

We discovered that throughout history alchemists were trying to find that same 'point of infinity' – seeking to be present in all cycles, waves and oscillating systems. We should note that *everything* is oscillating, and the zero-point in the cycle, everywhere and in everything, is what provides the regular pulse. It was this source of energy that the alchemist sought – this was the famed Philosopher's Stone.

Did the alchemist – like the shaman – understand that this zero-point in every wave and cycle reflects the same point at the centre of everyone's consciousness? Did he see that everything is being driven by this centre? Did he have this same insight, like the shaman before him – an insight that only comes through the enlightenment experience?

If it is true that we live in an 'information universe', whereby everything is made up of energy/information, as 'Molecular Information Theory'[9] states, then in effect, by reaching into the source-centre, the collective unconscious – and doing so *consciously* – the alchemist would have been able to transform his own consciousness. Eventually, because of the dramatic alteration of his own psyche, the energy/information patterns of the material world that he was experiencing would also change, even dramatically. This is why Paracelsus, one of the most renowned alchemists, said: 'No one can transmute any matter if he is not transmuted himself.'

Now the significance of all this is far-reaching indeed: it means that the patterns of the reality around us are composed out of our own projected energy and that most of the time we are creating and recreating these patterns *unconsciously*.

It is because most of us are unconscious of the process that we cannot control our creations. This is why we feel that we are mere 'pawns' in a 'game of chance', unable to control events or even our own experiences… Things just happen to us. The Shining Ones knew differently.

The Labyrinth and the Brain

The traditional labyrinth design, which can be found all around the world, consists of seven circuits. These circuits must be thought of as an ascending and descending process but also an inward and outward process. As regards frequencies of energy, there are seven major steps to climb in frequency before reaching the zero-point centre.

Figure 14: Labyrinth
In this medieval Spanish labyrinth, note the seven folds counting down from the top to the centre.

Below is the labyrinth design, schematized. This illustration shows how each inner level of the labyrinth is associated with the one colour in the ascending sequence of the electromagnetic spectrum, and similarly one of the seven chakras that align the human spinal column, one of the seven notes of the musical scale, as well as one of the seven levels of an atom and subatomic particle. We can reveal now that the classic labyrinth design is really a simple drawing of the brain – the spiralling convolutions of the labyrinth making a correspondence with the convoluted folds of the brain.

The centre is white – which in terms of light is composed of all the colours of the spectrum. This is just what we would find with this point in the brain, which is akin to the source-centre of consciousness itself.

The labyrinth showing the ascending colours of the spectrum is interesting in light of recent research into brain activity and the synchronized frequencies of the left and right hemispheres. The illustration below is a picture of the brain at the moment of synchronization brought on by meditative techniques.

This picture is taken from the late Robert Monroe's 'hemi-sync' website. Robert Monroe was the author of *Journeys out of the Body* –

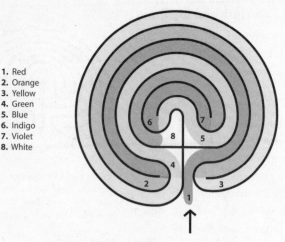

1. Red
2. Orange
3. Yellow
4. Green
5. Blue
6. Indigo
7. Violet
8. White

Figure 15: The Labyrinth as an Image of the Human Brain.
This representation of the labyrinth shows how it relates to the seven principal colours of the spectrum, beginning with red at the bottom and tracing the path around the seven layers to violet. Note the echo of the Egyptian ankh (incorporating the tau-cross and *ru* "gateway") in the centre, as if we are being told that the *ru* is at the centre of the brain.

one of the first books that included detailed accounts of Out of Body Experiences (OBEs). Monroe had described the very same sensations that yogis describe with regard to the trance states that can lead up to the kundalini experience. In Monroe's case this had occurred prior to his first OBE. These OBEs then became a regular occurrence for him – so much so that he was later able to induce them and control them at will.

The Hemi-Sync Process

Hemi-sync, first developed by Monroe, assists meditation and helps the subject to access the hypnagogic state – the precursory state which leads to psychic abilities and the experience of OBE phenomena. Hemi-sync encourages coherent brain-wave activity through the

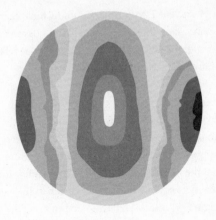

Figure 16: Hemi-Sync Brain Patterns
Wave Patterns of the two sides of the brain synchronized via the Hemi-sync
process reveals a harmonious pattern with emphasis on the centre of the brain
– the area of the thalamus.

synchronization of the left and right hemispheres of the brain.
Different frequency sound waves are transmitted to each ear through
a set of headphones and these waves entrain the frequencies of each
hemisphere to reach a point where both are harmonized and synchronized so as to create a centred state in consciousness.

We would add that in effect, the hemi-sync process has really been
designed to lead one's consciousness into the hypnagogic state – the
borderline state between waking and sleeping consciousness. As we
have seen, the hypnagogic state is responsible for many kinds of paranormal phenomena – including OBEs and remote viewing – but if
sustained by one remaining non-fearful and non-judgmental – i.e.,
calm, neutral and indifferent to all that is going on in this state, it can
lead one to experience the ultimate 'centre point' in consciousness: the
enlightenment experience known as the kundalini awakening.

It is obvious now that the ziggurats of ancient Mesopotamia and the pyramids of ancient Egypt, America, and China, represented the 'world mountain' which illustrates humankind's desire to access this centre, as shown in the labyrinth – which seems to be related to one's energies reaching the centre of the brain.

The Ear of the Goddess

We discovered that a detail in a Christian legend about the conception of Christ through the 'ear' of Mary (*see Chapter Eleven*) had been taken straight from Sumerian texts, thereby giving more support for our theory that the human ear was used as a metaphor for the spherical toroidal energy vortex. The toroidal vortex in this context is the head and its power points, and relates to one entering the underworld and the 'higher worlds' associated with the seven-levelled frequency-spectrum as related to the seven chakras (*see above*). For example in the Sumerian texts we have the words:

'From the Great Above, Inanna opened her ear to the Great Below.'

'The Great Below' is of course the underworld. As mentioned earlier, before one can reach the 'higher worlds' related to the centre of the sphere, one has to descend into the 'underworld' – which was believed to be 'inside' or 'under the earth' – that is, down through the levels of human consciousness related to the seven concentric layers which surround the centre of the sphere.

In the Sumerian story of Inanna's descent into the underworld, we are told that the goddess gathered together the 'seven attributes of civilization' known as the *me*, which she then transformed into adornments worn by her as protections. Beginning from the base of the spine, these were:

1. The lapis measuring rod and line (first chakra).
2. Her royal breechcloth (second chakra).
3. Her golden hip girdle (third chakra).
4. Her breastplate called 'Come, man, come' (fourth chakra).

5. A double strand of beads about her neck (fifth chakra).

6. Two earrings of small lapis beads (sixth chakra).

7. Her crown (seventh chakra).

As indicated, each of these adornments really represented one of the seven chakras because they were worn at the level of each relevant endocrine gland (see above). The two earrings are associated with the pineal and pituitary glands, which are again associated with the opposites as well as the two sides of the brain.

We are told that as Inanna reached the portal of each of the seven levels of the underworld, she had to shed an item of clothing in order to go further. We see here an allegory of the rising serpent energies, which ascend the spine through each of its chakra levels.

The ear with its convolutions, which to our ancestors must have resembled what they saw as the inward and outward spiralling path of energy that forms a vortex, is used here as the symbolic portal into these realms associated with the underworld.

In Sumerian, the word for 'ear' and 'wisdom' are the same and wisdom is an epithet of the serpent. But this is not all: Enki, the Sumerian god of wisdom – known also as Ea or Hea, and probably one of the Shining One 'fish-beings' like Oannes – *see Chapter Nine*) is said to have 'his ear wide open' – again, meaning that his ear is a simile for the 'vortex portal' into the spherical, toroidal vortex and into its core-centre, or nucleus. That the ear is used here to symbolize the vortex is interesting, since the inner ear is referred to as the 'labyrinth' by physicians – for example, bony labyrinth and membranous labyrinth – and the labyrinth is associated with the spiral vortex.

The Earth-sphere would have been seen to correspond to Ea's head – and the nucleus of the Earth to the centre of his head. In other words, we are being told that the centre of Ea's head and the centre of the Earth are the same as the centre of all creation – this being referred to as heaven. But more importantly, we can clearly see that the labyrinth

59

Figure 17: Spherical Standing Wave
A representation of an electron – a subatomic particle that is really a spherical standing wave. We are presented here with an image of the 'primordial mound' or 'world mountain' rising from the primordial waters of creation. Reality is a process of permanent and universal re-creation. Drawing based on images presented by Dr. Milo Wolf.

design was also adopted from the coiled serpent – which relates also to the lizard that enters the head of the goddess in Sumerian myth.

We conclude that all these Sumerian concepts and metaphors are really shamanic in origin. It is possible too that if the ancient shaman, while in trance, was able to reduce the focus of his consciousness down to cellular and molecular levels and even perceive his own DNA, he was also able to reduce his consciousness down to the atomic and sub-atomic level, as discussed earlier in the chapter (*see page 50*). The symbolism associated with the winding, spiralling, coiling serpent, also makes a correspondence with the theory, first proposed by Dr. Milo Wolf, that all matter is structured of spherical wave centres – that is, spherical standing waves, and who tells us that the physical structure of charged particles really involves inward and outward spherical quantum waves.

Our theory is that evolution is really a two-way process – much like a standing wave, and here we mean that we can apply the 'standing wave' to time itself. This means that time and also evolution as we see it, and as regards the collective consciousness, are really arranged within and along a standing wave – information patterns appearing as interactive phenomena and events moving from past to future, but also from future to past.

Now the evidence we have found through cross-referencing the data relating to many different disciplines – physics, philosophy, eso-terica, metaphysics, psychology, parapsychology, shamanism, Egyptology and other ancient cultural studies – suggests that we only see and experience half the process – being the *material* half of the process – what we observe in the biochemical and biomolecular world of atoms and subatomic particles. According to Wolf, these so-called 'particles' are really 'wave centres' – what we see as 'point particles' like electrons for instance, which are being formed from these two-way standing waves – all of which produce and compose the world of phe-nomena in which we experience ourselves and everything, as slowly moving from past to future *(see fig. 19)*.

The other half of this process – being the flow of energy/informa-tion coming from future to past, and which could be described as the continuous 'echo' from, let's say, the 'omega point' in the future, is to us subjective and in our minds, subconscious, and so most of the time we are oblivious to this other half of the process – except those rare times when we may accidentally and consciously tap into this 'backflow' of energy/information by spontaneously entering the hypnagogic state – how one experiences precognition or precognitive phenomena. So, then, it is the subliminal information flowing from the future to the past that is always steering the path of evolution to its 'goal'.

Evolution has to have a 'goal' – a 'final complete picture'; and surely that 'ultimate result' must already exist. As we know, when assembling a jigsaw puzzle piece by piece, we already have a picture to work to. That 'final picture' or 'goal' would be what the mystics refer to as the 'Eternal Now'.

The Eternal Now

There is only really the 'Eternal Now' and that 'Now' exists in the beginning and also the end of the standing wave that we call physical existence and evolution, which means that time is cyclical. The now is the 'alpha-omega' of the cycle – as symbolized by the point where the symbolic Ouroborus snake is biting and swallowing its own tail. However, that Now is also the 'zero nodes' in the standing wave, and in all standing waves.

This means that if the Now exists in any and all cycles and standing waves from the macrocosm to the microcosm, then it also means that the Now can be 'accessed' at any time along the path of evolution and this means at every instant during the cycles of our own lifetime or timeline.

How does one do this? Well that takes us back to what the shaman is attempting to do through sustaining conscious awareness in the hypnagogic trance state, which can ultimately lead him to reach the point of enlightenment. Within the Now is all the information we need and it is also within us, which is why the shaman goes inside himself.

The Now is simply found within the 'transliminal phase point' of each and every cycle, 'where' and 'when' the positive crosses into the negative, and vice-versa, as in travelling waves, and also the nodes in standing waves. This also means that it surely exists within our own consciousness, which is also cycling – oscillating many times a second – and therefore the Now is really the moments in the cycle 'where' and 'when' we become unconscious.

The shaman attempts to become 'conscious of the unconscious'

Figure 18: Dual Ouroborus
This variation of the symbolic serpent that devours itself clearly shows the two points in the cycle where positive (male) crosses over into negative (female). The female is the winged, crowned serpent. Again, these opposites also apply to the day/night cycle and also the waking/sleeping cycle. The tree in the background symbolizes the *axis mundi* – the earth's polar axis and also the human spinal column.

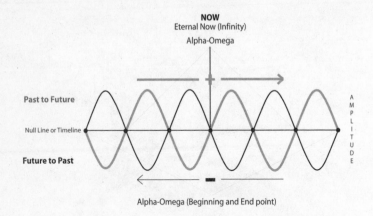

Figure 19: Time and Evolution as a Standing Wave
A 'standing wave' is a wave of energy that has become trapped between two points: when the travelling wave hits a point where it can go no further, it turns back on itself, becoming a two-way wave of energy-information.

and in doing so he experiences and becomes the Now – like Jesus, who said that he was the 'Alpha and Omega'. Of course this is a rebirth, and it is through this kind of rebirth in the Now, and during his lifetime, that the shaman then begins to understand the cyclical process, and how the life-death cycle is really a larger version of the waking-sleeping cycle. By accessing the unconscious in the waking-sleeping cycle via hypnagogia, one also accesses the unconscious knowledge of the life-death process.

As in the waking-sleeping cycle one is often unconscious at the point of death, and if so, then the cycle will repeat, with one having no knowledge of any previous lives, or indeed that one is creating one's reality and is trapped in the cycles one is actually creating.

However, becoming conscious at the point of death, as one would in the hypnagogic state in the waking-sleeping cycle, one becomes aware, and with full knowledge of one's condition, and so one becomes the Akh, a Shining One: sentient, superconscious. Everything collapses into the Now and one can choose either to exit the cycle, or to reenter it – but with full knowledge of one's condition, allowing one to create consciously and be able to awaken others.

It is interesting that the Mexican Nagals are called the 'Now Shamans' (*see Chapter Six*), which also reminds us of the 'Present Moment' associated with the ancient Egyptian god Aker, who like the Roman Janus, and also Baphomet, looks to the past and to the future.

Look again at the caduceus (*see page 50*) – is that not a standing wave diagram? And what is the caduceus associated with? The kundalini enlightenment experience, by which one experiences the Now – the superconscious.

Moreover we could say that everything we are and experience Now – meaning our very existence in material reality – is being held in balance between these two waves – much as the electron is continually appearing at these wave centres and is held for a moment in time. Of course this phenomenon at the subatomic level, of millions and millions of wave centres, appears as built-up static objects at our level of perception and experience. So again, we could say that even our very physical existence is at the 'midpoint' – but because we rely mostly on our left-brain perceptions, which are related to the flow of energy-information moving from past to future, we are only seeing half the effects, and so we build up a picture of reality from only having half the facts.

We would state, though, that the information in the future and the 'goal' of evolution itself, is not static but can be altered and changed, and that all the possibilities are given to us in that 'return wave'; we make our choices subliminally based on our internal dialogue, which is why the patterns we experience will tend to repeat and stay the same. Evolution is also a cyclical process of which we are subconscious (female and related right-brain) as well as a linear one, of which we are conscious (male and related left-brain).

We can see then that the phenomenon of physical reality – its actual creation at every point in its fabric, and so its very existence – depends on the friction between Yes and No, the two-way flow of energy information we find in the standing wave, and that it manifests and exists in that friction.

The lizard myth is a perfect example of how a great deal of such information can be conveyed through a simple allegory. As explained below in Chapter 11, Mary conceiving her child via the 'lizard entering the ear and exiting the mouth' is a metaphor not only for the rebirth of an enlightened individual, but also conveys the processes behind the creation and recreation of reality as well as the process behind the life-death-rebirth cycle known as reincarnation.

The 'lizard conception' of Christ is something which many of us would find confusing. However, this was intentional, as this information was being conveyed to only those who understood the processes, as explained briefly for the first time here, and because they had actually *had* this experience. It was the means by which such people could be recognized and brought into the 'higher initiatory fold', which had infiltrated the early Church – the same institution of power which had plundered and exploited this shamanic-pagan knowledge of the ancient Shining Ones – corrupting it in the process.

In other words, the 'shaman saviour' – being an example of shamanic and pagan power – was employed by the Church as the 'son of God' for which the Church conveniently acted as mediator for the masses. But at the same time, the wider knowledge of the internal processes by which one could actually become an enlightened 'god', by realizing the crucial point in the creative process and therefore taking control of it, was forbidden and all mention of it suppressed and eradicated.

Does this mean that the Pope himself was an initiate of the 'serpent cult' who played his part in the encoding of this knowledge? It goes to show just how deep, and how high, the Church had been penetrated.

This does not mean that popes understood this knowledge in the way that we have interpreted above. We are also using contemporary language to communicate these concepts. However, it is possible that the Shining Ones – the originators of this encoded knowledge – understood it in the same way or similarly, using the symbol of the 'serpent' to convey energy in the form of 'frequency waves' and themselves as the 'fish' that swim in these waves (the waves being the 'astral sea' of what we would call the higher frequencies of the spectrum).

This is why up to seven levels or more of the spectrum were depicted in the temple-pyramids of Mesopotamia – the ziggurats – and also the step pyramids of Egypt and America. Above all, we would say that the complex details given above, and conveyed via myth and religious allegory, are shamanic in origin and underline the 'Shining' enlightenment process which the shaman employs. *(See also Appendix.)*

Light from Darkness

The Power and Influence of the Shaman

'Live in joy and in peace even among the troubled. Live in
joy and in freedom as the Shining Ones.'

Verses from the *Dhammapada*, an ancient text attributed to
Gautama Buddha that serves as a spiritual resource for all Buddhists

Why do mystics of the modern world find it relatively easy to
convince us of the ancient wisdom? The answer to this question
comes from the realization that we are more in touch with the universe,
the Earth and the hidden forces around us than we comprehend.

Our modern sensibilities and rationalism have taken us away from
these astounding ancient insights. We no longer believe in the sun as
the god of light and life and yet in some respects we understand that
this is true. The sun does give us light and without it we would die. The
word 'god' is simply a term used before the existence of modern
science.

The beliefs of ancient humans came about through their understanding of the world around them. There was no science book to
learn from – they simply had to work things out for themselves and
give their own interpretation to the natural phenomena around them.

Since prehistory, shamans have exercised control by seeming to
know exactly what people were thinking, what worried them and what
pleased them. Most importantly, they knew how the environment

affected people. They understood how the mind worked.

The brain reacts strongly, though elusively, to cyclic patterns in the environment, although we are yet to fully understand this. Functions such as sleep, consciousness, memory, imagination and creative ability are all extremely complex and poorly understood. They too are affected by our reaction to cyclic patterns and the Earth's electromagnetic radiation.

Of course, ancient humans had no modern scientific understanding of the cycles of life and the electromagnetic currents around the globe. They understood these in their own way, through their rituals and sacred dramas. Over time they began to organize into specific groups and utilize 'special' people, shamans, to whom they sometimes attributed powers of foresight, the ability to predict weather patterns, water divining or energy dowsing and understanding foreign languages.

Earth Energies and the 'Paranormal'

It has been said that shamans were the first to interpret the 'secret currents' or 'ways' of life.[1] This could be interpreted to mean the Earth's ley lines – energy currents, or meridians[2] – and also the energy currents in the body, the opposite forces, which could be balanced for healing and good health. This healing was sometimes effected by the use of herbs and other plants and sometimes by the 'secret ways' of the shaman. These secret ways used the knowledge of electromagnetism, the Earth energies and possibly acupuncture as well as the venom and blood of the most sacred of Earth's creatures, the snake. The shamans would have understood the cycles and the balances required, and apparently could miraculously heal their patients. Today, holistic practitioners use electromagnetic meters and electric impulses to monitor, measure and administer healing in similar ways.

If the ancient priesthood of the Shining Ones knew the secrets of cycles and magnetism, they would also have had an understanding of the mind and how to influence it. Looking back at everything we have seen thus far, it is no surprise to find that a synchronization of the frequencies of the two hemispheres of the brain is conducive to psychic experiences. This synchronization or balance is brought about through hypnagogic trance. Hypnagogia is really a form of self-hypnosis. As we know, hypnosis and self-hypnosis have been used and abused over the centuries to great effect. The speeches of Hitler, for example, produced a kind of mass hypnosis on a grand scale. This is an example of how understanding the processes of the human mind can help those who want power.

If the Shining Ones used control for their own ends, perhaps this was how tens of thousands of people were fooled into believing that someone, say a pharaoh or king, was a god.

The term 'mesmerize' derives from the Austrian physician Franz Anton Mesmer (1734–1815), who believed the human nervous system to be magnetized. He coined the phrase 'animal magnetism' and claimed that magnetism from the planets had actually brought about healing at one church in Austria. He developed a therapeutic regime that incorporated iron magnets, magnetite and the laying on of hands, and built up a large following, many of whom claimed to have been healed by his animal magnetism.

Although using magnets on the body to achieve a therapeutic response is still a relatively untried method, there is some evidence that our ancestors dabbled in it. Also, as the Methodist founder John Wesley (1703–91) said, 'Consider how far bodily disorders are caused or influenced by the mind.'[3] If many illnesses are caused by an imbalance of energy such as electromagnetism, then perhaps the brain can help to cure the body by utilizing or balancing out this disparity. Alchemists hinted at this many centuries ago. It also seems that the ancients utilized the Earth and the energy of electromagnetism for specific healing purposes and thus made themselves 'gods before men'.

Science is currently looking into some of the more common paranormal experiences in relation to the brain. Extra-sensory perception, or ESP, is one such area. This is where information is supposedly transmitted directly between one brain and another. Scientists have as yet been unable to prove the existence of ESP, although they have had some unusual and unexplainable results.

As we write, scientists in Beijing are working on the 'Quantum Entanglement' theory. In this scenario, they put two people into separate rooms and connected them up to scientific apparatus. One person was flashed 100 times with a bright light while the other person's reactions were monitored. Amazingly, the results showed beyond doubt that the reactions triggered by the flashing lights had transferred to the other chamber and into the mind of the second person. The scientists have called this amazing effect 'Quantum Entanglement' and they are even now researching how it can be used in communication devices.

Bird Navigation

Man has always revered birds. From the shaman flying in a trance state across the land to the artist's depiction of 'winged angels', something has always attracted us to winged creatures. Maybe it is the idea of taking flight and disappearing. Maybe it is a shared understanding of travel and migration which speaks to our nomadic hearts. Or maybe it is the desire to join the great sun god in the sky, who was often depicted with wings. In ancient times the human soul was depicted as a bird and the ancient Egyptian *ba* was a human-headed bird *(fig. 23)*.

Birds are basically reptilian and therefore lack a mammalian cortex and mid-brain. Their migratory instinct comes from the cerebellum or old brain, which in humans governs our instinctive and spiritual element. It is claimed that many birds navigate using the sun and moon, while others use the north star. Lately it has been shown that they also follow roads, however this is due to the fact that roads are often built on ancient trackways or ley lines and in all likelihood also have electromagnetic properties imparted by their very structure. Research has shown that birds are sensitive to the Earth's magnetic field.

In an experiment, a homing pigeon was blinded by frosted glass contact lenses and taken 1,000 kilometres away from home, yet it made the return journey without error. The reason for this is that between the eyes of a pigeon there is an area of tissue with over a million bar-shaped pieces of magnetite or lodestone.[4] Magnetite is a magnetized mineral of iron oxide and was used by the ancients as a compass because it naturally swings northward. The ancient Chinese knew of its properties and thought it magical. They used an implement containing magnetite in the shape of the Plough (or Big Dipper) constellation on boards for divining the future. Although we have not yet discovered exactly how pigeons use the magnetite, we have seen that amazing feats of navigation are possible. In theory, the magnetite picks up the Earth's magnetic currents and triggers directional messages to the bird's brain. These are the same magnetic currents that the ancients discovered and built upon at node points or crossover points.

In 1970, Dr Robin Baker of Manchester University experimented on people to discover whether they could pick up these energy currents. Blindfolded volunteers were taken from their homes, disorientated and then asked to point the way home. A majority – above the accepted mathematical probability – pointed correctly. When, in later tests, bars of magnets and brass were attached to the volunteers' heads, only the ones wearing brass could point their way home. The magnet had affected their ability to 'see' the way.

A Czech physicist, Zaboj V. Harvalik, found that a percentage of the people tested could actually detect changes in the magnetic field as small as one thousand-millionth of a gauss. A typical child's magnet is 1,000 gauss. If, in our ancient past, we actually did have this directional compass within us, would it be possible to get it back?

The Anima Mundi

Maybe we have actually tried to retrieve it. In alchemy there is the idea of the 'spirit of the world', or *anima mundi*, a worldwide spirit which gives us information, including our whereabouts and way home. Relate this to the idea that the real truth behind alchemy is something akin to the kundalini enlightenment experience, which is in turn related to the spectrum of electromagnetic frequencies, and we can begin to see what the ancients were really talking about, especially in regard to the Hermetic tradition and the teachings of Pythagoras. The *anima mundi* is indeed *electromagnetism* and indeed, in part, alchemists were talking about a method of understanding the greater world around them.

Many para-scientists have recorded electromagnetic effects emanating from ancient standing stones. The Dragon Project, which was set up specifically to monitor energies from such structures, found that all stone circles in England and Wales occur within a mile of surface faults, which are known to cause certain electromagnetic effects. Where these energy lines cross ley lines and other ancient energy centres, many strange phenomena occur. A large cross-section of scientists and para-scientists have reported that people can experience peculiar effects at these sites due to the radiation produced. These include dreams and psychic abilities, seeing lights and hearing noises. All of these occur more frequently at times of greater importance such as the equinoxes and solstices, and they are heightened by solar activity: *the great 'sun god' in the sky aids our enlightenment process!* No wonder ancient man worshipped the sun god as the highest of deities. However, we shall discover that other celestial bodies also have effects upon us.

Dowsing and Geomancy

Our connection with the Earth's electromagnetism can also be seen in the ancient practice of dowsing. Today we use dowsing to discover underground fissures, water, artefacts and minerals. The dowser uses rods or a weighted pendulum and walks across an area. The rods or pendulum then move accordingly at the precise spot. Dowsers say that the instruments are incidental and react only to the vibrations, waves or electromagnetism that is being picked up by their bodies.

If scientists have shown that some people are sensitive to one thousand-millionth of a gauss of magnetism, there is a strong possibility that dowsing is a practical and measurable skill. This would explain how the ancients could plot ley lines and understand 'dragon paths' or *feng shui (see below)*.

There is much evidence to show that ancient peoples practised dowsing, or radiesthesia, in one form or another. In the Tassili-n-Ajjer caves in the Sahara, south-eastern Algeria, there are pictoglyphs approximately 8,000 years old which show what appears to be dowsing. Thoth, the Egyptian god of wisdom and writing, and the Greek magician-craftsman Daedalus are credited with its invention.

The Chinese, the masters of *feng shui* (Chinese geomancy), have also been credited with the invention of dowsing, in the third millennium BC. In the Bible we find that Moses (the patriarch who, according to Acts, had all the knowledge of Egypt) was adept at finding water with a staff or rod. However, the writers of the Bible vehemently opposed the tradition of dowsing (for example, Hosea 4:12). This was due to the fact that just about any layperson could dowse and therefore could take the secret knowledge away from the priesthood and reduce its power.

Later, the Catholic Inquisition found it necessary to stamp out dowsing once again, although many abbots, monks and clergy continued the practice in secret and even wrote extensively on the subject, albeit symbolically. What would be the reaction of the Church if the people were to find out that their own prophets, including their supposed Saviour, practised divination? As we shall see later, they simply choose to ignore the fact.

Geomancy is also a global phenomenon. It is the ancient form of reading messages from the Earth. The word comes from the Greek word for the Earth, *ge* or *gaia*, and -*mantia*, meaning 'divination'. But Ge or Gaia is also Mother Earth, so geomancy is about gaining knowledge of and from the mother goddess.

Ancient Greek, Latin and Arab writers tell us about geomancy. It is also referred to in the Bible in some remarkable places. The timescale of the spread of geomancy across the globe is much debated. There is, however, no doubt that the technique was universally used and it shows a survival of ancient mother goddess traditions right through into Christianity.

In geomancy, the Earth may be drawn upon by hand or with sticks and a response received and read. Special codes or symbols may be used, which are known only to the initiated. The symbols are usually lines, dots or stars. The final symbol is probably the one we should remember, as this includes the symbol of the fish *(see Chapter Nine)*. The Arabs used random marks and read these. In other parts of the world, earth was thrown into the air and the shapes it formed as it fell on the ground were interpreted.

In Chinese tradition, the most complex form of geomancy is *feng shui* (literally 'wind and water'), the interpretation of the lines of Earth energy (which in China are known as 'dragon paths') and the use of this reading to discover where best to place tombs or temples. The Chinese use a similar technique of reading meridians on humans in acupuncture, a popular and effective alternative medicine. The Chinese called the powers of the Earth *yin* (female, negative) and *yang* (male, positive). We have already mentioned the positive and negative phases in cycles, and as we know, everything, including energy, matter and magnetism, has a positive and a negative polarity, so once again our ancestors were there before us.

Modern-day dowsing has shown that sites such as Stonehenge, Glastonbury, Newgrange, the pyramids of Egypt and the ziggurats of

South America are all situated on the convergence points of these Earth energy lines. This is yet another example of these ancient beliefs fitting in with existing cultures. The Shining Ones who brought this knowledge did not change the lifestyles of the general population, which is why it has been so difficult for archaeologists to discover their existence. Instead they simply passed on knowledge, sharing the power amongst themselves and the few who were chosen to become Shining Ones.

Rites of High Places

From the early days of shamanism, high places such as mountains and trees were important and were linked to the idea of getting closer to the gods or ancestral spirits, sometimes by hanging on a tree. To this day some North American shamans bring on trance by being suspended by their wrists, hooked through the flesh in the style of crucifixion. The pain of this action is believed by many ancient cultures and mystics to move one closer to a knowledge of God. In Norse mythology *and on the opposite side of the Atlantic*, the god Odin attained knowledge via the same method of self-sacrifice as he hung from a spear impaled upon Yggdrasil, the 'tree of life'.

According to one writer on shamanism, Mark Dunn:

> 'The "Ód" part of the name Odin refers to an altered state
> of consciousness such as for example ecstatic trance states,
> as well as out of body experiences and the experience of an
> internal spiritual light. The "in" part of the name refers to
> "mastery" over whatever "in" is applied to. Odin visited the
> Underworld for this knowledge, and gained powers of
> raising the dead, prophesy, shape-shifting and flying.'[5]

The parallels are obvious. Christ was 'flogged' before his 'death', then he 'resurrected' – transformed, shapeshifted – and could foretell the future. The ritual flogging he is supposed to have been given is symbolic in that flogging also induces the trance state. The whole mythos of the Jesus story is an amalgamation of sun-god rituals and beliefs centred on the 'Shining' kundalini enlightenment process.

The ancient Egyptian *Book of the Dead* has many images of light and darkness, with three streaming rays of sunlight hitting the 'Shining Soul' of the initiated. The seating arrangements described for initiation are also similar to Christ's words, 'I come forth to Heaven and I sit myself down by the God of Light': 'I have made my form like his divine form.' In other words, 'We are the same.' 'Christ' is the title of one who achieves internal solar enlightenment and therefore appears like his father – the sun.

In the chapter 'Making the Transformation into God who Giveth Light in the Darkness', we find a familiar 'Christian' aspect to the text: 'I have come to give light in the darkness, which is made light and bright...'

This light/darkness aspect was not solely a later Christian teaching. It was used all over the world and had been for thousands of years. It is clear here that the teachings of Jesus, given by those who had spent time in Egypt, were influenced by other cultures, or by the Shining Ones themselves.

The Egyptian *Book of the Dead* will become more important to us as the wheels of history turn. Much like the Bible, the book is a collection of various texts written over a considerable period of time (roughly 2400 BC to 1600 BC) and its real name is more closely translated as *The Chapters of Coming Forth by Day.* Parts of the book, or whole versions, were placed in the grave of the deceased so that they could find their way to the 'light' of the blissful hereafter. The book offers advice on how to get there and how to answer the judges of the otherworld once there. There are also many hymns, potions and magic spells, said to have been written by the god Thoth.

Thoth was traditionally the deity of wisdom and of the moon, like Isis. His aspect of the moon was the reckoning and calculation of time.

He invented writing and was associated with magic, alchemy and medicine because of his power over writing and time. He acquired the Greek name of Hermes when Egypt was under Greek rule, hence the writings of the 'Hermetic' tradition dating from the second or third centuries AD, which were attributed to 'Hermes Trismegistus' or 'Thrice-Greatest Hermes'. The Hermetic works call upon people to become initiated and to receive wisdom and personal vision of the light of God to attain rebirth – in other words, to become 'Shining Ones' *and attain the enlightenment experience.* These works survived and influenced a whole host of Gnostic traditions from Christianity to Islam.

Another passage from the Egyptian *Book of the Dead* tells us: 'I have the power to be born a second time ... I am the Lord of those who are raised up from the dead ... He illuminates the earth ... I shall come into being in the form of the Lion-god.' The lion or sphinx was taken up by the Hebrews when predicting the future coming of their Messiah and, as we know, the lion is also symbolic of the sun. This second birth is literally the discovery of the inner sun – the illumination of the mind, the self-creating universe.

Jesus visited the underworld during his symbolic death, as the sun drops below the horizon as it sets, and following his 'otherworldly' ministry he 'flew' off to heaven and then came back. *The Book of the Dead* was quite specific that such symbolism was to be taken as pertaining to this life, and many Christian Gnostics also assumed Christ's teachings were saying the same thing: that we can symbolically have this second life of heaven on Earth here and now. This is the way to the inner circle of the initiated. To be reborn in the current body, which Christ spoke of to Nicodemus, can only be the spiritual awakening associated with the kundalini experience. The constant cycle of rebirth starts *here and now*, with 'chosen ones' becoming Shining Ones.

Shaman Power

Early European explorers of America called the shaman a 'medicine man'. 'Medicine' in the context of Native American shamanism obviously refers to healing, but it encompasses far more than this – it embraces all the powerful forces, or 'magic', at the shaman's disposal. The magic of the shaman is the ability, or seeming ability, to manipulate nature, and from this also came *the ability to manipulate man*.

Many shamanic ways were highly reminiscent of alchemy. In Greece, *circa* the sixth century BC, the shaman was called *iatromantis*, which means 'physician and soothsayer'. The ancient Greek shaman was also known as a 'purifier', the obvious term for his baptismal skills; *thamaturgus*, which means 'miracle worker' and was applied to the Christian saints in later years; and 'speaker of oracles' for his prophetic show of knowledge.

Like the Essenes of later years (*see Chapter Thirteen*), these shamans abstained from alcohol and sex and lived an ascetic life. To control their hunger they ate a plant called *alimos* (meaning 'not hungry'), which has been compared to the coca leaf of the Peruvians. They believed the soul travelled to the 'place of Apollo', i.e. the sun. In esoteric terms, this is again the inner sun. They carried out their healing by entertaining the power of the spirit of Apollo to keep the body alive. Falling out of favour with the god would bring illness, and only the shaman could restore this favour.

Not surprisingly, the earliest known Shining Ones from Sumerian myth, whom we will be looking at later, were also known as physicians – 'serpent' or 'shining physicians'.

However, being a healer was just one aspect of the shamanic role. It may have been that at some point in the past these various aspects were split between the priesthood, as they were in Hebrew tradition. According to some, archaeological finds reveal that all humankind's ancient myths are summed up in the role of the shaman.[6]

Cave paintings dating as far back as 17,000 years ago show the rituals and trance states of the shaman. The tribe or group would go to a dark cave, symbolic of the womb, and enter an ecstatic state via dances. The hypnotic and evocative sounds of the leather drums, the eerie flickering light from a single flame and the shaman's mystical chanting would all add to the mystery. Often these vision-inducing trances were brought on by fasting, and here we are reminded of the biblical prophets who went away into the wilderness, sometimes into caves, and fasted for many days. Later they would return with some great and mystifying word of God.

Another aspect was that during a vision, a shaman could understand the words spoken by a foreigner. Trilles, an investigator into shamanism, noted:

> 'During one of our voyages with Le Roy, we arrived at a village [in India] one evening and met a witch doctor who described to us in detail the route we had taken, the stops we had made, various meetings, the food we ate and even the conversation we exchanged. Here is a typical example: On the way we came across a small tortoise and Le Roy said, "There's tonight's dinner," and because we were very hungry, I added, laughing: "And if necessary we'll add the guide's head to it!" We were speaking French, so the witch doctor could not have understood a word, yet, without budging from his village, he had seen us in his magic mirror and repeated everything we said.'[7]

Trilles also tells us how 'tribal unity and awareness could be much stronger than we think, sustained by the activities of the priests, magicians and singers who go from tribe to tribe, rediscover them, visit them, as if called in some unaccountable way – through their mysterious sciences'. Shamans travelled widely, were respected, maintained tribal unity and used the 'mysterious sciences'. The people were in the service of these shamans and self-elected priest-kings, and this may explain how such monuments as Stonehenge and the structures of Central and South America could have been built.

Shamans also used words and names as if they were sent from God. Simply naming a man would have him dead, and this idea of the 'Word' as an effective physical creative or destructive power carried on explicitly in the Bible, as shown by the prophets and the account of Jesus casting out demons with just a word. Indeed, Jesus came to be seen as the 'Word' itself – the Demiurge, the active power of God on Earth and in the cosmos.

In the Bible too we have the shamanic interpretation of languages in Acts, when the spirit came down upon the disciples. This was related as flames appearing upon their heads – a distinct reference to the enlightenment aspect associated with the top of the head and with the symbol of the sun. This shows that the prophets and apostles were more than just inheritors of the shamanic knowledge – it was this knowledge that actually gave them their prophetic and apostolic powers.

According to Deuteronomy 6:8, the priests of Israel wore a phylactery on their foreheads – a blackened square case containing biblical passages – and in ancient Egypt we find the royal *nemes* headdress – a piece of striped cloth with the *uraeus* serpent insignia at the centre of the forehead – mimicking the serpentine kundalini aspect of the chakra system.

In many Christian cathedrals, there are portraits of Christians with strange marks on their foreheads. At Lichfield Cathedral in England, for instance, stone statues with circles, diamonds and triangles on their crowns or hats are everywhere.[8] No explanation is given for these images, no reason given for these marks, they are just there and in some very symbolic positions. The pictures of bishops are enhanced with the marks and face a large mystical image of the Virgin Mary with the bright rays of the sun shining from behind her. This can only be a symbol for the illumination – an emblem of the sight that is perceived through the 'third eye'.

Reflecting on all this, could it be that we use more senses than we know? Is the dowser's skill simply the result of being more acutely in touch with the world? As we move forward through the evidence, the answers to these questions will arise.

On Fiji they eat a delicacy called the *masawe* root. The cooking of this root is called the *vilavilareivo* ceremony, which means 'he who enters the furnace'. Many other tribes around the world actually do enter real flames in the practice known as fire walking. Initially, this was the role of the shaman, who would amaze people with his powers over nature. There is an example of this in the story of the three magicians in the biblical Book of Daniel. Shadrach, Mesach and Abednego, great magicians for the Lord, were bound and tossed into the heated flames of a furnace but emerged completely unharmed. Shamans are said to be able to control the laws of physics and simply cast off the pain of such a torment. This belief is a direct result of solar-linked myths. The effect is to show that the shaman is really the great Shining One on Earth and cannot be harmed by his own flames.

In Inuit shamanism, to become what is known as an *angakoq (see Chapter One)*, a shaman must call down the positive power of God – the solar divinity. This powerful spirit comes upon the shaman and is called *gaumanek*, which means 'illuminated' or 'shining' – the shaman literally becomes the Shining One on Earth.

There is nothing different here from the experiences of the biblical prophets, the Egyptian priesthood and Hindu and Buddhist monks. The shamanic trance state and the kundalini enlightenment, its psychic effects and resulting paranormal abilities and events are experienced in much the same manner the world over.

As mentioned earlier, the shaman also regularly takes himself away into solitude for a period of contemplation. This is common to many of the faiths of the world. Even today, we have pastors and priests who go away on retreats to be alone with God and to exchange ideas with like-minded initiates. Shamans, too, may use this time to meet up with others of their kind who have also withdrawn to the 'wilderness' – a term or phrase that can easily double for the shamanic underworld and the subconscious.

Many shamans claim to have moments of great spirituality. They experience times of joy and sadness comparable to those experienced by Christians in the Western world, the ecstatic experience of the Toronto Blessing being a perfect example.[9] In the midst of these experiences they gain their *gaumanek*, their enlightenment or 'shining'. Whilst contemplating beneath a tree (again, a metaphor for the spine and the chakra system), Siddhartha Gautama became the Buddha, or Enlightened One. Jesus took himself away to Gethsemane the night before his 'death', the beginning of his process of 'rebirth' when he became enlightened.

Like Moses in the Bible, the historical shaman was not just a prophet of the 'most high God', he was a magician and sorcerer with his caduceus staff and divination skills. He was able to descend to the depths of hell, as was Jesus, and return once again. And, like many a prophet of other future faiths, he could ascend to whichever of the seven stages (chakra levels) of heaven he needed to go. Celtic representations of meditating man and other Druid similarities show us that this shamanistic and 'Shining' belief spread throughout the known world, and this is basically why future additions to the tenets of the shaman – such as Christianity – were readily accepted worldwide.

Shamanistic belief takes the form of a duality of good and evil, light and dark. This carried on into the major religions, all of which have this dualistic belief at their core.

Shamanism is still alive today in the Native American and South American cultures, and in Africa, Central Asia and Siberia. Here shamans perform their roles and their souls ascend ritualistically to heaven during an ecstatic experience (Greek *ekstasis*, 'standing outside' oneself) probably brought on by narcotics, meditation or sacred dancing.

Subtle hints, missed by orthodox history, are beginning to reveal an ancient hierarchy of special people whose beliefs were shamanic in origin. We can see that they may have understood natural cyclic phenomena, that they created creeds and dogma around celestial cycles and that they used this superior knowledge to manipulate humankind. There are many belief systems in the world, but they all come from one basic and undeniable core, invented and developed by the Shining Ones.

In the following chapter we will try to piece together the riddle of where this elusive priesthood came from.

The 'Source Civilization'?

The Origin of the Shining Ones

'Serpent mythology is arguably the most widespread mythology known to mankind.'

The Divine Serpent in Myth and Legend, Robert T. Mason, PhD, DD

What do we know of the Shining Ones' origin? As we can trace their movements from one place to another, it would seem that they were a nomadic people. Yet, as we can see from the wisdom that has been passed down to us, they were too advanced to have been purely nomadic. Although their roots lie in primitive man, their level of development could only mean that at one time they had become isolated from the rest of humankind. It is possible that this seclusion period preceded a global catastrophe of some kind, which destroyed their homeland, forcing them into a nomadic way of life. This of course forces us to re-examine some familiar theoretical territory.

Throughout the 1990s we have seen a resurgence of the 'source civilization' theory – really an old theory that has evolved through many different forms, maintaining that an advanced civilization once existed on Earth and its people 'seeded' the world's civilizations with their sophisticated knowledge.

Spearheading this renaissance are author and journalist Graham Hancock and author-engineer Robert Bauval, who have not only provided new inspiration for regular readers of this genre but have also offered up this stimulating theory to a new generation of enthusiasts, revitalizing a subject that hit a previous peak in the late '60s to early '70s. At that time the 'advanced civilization theory' was placed alongside the 'ancient astronaut theory' made popular by the book *Chariots of the Gods* by Erich von Däniken. Naturally, interest in these theories emerged in the wake of the first moon landing in 1969 and the good timing of Kubrick's film *2001: A Space Odyssey*, based on the novel by Arthur C. Clarke. Throughout the '80s readers of the genre were kept satisfied by a series of books written by author and self-acclaimed scholar Zecharia Sitchin, who synthesized the two theories together. However, in all seriousness, the two books that really achieved a revival of the 'advanced civilization' theory were *The Orion Mystery* by Robert Bauval and Adrian Gilbert (1994) and Graham Hancock's book *Fingerprints of the Gods* (1995).

We would indeed endorse these authors' theories to a certain extent, as we have actually found more data that support them. But what these people may indeed realize but have so far failed to emphasize is that whatever scientific knowledge was passed on was originally based on fundamental spiritual principles and, more importantly, *one's attainment of the higher states of consciousness* – the spiritual awakening the ancient Hindus named kundalini.

This is not a reiteration of common phrases and words that have been overdone in the so-called 'New Age' literature. Our assertion is substantiated by the profound wisdom preserved in the world's esoteric literature and religious scriptures – much of which is ancient in origin. Of course not everyone who lived during this now forgotten epoch understood this knowledge – only those who had earned the position of 'adept' or 'master' understood it and utilized it, say a shamanic priesthood of some kind which we have now identified and who were known as the Shining Ones.

The Shining Ones as Global Phenomenon

What must be emphasized is that in-depth research into other civilizations and cultures does provide proof that the Shining Ones are indeed a *global phenomenon* in that this term or 'codename' is applied to certain intelligent beings that seem to have existed all around the world and *emerged at different periods in history*.

Indeed, the recurrence of the name is astonishing at first sight. It crops up in all cultures, though is often hidden, either through mistranslation or myth or intent. The Anannage or Anunnaki gods of Sumeria and Babylon, the Shemsu Hor or Akhu of the Egyptians, the Devas of Hindu myth, the mythical gods of the Americans and the Europeans – at face value, the names appear to be different from each other, but they all translate into 'Shining Ones' or versions such as 'Shining Father', 'Shining Soul' or 'Shining Sons'. The biblical Magi, for example, are from the land of the rising sun, the East; they are shamans, magicians – Shining Ones. The gods of the Jews, the Elohim, are the Shining Ones – the list goes on and on.

There is an understanding in all religions, by priests, pastors, rabbis and witches, that the Shining Ones have been there all along. Adherents of each individual religion have known about them in their own particular area, but because their outlook has been insular they have not made the global connections.

The Feathered Serpent

Like the name 'Shining Ones', 'feathered serpent' or 'plumed serpent' is also a worldwide appellation given to specially instructed beings who came from a mysterious land beyond the sea. It is the meaning of Quetzalcoatl, the Aztec name of the great pre-Columbian Mesoamerican creator god, the god of air and water. Quetzalcoatl (called Kukulcan by the Maya) is the essence of a shaman. His magical and creative abilities in the use of blood and sacrifice and in his clothing, all show his origins. He is the great white man with a red beard –

a symbol of the evening or morning sun. He is said to have come to the Central and South American shores in prehistory and it is very likely (especially with the travels of Thor Heyerdahl) that this solar priest travelled from Europe with a retinue and brought the ancient traditions with him. In fact, it is more likely that somebody took the beliefs of the Shining Ones and created the myth of the god-man of Quetzalcoatl, who is just another serpentine solar god.

Quetzalcoatl was called 'feathered serpent' possibly because of his 'astral' or 'psychic' abilities. Some have attributed these otherworldly powers to ancient spacemen or extraterrestrials, but it is more probable that we are dealing with people who had become enlightened through the kundalini experience and had formed a priesthood. Then, after what may have been a global cataclysm, those Shining Ones who survived dedicated themselves to the task of instructing the rest of mankind in their knowledge so that it could be preserved in the event of future catastrophes – hence the scientific and metaphysical knowledge which seems to have been encoded in many of the world's myths and legends.

The Serpent People

Foremost, these people were seen as gods, and because of the worldwide snake or serpent symbolism we are certain they are the adepts who were also known as the 'serpents' or 'serpent people'. There are many reasons for this and we are immediately faced with concepts that are both complex and multifaceted but that soon become laced together by the snake – archetype of the Shining wisdom. We now know that the various 'serpent' or 'snake cults' we find entrenched within different cultures around the world really originated from the profound knowledge and wisdom of the Shining Ones.

The 'serpent people' were so called because of their use of the snake for healing and to reach altered states of consciousness, and also because the snake's serpentine form could be used as a universal symbol to convey information about the hidden processes associated with the body (the microcosm) and the Universe (the macrocosm). After all, it was the 'serpent' – the kundalini experience, the evolutionary energy in man – that had granted them this knowledge in the first place.

What we have learned regarding the use of the two properties of the snake – snake blood mixed with venom, the original elixir of life[1] – is merely symbolic of the fusion processes by which one can attain the ultimate goal of enlightenment, illumination and immortality.

It is also possible that the consumption of the snake – which is very rich and high in protein – could have deformed these individuals via genetic mutation over hundreds of years so that they looked like snakes or serpents. The elongated skulls that have been found in several places around the world are evidence of this. It may be that these people even helped this deformity from birth onwards by placing planks of wood on the malleable structure of the head and wrapping bandages around it, thus forming the peculiar-shaped heads which the likes of Erich von Däniken, thousands of years later, would claim as proof of alien visitation.

Looking more deeply into the effects that would have been caused by this abnormality, we discovered that not only would the pressure on the brain have caused severe pain, but it would also have had amazing effects upon the very areas of the brain that we believed were responsible for the shamanic trance states. It seems we had found real people in history who were 'natural' shamans. They had either become 'snake-like' via the venom protein or they had transformed themselves by using it. They had experienced the enlightenment experience and so been seen as special, illuminated, 'Shining'. Their bloodline would have been very special indeed.

Anthropologist Jeremy Narby, who has studied the shamans of the Amazon, found that while in trance a shaman will very often see 'shining, giant snakes' that talk to him. And if he requests it, these serpents will pass on profound knowledge. Narby believes that these giant snakes are really the shaman's own strands of DNA – which are indeed serpentine and form a double-helix pattern similar to the two snakes on the caduceus staff. In effect, it would seem that while in this altered state the shaman is able to compress the focal point of his consciousness right down to the molecular level and beyond. If Narby is right, then it is no wonder that the serpent people held snakes in such high esteem, especially if they were always seeing and interacting with them while in a trance.

Certainly people are going to take issue with these explanations. Nevertheless, something that cannot be discounted is that the serpent people were linked with the worldwide worship of the snake – and we have to ask why.

Another writer who has researched into the worldwide serpent mythology is Mark Pinkham. In the introduction to his book *The Return of the Serpents of Wisdom* he writes:

> 'I have discovered a subtle thread linking most religious traditions together like tightly strung beads on a resplendent necklace. The uniting thread I refer to is the ubiquitous symbol of the world's spiritual traditions. Traditionally these diverse masters have been intimately connected with the snake, serpent or dragon and referred to by regional names denoting "serpent." They have been called the Nagas ("snakes") in India, the Quetzalcoatls ("plumed serpents") in Mexico, the Djedhi ("snakes") in Egypt, the Adders ("snakes") in Britain, and the Lung ("dragons") in China, to name a few. Collectively they have been called the "Serpents of Wisdom" and associated with a worldwide network of spiritual adepts known as the Solar or Great White Brotherhood.'[2]

Pinkham then goes on to say that this race of people first manifested on 'dual motherlands', two large continents which once existed in the western Atlantic and eastern Pacific – maybe Atlantis and Lemuria (otherwise known as Mu).

Atlantis, he says, was predominantly a materialist culture and Lemuria a spiritual one. If so, they would, of course, be examples of the duality which exists naturally in human consciousness and human creations. Looking at the world today, this would also in some way explain why the West is predominantly materialist and the East is predominantly spiritual.

Pinkham also writes that it was from these two landmasses that the serpent people 'disseminated the sacred knowledge, which would assist fledgling humankind in its quest to achieve spiritual enlightenment':[3]

> 'When their Motherlands eventually collapsed and began to sink to the bottom of their respective seas, the Serpents of Wisdom bundled up their ancient wisdom and migrated to various parts of the globe, where they were welcomed by the indigenous people as "Serpent" prophets. Under their guidance numerous "Dragon Cultures," which were comprised of colossal pyramids, multitudinous serpent motifs, and ruled over by Dragon Kings, eventually came into existence. These Dragon Cultures continued to survive for many thousands of years.
>
> 'Beginning approximately two thousand years ago, the Serpents of Wisdom and their Dragon Cultures encountered an inimical foe in the Christian Church. The patriarchs of the new Christian faith judged the old serpent wisdom to be heretical and began an initiative to completely stamp it out. Fortunately, before these upstarts were successful in their iconoclastic campaign, many of the Serpents disappeared "underground" and were able to safely preserve ancient knowledge. They later resurfaced as

the Islamic Sufis and their eventual heirs, the Templars, Freemasons and Rosicrucians, who kept the flame of serpent wisdom alive while inspiring and organizing the revolutions which have slowly precipitated a democratic world.'[4]

While we would agree with much of what Mark Pinkham has written, we are aware that his book also reiterates many of the same old themes that have become part of the 'New Age' culture. The connection with Atlantis is a cliché many of us have grown tired of hearing about. The time period connected with this ancient continent is so far back in our past that these things cannot really be determined. We can only look at the overall pattern, and this is one of the purposes of this book. We are certain, however, that with further research these issues will be resolved one day.

It does not matter at the moment if these people came from Atlantis, Lemuria, Mu, Thule or Hyperborea. What matters to us now is the nature of the knowledge they retained and utilized, the knowledge that set them apart from other mortals.

Clues as to why they were seen as different and revered as gods can be found in contemporary accounts of the paranormal experiences in which they were involved. All of these seem to be varying conditions of the kundalini experience. All the accounts describe an underlying 'energy' – a phenomenon that seems to be generating these paranormal experiences. It is possible that it generates *all* our experiences, and for that matter *our very existence*.

There is a part of our consciousness – call it the 'unconscious' – which is responsible for the autonomous processes that are happening within us all the time. Most of us are unaware of these processes, but these people became aware of them and therefore of that part of the psyche that runs the whole system. Based on the reports of the enlightenment experience throughout history, it seems to be a fact that we can achieve this. Perhaps at one time, say during the legendary 'Golden Age' that appears over and over again in ancient myths and legends, many people experienced it and man's consciousness was more in balance.

In any case, over time people began to understand what this experience was and then, possibly over hundreds of years, those who had experienced it formed an alliance and developed their understanding into a system of knowledge which gave them influence and power. This is all hypothetical, of course.

Where Did the Shining Ones Originate?

What we can say for certain is that the similarities that we find between cultures around the globe stem from Mesopotamia, or more precisely Sumeria, and from *a priesthood that moved around*. Sumeria will be discussed in detail later. But given that the cosmological beliefs of these Shining Ones clearly have a shamanic foundation, where do the roots of shamanism lie?

Some say that shamanism originated with the Tungus people in eastern Siberia, where the name 'shaman' itself comes from. According to Ward Rutherford, there is evidence to suggest that shamanism spread with the Bön-po religion of Tibet.[5] In the Bön religion, the shaman controls the three worlds or three 'cosmic zones' (underworld, Earth, heavens), so we could say that this may have been an early birthing place of the Shining Ones' belief system, and probably even the place where some of the original schools of the priests were located.

However, it could also be said that the Bön tradition, though extremely ancient, was not the origin of the Shining Ones, that indeed their home lay beyond, with the worldwide cult of the serpent. And when we say 'beyond', there is evidence to suggest that these people did come from a land now lost.

There are numerous legends of submerged lands or continents and we would suggest that although the Shining Ones' existence was contemporaneous with the Siberian and Tibetan shamans of old, their land was a unique centralized and advanced shamanic culture or civilization. They were a sophisticated people, isolated from the less developed world of their cousins, whom they no doubt ruled over. Indeed, our research also points to a Golden Age in the past when the Shining Ones were in the ascendant and the principles of the knowledge associated with the enlightenment experience were practised. This Golden Age no doubt produced the first ever religion or all-encompassing belief system, based on the concept of the *centre* – the inner sun.

Were the Shining Ones as scientifically advanced as we are today? Who can say that civilizations do not rise and fall in cycles – each time having reached the same level of technical advancement and sophistication?

Whatever the catastrophe was that ended the so-called Golden Age and the Shining Ones' reign as 'gods' and 'shepherds of men', according to the ancient texts the survivors came ashore in different parts of the world and were forced to live with their more primitive neighbours and so taught the rest of humankind their knowledge.

The Shining Ones and Atlantis

While we do not necessarily accept the theory that the legendary Atlantis was the homeland of the Shining Ones, there are some details concerning the lost continent that do interest us. These details seem to be some kind of symbolic encoding associated with the metaphysical principles we have already outlined, which we say have their origin in the Shining Ones.

The story of Atlantis has come down to us via the Greek philosopher Plato (427–347 BC), who wrote of it *c.*370 BC in two of his dialogues, *Timaeus* and *Critias*. One of the details that interests us

94

concerns the stone that was said to have been quarried from Atlantis. Plato tells us that one kind of stone was *white*, another *red* and a third *black*, and that the hillsides displayed veins of red, white and black marble alongside deposits of every kind of precious metal. We are told that Atlantean architects used this red, white and black marble to design their buildings, with these same three colours tastefully combined and contrasted.

Have we discovered the original source of the red, white and black theme which we keep encountering on our journey through these myths and legends? Not necessarily. Remember that these descriptions were given by Plato, who could be part of the code we are now unravelling.

As we have seen, the theme of red, white and black is related to different states of consciousness based on the triad. The red and white are interchangeable but relate to the male–female, positive–negative opposites of the triad *(fig. 6)*. The black relates to the neutral midpoint found between the opposites and also at the apex of the triad. These three colours also relate to the kundalini-chakra system and the principal nerve channels: the male *pingala* (red), the female *ida* (white) and the central *sushumna* (black) *(fig. 10)*.

We therefore cannot rule out the possibility that these colours *were* actually associated with the sunken land of Atlantis, which may have once existed, and may have even been a centre for the serpent people or Shining Ones. If so, then the colours were made to correspond with these esoteric processes, or vice versa, so that the code could encompass several themes at once, concerning not only the nature of reality and the place where the knowledge originated but possibly the very nature of the catastrophe that had lost them their foundation or centre.

The existence of Atlantis remains inconclusive. However, the fact that in the Hindu cosmology the god Shiva is red, Vishnu-Krishna is blue-black and Brahma is white reveals that we are dealing with a worldwide code, and obviously from the same source. Furthermore, the Hindu myth of Manidvipa is said to be an allegory pointing to the destruction of Atlantis by a flood and the survival of its three races – red, white and black – in a special kind of ark. The Hindu trio Shiva, Shava and Shakti are often depicted fleeing their destroyed world Manidvipa, the 'Island of the Jewels'. But could this also be interpreted to mean that this knowledge was rescued, preserved and carried over?

We are told that the Hindu trio also correspond to the three sons of Noah, who symbolize the three races of humankind. Again, we can see the symbolic device of the triad being used both on an individual level, as regards the three aspects of consciousness, and also on a collective level as the three aspects or 'races' of humankind.

We would note too that in ancient Egypt, where, as we will see later, the surviving Shining Ones migrated after landing in Sumeria, the land was divided between Upper Egypt in the south, which was signified by the colour white, and Lower Egypt in the north, which was signified by the colour red. The Nile itself and the fertile alluvial soil along it were black – as the ancient name of Egypt, Khemet, which means 'black land', testifies.

Plato's Atlantis contains another detail that points to shamanic ideas. In *Critias*, we are told that Poseidon, the Greek god of the sea and also of earthquakes, was given Atlantis, and there he fell in love with a mortal maiden called Cleito. She lived on a hill, and to prevent anyone reaching her home, Poseidon encircled it with alternate rings of land and water, 'two of land and three of water, which he turned as with a lathe'. He also laid on abundant supplies of food and water to the hill, 'bringing up two springs of water from beneath the earth, one of warm water and the other of cold, and making every variety of food to spring up abundantly from the soil'.

People tend to take the Atlantis story seriously and literally. It is true that we cannot really discount the reality of it, as the details may have been based on some truth. However, like the three colours of the triad, we can also interpret this concentric ringed hill as symbolism, as it surely points to the shamanic concept of the seven-levelled concentric sphere we saw earlier associated with the 'sphere of consciousness'.

The hill on which Cleito lives encircled by alternate rings of earth and water is obviously based on the shamanic world mountain or primordial mound of creation, as we have seen with the Stepped Pyramid in Egypt, the Mesopotamian ziggurats and even the prehistoric mound Silbury Hill in England. Moreover, in Hindu and Buddhist cosmography there is a central mountain called Mount Meru. Around this mountain, which acts like the hub of a wheel, there are again seven concentric circles of water, each separated by seven circles of land, including a range of golden mountains.

Returning to the Atlantis myth, the earth and water correspond to the male and female opposites, and the two springs, one warm and one cold, correspond to the two opposite *nadi* nerve channels – the *pingala*, which channels the hot, active 'fiery' energy related to the male, and the *ida*, which channels the cooling energy related to the female.

Interestingly, we see these same motifs associated with the trance state and the enlightenment experience in the town of Glastonbury, England. Legend says that after the crucifixion of Jesus, Joseph of Arimathea brought the Holy Grail to Glastonbury. Earlier we mentioned how the processes associated with the kundalini are literally 'drawn' on the landscape. We see this in the account of the mythical Atlantis, but unfortunately we cannot confirm it on the ground. However, we can confirm it at Glastonbury.

The name 'Glastonbury' translates as 'glass borough'. It was known as 'the Isle of Glass' due to the calm, still, glass-like appearance of the waters or lake which once surrounded the town and its central mound, the Tor. The deeper significance of Glastonbury and its Tor also stems from two unusual springs, which are said to have emerged from a cave entrance under the Tor. One of these springs is known as the White Spring, as it contains mineral deposits which give it a milky-white appearance, and the other is known as the Red Spring, due to its rust-red iron content. Like the blood of the snake, the Red Spring is said to have regenerative properties. Here we have yet another reference to the familiar theme of the red and white, but this time we see it in the real phenomena surrounding Glastonbury Tor – which is said to have been a place of initiation for the pagans and Druids of the region in Celtic times.

In Glastonbury Tor, we have a 'primordial mound' surrounded by seven concentric rings or levels, which was once surrounded by waters, and an upwelling vortex, along with two energy springs like the pingala and ida 'serpents' or nerve channels.

The significance of this was not lost on the pagan priests, who obviously believed this place to be the perfect 'gateway into the underworld, given that it reflected the fusion that goes on in the mind and body during the enlightenment experience. In the Grail romances this fusion is the 'healing' of the division, as in the Fisher King whose wound will not heal until someone reminds him of this division by asking the question 'Whom does the Grail serve?', thereby bringing the feminine principle to his attention, which then heals and illuminates him.

In a strange way this may explain why Cleito lived on top of the hill – as if, like the archetypal goddess, she represented the wisdom of the risen kundalini – and also why Poseidon prevented anyone from reaching her, therefore denying them this knowledge and wisdom. Could this knowledge have anything to do with the catastrophe that had befallen the Earth and resulted in the destruction of Atlantis?

Perhaps we will never know where the true homeland of the Shining Ones lay. However, many further clues regarding the migration and rebirth of the Shining culture are found in the symbolism associated with the world tree. This is what we shall look at in the next chapter.

The Tree and the Cross

Symbols of Spiritual Rebirth

'Nine whole nights on a wind-rocked tree,
Wounded with a spear.
I was offered to Odin, myself to myself,
On that tree of which no man knows.'

'Odin's Rune-Song', from the Icelandic *Elder Edda*

The tree figures in folklore throughout the entire globe and is central to all world religions. In Europe, India, America, Australia and Africa the worship of trees is so deeply ensconced in traditional beliefs that everybody must now wonder how these beliefs came to be so universal and so similar.

The Sacred Tree

A tree has strength, longevity and hardness, useful for buildings, weaponry and later ships, but of course it has esoteric significance too. Indeed the ancient Celtic word for 'sanctuary', *nemeton*, means 'grove' or 'woodland glade'. The term 'Druid' may derive from a word meaning 'tree'. The oak was very important to the Druids, who are said to have worshipped it as the world tree. In Greece it was the tree of Zeus and the Earth goddess Cybele.

We saw earlier how the shaman would climb the tree, axis of the three worlds, representing not only the Earth's axis but also his or her own spinal column and the seven chakras. Siberian shamans even mark the centre poles of their tents with seven notches. Among the Tsimshian people of the Canadian north-west coast, the shaman cuts holes on a totem pole; this serves as a ceremonial route which allows access to the house of Haidzermerh, the creator. The shaman then makes contact with the creator through a hole in the sky.

The Norse Yggdrasil, the world tree, is an evergreen ash which supports the Universe. The highest branches of Yggdrasil shade Valhalla, the Norse heaven, home of dead warriors. Sacred streams of living water feed the tree from three sources. It has three roots, which in one version extend into Niflheim, the underworld, Midgard, the human realm, and the world mountain of Asgard, the realm of the gods. These three were the three worlds of the ancient Norse people.

Trees, Death and Rebirth

The tree as the image of death and rebirth is universal. In South America, sacrificial victims were invariably fastened to tree trunks. In China and Japan there are sacred groves and trees standing at or just outside the entrance to villages; offerings are pinned to the trunks of these trees. In China, the tree was trained into the now familiar bonsai. The practice, which dates back as far as 1600 BC in the Shang dynasty, is an attempt to slow down the life of the tree and therefore render it a symbol of immortality – just as it was in the rest of the world.

In China, the elusive 'Eight Immortals' of Taoism, the Hsien, were believed to live in the sacred mountains and hold the secrets of life. They looked into the nature of trees as being connected with the elixir of life, a practice remarkably similar to that of the alchemists of Europe and the Middle East

In India, Vishnu was born beneath a banyan tree and was a reborn and enlightened being, like the Buddha, who was both born and obtained enlightenment (rebirth) under a tree. There are myths of gods being pinned to the tree or hanging from the tree. As we have already seen, the Norse god Odin (Ódhinn, Wotan, Wodan or Wodhanaz) the 'Great Shaman', was sacrificed on Yggdrasil; he was impaled there by a spear and hung for nine days to win the secrets of immortality and wisdom, while the Midgard Serpent gnawed constantly at its roots.

To be born again, the shaman sacrifices himself to the True Self, the inner sun – and the sacrifice is his own ego. Take for instance the image of Jesus on the cross (actually probably a stake or 'tree'). The biblical meaning of 'born again' is 'change of heart' or 'enlightened'. For Jesus, his True Self within was the 'Kingdom of God'. Like Odin, he too was pierced by a spear in the right side. Instead of nine days, Christ was three days resurrecting, and on either side of him hung a thief on a cross or tree – three crosses in all – on the hill (primeval mound) of Golgotha, the 'Place of the Skull'.

The worship of trees is fundamental to an understanding of the supposedly mysterious images from the past. Many have pointed to the structures of pyramids and other monuments, but archaeologists have not noted their connections to the universal tree symbolism, as well as to the primordial mound or sacred mount symbolism. The weight of similarities seen in the ancient world are staggering – not just in the buildings or the language, but also in the belief systems and the rituals which surround them. The tree was commonly used throughout the ancient world and for the simple reason that the belief and rituals of that world were spread by an ancient sun- and serpent-worshipping cult – the Shining Ones.

Even now, every December those of us who live in predominantly Christian nations will have a 'Shining One' in our own living rooms – either an angel or a fairy or a star positioned on top of the traditional Christmas tree, a pine or fir tree that also illustrates the inclining shape of the world mountain. The star is sometimes the pole star, or Sirius, the Shining Star of Bethlehem, symbolic of the reborn Shining Father

– the sun or sky god, risen above the tree of life and knowledge, and giver of the same. The angel is the supreme god that sits at the top of this tree. This Great Shining One, who personifies the source-centre of creation, also represents those who can reach him at the apex. The Altaian shamanic traditions say that the first shaman, Bai Ulgan, is 'seated on top of the mountain'. The fairy or fairy godmother represents the mother goddess of wisdom (the risen kundalini energy) who once held this top position. This goes right back to the earlier goddess cults, before the shaman (represented by the 'father god') usurped her and took her power.

The Cross

Like the tree, the cross is an archetype found in all cultures, mostly in a magical context, where it has power as the route to enlightenment – the 'serpent fire' – and as a symbol of the inner solar power.

The cross is unique in its all-inclusive symbolism, which covers cyclic or vortex patterns, the sun god, the Earth goddess, the life-giver, the great tree and the Earth energies. The symbol of the Aztec creator god, Quetzalcoatl, the feathered serpent, was a cross. The Aztec weather goddess also carried a cross, and at Cozumel it was an object of worship. Native Americans marked their boundaries with a magic cross.

In many cultures a cross was placed upon an initiate's chest as a symbol of rebirth. In around 100 BC, crosses were set up above the graves of the elect by the ancient Scandinavians, who also used them as boundary markers. The staffs of the Norse priests were crosses combined with the caduceus.[1] In many doctrines the four branches of the cross stand for air, earth, fire and water. The permanence and alchemical significance of this is obvious to the enlightened.

Forms of the Cross

There is an enormous variety of cross forms, all of which come from the same root – the most basic of altars, the sacrificial tree. The tau-cross, shaped like the letter 'T' (*tau* in Greek, hence the name), or *crux commissa*, is probably the oldest type. It is the cross of Thoth (the Greek Hermes), who became the god of the alchemist, the magician, the inheritor of the Shining Ones' legacy.

The Egyptian *ankh*, or *crux ansata*, consisting of a T-shaped cross with an oval loop known as the *ru*, represented life, and was held by a deity or king as a sign of his power to issue life. When it was held to the nostrils, life returned to the departed, in a similar way to the breath of life being breathed into the nostrils, as noted in the Bible and just about every other creation myth. Without the loop, this cross repre-sented eternity to the Egyptians, and this symbolism predates the Christian cross, which was introduced into Christianity *300 years after the supposed death of Christ*. The reason for this was so that this new Shining One, the enlightened king-priest-deity, could be linked with the old traditions, just as he was in so many other ways. Those with the eyes to see and the ears to hear would have understood the *vital sym-bolism* involved with this link.

The Bible never mentions a cross – the original word was 'tree', and almost all early Roman crucifixions were on trees. People were also often impaled or nailed to a pointed stake or tree, called a *stauros* in Greek, and left to die. So where did this idea of a cross come from? And

Figure 20: Forms of the Cross
Left to right: Tau Cross; Ankh; Latin Cross; Celtic Cross; Swastika.

who added it to the Christian Passion? The answer lies in the cult of Thammuz.

Thammuz (Tammuz) was a Middle Eastern god who died every year and rose again in the spring (at the same time as the Christian Easter or rising of Christ), matching the cycles of the sun. He is equated with Thoth or Hermes, but that's not all. He is also identified with other Middle Eastern resurrecting gods, such as Adonis and the Babylonian Marduk. The Jews obviously knew about the cyclic nature of Thammuz, as he is spoken of in the Book of Ezekiel, where there is a mention of 'women weeping for Tammuz'. The early fourth-century Gnostics took his symbol, the tau-cross, representing the sun, the Earth and the cycles of life, and made it represent the man who was to symbolize all these things and more. Jesus may have died on a 'cross', but symbolically he died on the shamanic world tree – the *axis mundi*.

In the Christian mysteries, the Latin cross, *crux immissa* – the cross of Christ and the most widely known cross in the Christian world – is symbolic of the universe, the cyclic patterns of life and death and space and time. It tells of the coming of the next 'man of light' or Shining One and in this respect is similar to the swastika *(see below)*.

The Celtic cross resembles a Latin cross with a circle around the junction of the four arms of the cross, but is a pre-Christian solar symbol in origin. It is remarkably similar to the majority of stone circles when viewed from above. There is a long alley or passageway through which the sun (or kundalini serpent) rises up in new life-giving vigour to the altar at the centre of the circle, which is the place of the thalamus and the chakra power centres within the head. The centre of the circle is the seed-point, the place of the sacrifice and the place to receive new life. This is also the point of intersection (neutral point) as regards the two beams of the cross, which represent the two opposites, and this is where the head of Jesus is located on the cross. Therefore, as above, so below, the sacrifice on the cross is found in the rituals of the stone circles on the ground.

Crosses and Sacred Architecture

Many cultures the world over, from Hindu to Aztec, with or without a connection to Christianity, have set out their sacred buildings in the form of the cross, all in the same style as the circles and the pyramid with the ritual centre at the head of the cross.

Many of these cross-shaped buildings, especially in the Americas, are built that way to reflect the four elements – earth, fire, air and water – and the four corresponding directions of north, south, east and west.

Many burial mounds around Europe are also laid out in a cross-shaped pattern, obviously due to the rebirth aspect of the cross. West Kennett longbarrow in England is cross-shaped, with the entrance facing the rising sun, symbolic of new life. Carrowmore, Newgrange and Knowth in Ireland are the same, and there are many more.

The Swastika

The swastika cross, also called the *fylfot*, *manj* and *Hakenkreuz*, resembles four Greek letter gammas (Γ) joined together, hence its Latin name, *crux gammata*. Originally this symbol depicted four serpents chasing one another's tails. It was widely used in ancient times and is found on many monuments around the world. Regarded as a symbol of good fortune ('swastika' is from the Sanskrit *svastika*, 'of well-being' or 'blessed'), it has been used by Mesopotamian, Cretan, Mayan, Navajo, Celtic, Hindu, Jain and Buddhist cultures. It was originally a sun and snake symbol, a symbol of the Shining Ones and of the Earth mother, the two important deities coming together in one symbol.

Also called the 'rotating cross', the swastika is believed to represent the movement of the sun through the heavens and the cycle of life. It symbolizes the oscillating vortex of creation (the clockwise-rotating swastika) and destruction (counterclockwise) and conveys the message that everything is pulsating, oscillating, from the macrocosm of spinning galaxies to the microcosm of spinning atoms and sub-atomic bodies. Indeed, the Universe itself is going through the same expansion and contraction process – each half of this cycle taking billions of years. Under the Nazis, the 'Aryan' swastika (German *Hakenkreuz*, 'hooked cross') became a symbol for German dynamism and renewal. Hitler first observed it on an Austrian monastery doorway and it became the symbol for his Thule Society, one of the roots of the Nazi movement.

The Sacrificial Tree-Altar

The symbolism and power of the tree and cross come together in the ancient stone circle. In prehistoric times, worship – especially more sacred and secretive worship – seems to have been carried out in groves. A natural grove or glade would have been modified, with a sacrificial tree being placed at the centre or entrance. Upon this 'tree-altar', the king-god or son of the king-god would have been sacrificed.[2] Also, the sun would have penetrated the glade, like the male impregnating Mother Earth.

Such locations would have been carefully selected by a dowser, who would have been able to sense the positive and negative telluric currents of energy – the Earth's magnetic 'lines of force'. These sacred places marked points where these positive (or male) and negative (or female) forces crossed and cancelled each other out. These crossing-points are small vortices in the Earth's magnetic field, rather like the chakras in the body, and all kinds of paranormal events happen there. They were therefore seen as perfect gateways into the other worlds.

A grove which marked a vortex would originally have been ringed with posts, poles or trees and these would eventually have been replaced by more permanent stone circles. At this stage, the tree-altar or sacred tree would have been replaced by a large monolith that was the focus of the circle. The movement of the stars and the cyclic patterns of nature would have been taken into account – and suddenly we would have had the most useful temple in existence.

Centres of Shining Wisdom

Around these magical circles arose great centres of learning, Stone Age 'universities' of the initiated. People would come from miles around to pay their tithes to the sacred priesthood, hear the prophecies, enact the rituals and learn.

Archaeological evidence confirms the existence of these great centres. In places like the late Neolithic site of Skara Brae, a Shining centre in the Orkney Islands, the buildings alone show that the inhabitants were no ordinary farmers. There were few trees on Skara Brae 5,000 years ago, so the buildings were made from stone and therefore have not disappeared over time. Further south, the great white horse carved into a chalk hill at Uffington in England, for example, signposts the way to the Shining centre of Stonehenge.

There are many other such sites, and even larger ones, around Europe. Chysauster and Carn Brea in Cornwall show the south of England as being important, probably because the priests could cross easily from this popular tin-mining area to the European continent. The most famous priest of all time, Jesus Christ, is said by tradition to have visited Cornwall with Joseph of Arimathea, who himself is reputed to have owned Cornish tin mines. Did they visit the old universities of the Shining Ones?

The bottom line is that the tree-altar at the centre of the circle or cross in such ancient structures represents the individual in the neutral-point trance state, the point also between life and death. This is the eclipse or quantum state, and the eclipse aspect is portrayed by the discs of the sun and moon often depicted on either side of the head of Jesus as he hangs on the cross. As we know, the trance state can lead to the kundalini enlightenment associated with the spine – hence the tree.

In the Hall of Ma'at scene in the Egyptian *Book of the Dead*, the deceased is judged before Osiris, the god of resurrection and rebirth. The cross is the judgement scales, with its extended arms and the head of Ma'at, the goddess of wisdom, representing the risen kundalini, at the top of the central column. The dead person is being judged by how balanced they are – to make it into 'heaven' they have to reach that fine point of balance between opposites.

There is another archetype associated with the tree, one associated with creation, and this is the phallic stone pillar or column – the world pillar. The most famous examples of this are the obelisks of ancient Egypt. To really understand the significance of the world pillar in connection with the Shining Ones, we must also study the myth of the phoenix.

Figure 21: The Scales of Ma'at

The Egyptians believed that after death, the heart of a deceased person was judged by being weighed against the feather of Ma'at, the goddess of justice. The feather symbolized purity and truth: only those whose hearts were free from the weight of sin would balance the feather and be admitted to paradise. The baboon form of the god Thoth, who records the verdict, is on the right.[3] Drawing based on ancient Egyptian original.

The Myth of the Phoenix

The Bird of Enlightenment

'To the ancient mystics the phoenix was a most appropriate
symbol of the immortality of the human soul, for just as the
phoenix was reborn out of its own dead self seven times
seven, so again and again the spiritual nature of man rises
triumphant from his dead physical body.'

Manly P. Hall (1901–90)[1]

In his *Metamorphoses*, the Roman writer Ovid (43 BC–AD 18) gives
a description of the phoenix – a mythical bird that closely
resembles an eagle and is associated with resurrection and rebirth.
'Metamorphoses' means 'changes' or 'transformations' and the same
work also describes the mythical 'Golden Age'. As we discovered, the
phoenix and the Golden Age share a common source in the Shining
Ones.

It is said that the phoenix existed at the moment the Universe was
first created and that it knows all about life, death and reincarnation,
secrets that even the gods do not know.

The phoenix is related to similar sacred birds in different cultures
around the world. These birds are synonymous with the concept of the
immortal human soul, which in ancient Egypt – the ultimate source
of the Greco-Roman phoenix myth – was known as the *ba*.

Figure 22: The Phoenix
The Phoenix rises from the flames. Drawing based on a medieval manuscript.

Figure 23: The Ba
The Ba bird bearing the *shen* ring, the ancient Egyptian symbol of eternity (see fig. 27). Drawing after *The Book of the Dead of Ani* (*c.*1250 BC) in the British Museum.

The *ba* was depicted as a human-headed bird and represented the soul of the solar god Ra or Re, who was later combined with the god of creation, Atum, to become Ra-Atum or Atum-Ra. As regards the pagan pantheon of gods and goddesses, he represented the supreme father god. However, in terms of metaphysical ideas, he also represented the genderless, androgynous, neutral source-centre of creation and so Atum-Ra's soul was believed to exist within every immortal god and goddess on Earth as well as within every mortal man and woman.

The *ba*, and therefore the mythical bird of rebirth and resurrection, represents the spiritual life-force energy, the divine spark, the gift of God given to every living being – the soul which represents the spiritual source-centre.

The soul was considered to be above the duality associated with earthly existence and this, incidentally, reflects the belief that one's consciousness must first be in a balanced or indeed 'neutral' state to enter heaven, as symbolized in the scales of balance in the Hall of Ma'at. We can also see the meaning of the masonic plumb line in this symbolism. The plumb line is used to build a straight and stable wall, and therefore symbolizes balance, 'centredness' and moral 'uprightness'. in Egypt it was believed that this balance was necessary before one could pass on through the Hall of Ma'at to the heavenly kingdom.

Another ancient Egyptian sacred bird which symbolized the *ba* was the *bennu* or *benu*. This bird, depicted as a grey heron, ultimately represented the soul of the creator sun god Atum-Ra, but usually it signified the reincarnated soul of the god Osiris – offspring of Atum-Ra who first reigned on Earth. The hawk and falcon are also associated with the phoenix. Both represent the reincarnated soul of Osiris and of Atum-Ra that existed in Horus, the son and reincarnation of Osiris. Horus was later identified with Atum-Ra and ruled on Earth in his name, and both gods became one under the name of Ra-Horakhty.

All these sacred and symbolic birds lie behind the biblical dove, which came to be associated with the Holy Spirit aspect of the Christian Trinity and was used symbolically in the Grail romances; one of these, Wolfram von Eschenbach's *Parzifal*, also mentions the phoenix.

Although the connections are rather complex, we see here a distinction between the holistic source-centre of creation or godhead (Egyptian *akh*, spirit) and the divided, individualized *spark* (*ba*, soul), as symbolized by the bird, which flies back and forth between the source-centre and the Shining One, who was seen as a god because he understood this spiritual/physical process.

In church windows we sometimes find a picture of seven rays radiating from the dove, signifying the seven levels of creation from the spiritual source. Because it symbolizes the soul and 'astral vehicle' of a person, the dove is also depicted exiting the mouth of saints at the moment of death.

We will be looking further at the various attributes given to each of these birds in the course of our enquiry, but we will begin with the story of the phoenix.

The Phoenix Story

In our view, Ovid's descriptions of the phoenix, conveyed as they are through alchemical metaphor, are obviously part of a code, as are the descriptions of this fabled bird given by other classical writers and historians like Hesiod, Herodotus, Tacitus and Pliny.

We found that not only does the myth of the phoenix make symbolic references to the enlightenment experience, which is often described as a rebirth, but it also suggests the rebirth of an influential ancient culture, presumably after a worldwide catastrophe which possibly ended a Golden Age. Because the 'Shining' appellation given to these people turns up everywhere around the world, this culture could only be the Shining Ones.

The image of the newly reborn phoenix rising from its own ashes therefore conveyed a brand new beginning for those survivors who also understood the internal processes associated with the enlightenment experience – the 'rebirth' on an individual level. Indeed, in some ancient mystery schools, an initiate who had this experience was known as a 'phoenix', because it was believed he had been 'born again' like the legendary bird.

In brief, Ovid tells us that when the phoenix has lived for a certain number of years, it builds itself a nest on top of a palm tree out of odoriferous gums and resins. (In addition to Ovid's account, the Roman historian Tacitus said that the phoenix 'infused the nest with the germ of life'. This is an interesting clue as to what exactly this 'nest' symbolizes.) Ovid then tells us that the phoenix dies by *inhaling the odours from the nest* and that from the breast of the dead body a new phoenix is born.

Ovid's account, though popular, is not the original, and we find that by the fourth century AD the myth has undergone a few more alterations. For instance, in a Latin poem by Lactantius, we find that instead of dying by inhaling the strong odours of its nest, the phoenix bursts into flames from the heat of its glowing body and that its nest of spices, ignited by the rays of the sun, becomes a funeral pyre. In another version written in the twelfth century and attributed to the legendary Prester John, the phoenix catches fire because it flies too close to the sun. After three days – the same length of time that the shaman spent in the womb-cave and Jesus took to rise from the dead – at the rising of the sun the phoenix rises from the ashes of its former self.

The first-century Roman naturalist Pliny the Elder gives a different account again. This time a small maggot or worm (doubling symbolically as a snake or serpent) grows from the bones and marrow of the dead bird, and taking again three days, grows into the new phoenix.

Ovid adds that after gathering up the body and nest of its parent (former self), the new phoenix leaves its home in Assyria, Mesopotamia (in some versions it is Arabia), and carries the body to the ancient city of Heliopolis, considered to be the first ever city in Egypt. There, the phoenix sets the remains of its former self down on an altar in the temple of the sun. This part of the story remains the same in most accounts and seems to have originated in Egypt. Some 450 years before Ovid, the Greek historian Herodotus (c. 484–425 BC) was told by Egyptian priests that the newly reborn phoenix wrapped the body of its predecessor in an 'egg of myrrh' (myrrh was used in embalming) and then flew to their 'city of the sun' (Heliopolis), a city attributed to Atum-Ra, to deposit the egg on the altar there.

Going by what we now know about the ancient Egyptian bennu bird – of which more will be said later (see Chapter Ten), and on which the story of the phoenix was actually based – this altar would be the top of a pillar. This pillar was the benben, the column that once stood in the centre of the temple of the sun at Heliopolis also known as the 'Mansion of the Phoenix'.

The benben was the prototype for the pillars that Egyptians called tejen but which we know as 'obelisks', from the Greek obeliskos, meaning 'a prong for roasting'. The obelisk is an important part of the phoenix code and with a little research one finds that amongst other things it not only represented the axis of the Earth and the human spinal column, but in ancient Egypt also the phallus of Atum-Ra. Indeed, like the phallus, the obelisk is symbolic of the Earth's *upright* or *erect* axis – the ideal symbol and the ideal position – and means 'fruitful, fertile creation' and also 'rebirth' and 'resurrection'. It is no surprise to find that the obelisk is now an adopted masonic symbol found in many major Western cities – and many of them have been taken from Egypt.

Unravelling the Phoenix Code

Now that we know what the 'tree' of the phoenix represents, we can see that Ovid's descriptions of the 'tree' and the 'oils' made from the tree which are placed in the 'nest' at the top of the tree are highly symbolic – which is stating the obvious really.

Taking the individual level here, these items are more clues to the *physiological* aspects of the enlightenment experience in that they symbolize various components associated with certain unknown processes that take place in the spine. By all accounts it is through the 'burning' bright light of this *internal* illuminating experience that one is resurrected or reborn like the phoenix from the flames and knows that one is 'immortal'. In other words, one realizes that we live, die and are born again. The rebirth of the enlightenment experience is also associated with the shamanic trance state, as the trance state can actually trigger it.

Now if the 'tree' of the phoenix is the spinal column, then its 'nest' must be the human head or skull. This also means that the contents of the nest, i.e. the egg which contains the body of the dead predecessor as well as the oils, are symbolic of certain organs inside the brain. But what about the phoenix itself?

As mentioned earlier, the phoenix is the equivalent of the bennu bird of the ancient Egyptians and the dove of Christianity, but it is also the firebird of Russian folklore, the yel bird of the Native Americans, the ho-oo bird of the Japanese and the feng-huang of the Chinese – a bird that again symbolizes the union of yin (female) and yang (male) opposites. Were we surprised to find the story had so many parallels around the world?

It is evident that the symbolic device of the phoenix was used by the Shining Ones to communicate several themes at once, not only concerning their knowledge and wisdom but also the nature of the catastrophe that ended the Golden Age.

Going by the more popular accounts, at the point of death the mythical phoenix – whose gold or orange-yellow wings give it a flame-like appearance –'self-combusts', turning its nest into a funeral pyre. After being consumed by fire, it is then reborn from its own ashes in the form of a worm which grows from the bones of the dead bird and 'slithers' away, only then to mature into a self-reincarnated adult phoenix.

The *vermiculus* ('little worm' or maggot) that grows from the body of the phoenix in Pliny's account is a detail which was added later. This is an obvious clue – and further evidence that relevant information has been added to the myth at certain points in history, as if to nudge certain people in the right direction. Those people are the initiates who would understand it and so solve the mystery for themselves – that being the only way a person would believe it.

What processes are these things describing? The clues to this lie firstly in the 'fire' through which one dies and is reborn and secondly in the little worm, which is really the snake or serpent. They can only be the kundalini, the 'inner serpent fire' – an experience triggered by the shamanic trance state.

If the 'nest' is the head or skull, then we can see that the funeral pyre in the nest, i.e. the 'nest being set alight' by the sun, is the inner sun. This is an unmistakable reference to the climactic phase of the enlightenment experience – the 'fire' through which one is reborn, the bright white light explosion which takes place at the centre of the head at the point of enlightenment.

We would remind the reader that the Roman historian Tacitus said that the phoenix 'infused the nest with the germ of life', meaning that it placed something within the nest. This would be the egg containing its dead predecessor, and this reveals how clever this code is. The dead predecessor in the egg is a metaphor for the memories of the former self and selves which are being carried over into the next life. In other words, the egg represents the reincarnating soul.

What all this amounts to is that the egg in the nest (skull) at the top of the tree (spine) is the thalamus, which is located at the centre of the brain and has often been described as an egg by contemporary physicians. Esoterically, the thalamus represents the 'cosmic egg' of rebirth and regeneration.

We can see here the complexity and correspondences of the Shining Ones' code – a bird's egg has been crossed with the human ovum, also an egg, which contains the genetic nucleus. This nucleus is the 'stone' – a metaphor for the seed-stone found at the centre of a fruit. The spherical fruit would be the skull. The reason why the thalamic centre in the skull is identified with the 'cosmic egg' is because being at the centre of the head, it was seen as synonymous with the centre of the Earth, the ecliptic centre in the heavens, the centre of the Universe and the very centre of creation itself.

Furthermore, the spherical head, like the Earth, is associated with the feminine principle, as in the Earth being the body of the world mother. Again, these are shamanic beliefs, which means that the people who devised this code and have been adding to it throughout history were familiar with these shamanic principles.

If the spherical head is associated with the female, then the straight body or spine is associated with the male, and here we have the two binary symbols I and O, which are fused together in the ankh symbol, the *crux ansata*.

In summary, then, if the tree or world pillar on which the phoenix perches is the spinal column, and the apex or pyramidion of the pillar is the head, then the egg is the thalamus – the part of the body that was believed to represent the soul and the part that was passed over from incarnation to incarnation.

So we can see that the phoenix bringing the egg containing the ashes of its former self to the obelisk of the temple of the sun – has the Shining Ones' belief in reincarnation at its core.

As we know, the phoenix places the egg on top of the pillar. The bennu bird of ancient Egypt, on which, as already mentioned, the legendary phoenix is largely based, is associated with the benben pillar of Heliopolis and also with the miniature benben, or *benbenet*, the pyramidion (capstone) of the pyramid and obelisk. The pyramidion is the same as the capstone of the benben, and so the same symbolism can be applied to both.

This would also mean that the pyramid is a large-scale benben stone and therefore also a large representation of the skull or head where rebirth takes place. If the capstone represents the egg of the phoenix or bennu then it also represents the thalamus in the brain, which is associated with the centre of the seventh chakra point – the bindu point above the head, the inner sun.

It is said that the opening of the 'third eye' – seeing with inner vision – as associated with hypnagogic trance state, is really related to the thalamus, and that this awakening in the thalamus is activated by some kind of synchronization taking place between the pineal and pituitary glands in the brain which secrete chemicals – the oils of the tree. The awakening of the third eye – which is also the name given to the sixth chakra, located just behind the centre of the brow – can lead to the enlightenment experience.

It's interesting that the Egyptian word *bennu* sounds like the Hindu word *bindu* and that the benben stone signified the sun, as did the bennu bird. The root of *bennu* and *benben* is probably an Egyptian word meaning 'to rise' – a sense that links the rising sun, the phoenix (soul) that rises again and the rising kundalini.

We would note, though, that the capstone, or *benbenet*, of the Great Pyramid at Giza is missing from the structure. Perhaps, as conventional Egyptology has it, it has simply fallen off, like those of other pyramids, but if so, it has never been discovered. What if it was *never there in the first place* – as if emphasizing the point that in general man is unconscious of this spiritual source and these life-death-rebirth processes, and that his acknowledgement of them will initiate a collective rebirth? We would conclude that only then would be the right time to place the capstone on top of the Great Pyramid.

Overall, the phoenix myth and everything associated with it is a code that conveys the processes associated with reincarnation. The process of rebirth – kundalini – that can happen to an individual during his or her lifetime is being used to convey the message that this same process plays its part at the point of death and in the reincarnation of the self after physical death.

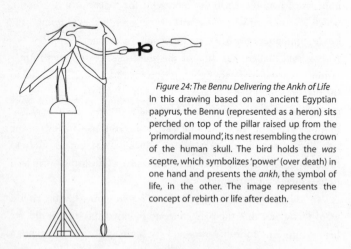

Figure 24: The Bennu Delivering the Ankh of Life
In this drawing based on an ancient Egyptian papyrus, the Bennu (represented as a heron) sits perched on top of the pillar raised up from the 'primordial mound', its nest resembling the crown of the human skull. The bird holds the *was* sceptre, which symbolizes 'power' (over death) in one hand and presents the *ankh*, the symbol of life, in the other. The image represents the concept of rebirth or life after death.

The symbolic phoenix device is also being used to convey the 'rebirth' of the Shining Ones after the 'death' of their people and the destruction of their homeland. It therefore also symbolizes the rebirth of the human race as a whole.

For those who are sceptical of our interpretation, we would like to stress that we have merely followed a logical path to this conclusion, using the clues we have been given. Moreover, we haven't finished yet.

The Caduceus, Roman Eagle Standards, Totem Poles and Maypoles

If we look again at the top of the caduceus *(fig. 12)*, we see the 'winged orb'. On one level the wings could be interpreted as belonging to the *ba*, phoenix or bennu bird which lands on top of the pillar or obelisk, here represented by the central staff of the caduceus. They could also belong to the dove, which in the Grail legends makes its appearance at the Grail castle every Good Friday – the Friday following the first full moon after the spring equinox, one of the two 'neutral points' in the annual cycle.

On one level of understanding, the orb also represents the skull, and at a higher level it is the egg of the bird which is placed inside the nest – again the skull. As we have seen, the egg is the thalamus, associated with the opening of the third eye and with the centre of the seventh chakra, the bindu point. On another level the bird is the human soul that is believed to leave the body during trance and fly out of the body as a pinpoint of light at the moment of death. The orb also represents this pinpoint of light, the egg which the bird carries. It is sometimes also depicted as a 'flying eye' – the eye of Horus, the god shown as a falcon or hawk, whose words feature in the ancient Egyptian *Book of the Dead*:

'I am the Dweller in the Egg. I am he who turns in the disc.'

In myth and symbology, the eagle can be equated with the phoenix, as they are described as similar in appearance. This is interesting, bearing in mind that the phoenix lands on top of the shamanic world pillar, as the Roman army used the eagle as its emblem and it stood perched on top of the standards that were carried into battle.

In the Roman army, each century, cohort and legion had its own standard and during battle it was held by an officer called a standard-bearer – a *signifer* or *aquilifer* – who, like the shaman, often wore animal-head skins on his head. The eagle standard-bearer would wear a lionskin headdress.

As the standards could be seen above the heads of the soldiers, they were used to keep them together as they went into battle. The standard was symbolic of the soul or 'life force' of the legion and also represented its achievements. To lose the eagle standard in battle was a terrible disgrace because it actually symbolized the spinal column of each man that accompanied it and therefore the life of the men – not that they saw it that way, as the symbolism is ancient and many would have forgotten the origin of the tradition. However, for these reasons, it was considered a great victory to have captured the standard of the enemy.

While we are on the subject of ancient warfare, perhaps we should mention the symbolism of the weapons used in battle. The attacking sword, spear and arrow are linear-shaped objects and are therefore associated with the male. The round shield used for protection is associated with the receptive female. The image we have of two armies, from ancient times up to medieval times, slugging it out using these binary symbols, one in each hand, reflects the struggle between the conscious self and the subconscious, the left brain and the right brain.

To go back to Roman standards, they were tall poles adorned with various insignia and symbols, some of which included many different types of animal, much like the totem poles of some Native American peoples, which display an ascending order of creatures with several carved figures (sometimes human) superimposed upon one another, topped by the mythical eagle-like thunderbird. The totem pole on which the thunderbird is perched, like the phoenix on the obelisk, with its wings outspread, is very similar to the caduceus, which symbolizes the kundalini-chakra system. The sacred bird, of whatever sort, represents the ascended soul of a person, which has risen through the seven levels associated with the material world.

In the totem pole, the chakras – or the points on the caduceus staff where the two snakes cross each other – are represented by the animals, mythical creatures or human-like figures in ascending order.

In the Hindu depictions of the seven chakras we find different animals portrayed in the centre of the chakra, each depicting a certain characteristic associated with the chakra level. These details reveal a profound connection between the traditional totem pole and Roman standards and the kundalini-chakra system associated with the spine.[2]

Another example is the traditional European maypole – a fertility symbol used during the ancient pagan spring festival of Beltane (1 May). On one level the maypole – often a fir tree stripped of its branches – represents the phallus, but on another level it is also the spine. The circular wreath placed at the top of the maypole makes a reference to the feminine principle, which is signified by curves, circles and spherical shapes. This is also the vagina, but on another level it again symbolizes the skull and the thalamic third eye – the 'egg' to be 'fertilized', opened, activated:

> 'The Maypole represents the phallus of the God [Atum-Ra].
> The wreath atop represents the vagina of the Goddess. As
> the Maypole is danced, the ribbons wind around the pole
> and the wreath lowers, symbolizing the Divine Marriage,
> the sexual union of God and Goddess [opposites].'[3]

The maypole has ribbons of two colours, again red and white, the same colours we see on the traditional barber's pole (barbers were once doctors, hence the healing aspect of the serpent associated with these two colours), and these ribbons are held by the male and female dancers, the males holding the red ribbons with their left sides to the pole and the women holding the white ribbons with their right sides to the pole. We should note that the left and right sides of the body are connected to the right and left hemispheres of the brain respectively. The male and female couples – four of them, making eight people in all – weave in and out, and over and under each other as they move around the pole, symbolizing the spiralling serpents of the caduceus, which in turn symbolize the pingala and ida nerve channels of the chakra system.

We are told that the maypole is sometimes anointed with oils such as myrrh. This is an interesting connection in regard to the phoenix's oils, which are symbolic of the secretions of the glands in the brain associated with the enlightenment experience.

We can see that such devices are all symbolic – encoded snippets of information to bring the initiate to the Shining Ones' system of knowledge based around the kundalini process.

The Eye of Ra

Godhead, Seed, Source-Centre and the Inner Sun

'Behold, oh ye Shining Ones, ye men and gods…'

The Egyptian *Book of the Dead*, Chapter 134

A s we have seen, the phoenix myth contains information about the processes associated with rebirth. In Egypt this was linked to the source-centre.

It is said that in ancient Egypt the simple circle with a dot at its centre was adopted as the sun symbol in that the dot depicted the sun – the Eye of Ra – at the centre of the solar system. Of course, for many years it was believed, as stated by the Church, that the Earth was the centre of the solar system. Then Copernicus proved that the sun is at the centre and the Earth merely revolves around it, but the ancients had known that all along. And even though it predates Copernicus by thousands of years, according to esoteric sources this interpretation of the ancient Egyptian sun symbol is correct. However, there are deeper

Figure 25: The Ancient Egyptian Sun Symbol
The dot in the centre of the circle represents the 'zero node' in consciousness, or psychic 'gateway' (see also fig. 1).

meanings to this symbol, which is evident in the clues presented in Egyptian art, and the original meaning goes deeper than anything suggested by Egyptologists and symbologists.

Through our research into esoteric literature and symbolism, we discovered that ultimately the dot represents the centre of all creation – the Absolute – the Godhead, the monotheistic God of various religions and the all-seeing Grand Architect or Supreme Being of masonic lore. But furthermore, we would say it also represents the 'inner sun', and in terms of how we would understand it today, it also represents the source-centre of the collective consciousness, where all energy is fused at a point – a 'point of singularity'.

If so, then the circle of the sun symbol, and particularly the space inside, represents the surrounding energy matrix where this same energy/information is measured (quantified) and spread out in space and time, i.e. the Universe and everything in it.

In terms of the physical universe, the dot at the centre represents the proto-atom that seeded the universe in the so-called 'Big Bang'. Scaling downwards towards the microcosm, it is therefore logical that it would also represent the centre of the Earth and the centre of the human brain as well as the nucleus of a cell, atom and subatomic particle.

This symbol therefore expresses the concept that everything is being created and recreated from its own centre – as in the universal model of the torus or spherical toroidal vortex, which scientists are considering to be the shape of the Universe.

We are told that the surrounding circle or matrix and everything in it represents what in Hinduism is termed *maya* (Sanskrit for 'illusion') – that the 'true reality' is that everything is really contained within this non-dimensional point, one's own centre, the essence of Truth itself. This dot or point is known as the *laya* or *shunya* (zero-centre) and is regarded as the source of all creativity and intelligence; the Supreme Void, the Godhead, the Absolute, the Eternal Now, where the energy-information of the time and space dimensions is fused to a point, while at the same time it is spread and divided outside that point. This point is the ultimate paradox, as it is nothing and everything at the same time. It is our understanding that this point is also not only nowhere – being non-dimensional and non-local to our senses – but also everywhere in space and time, i.e. localized and 'dimensionalized', as it resides at the zero-centre of each and every so-called 'elementary' particle.

The reader may have heard of the akashic records, a realm in consciousness where all the information of the Universe is supposed to be stored. Again, this abstract realm can only be what Eastern mystics refer to as the Absolute – the source-centre of consciousness, as illustrated by this dot at the centre of the circle.

This centre point is also the seed-stone that we find at the centre of a piece of fruit, the point that was cryptically named the 'stone', which has had people searching for a real stone ever since, even though it has been stated that it is a 'stone that isn't a stone'.[1] It was realized that the illusory circle of phenomena, the Universe that surrounds the source-centre, like the fruit that surrounds the 'seed-stone', was composed of a series of repeating cycles.

Atum-Ra and the Creation of the Universe

The Egyptian sun symbol has its origins in the most popular of the creation myths of ancient Egypt, the Heliopolitan version. This is named after the city of Heliopolis, which is closely linked with the phoenix, as we have already seen.

It is said that in the beginning, the Universe was a 'formless, watery void' named Nun or Nu. The god Atum, whose name means something like 'the All', existed before creation, 'floating inert alone in Nun' as one source puts it. Like the Tao of Chinese tradition, Atum-Ra, was neuter, an androgynous figure neither male nor female, but encompassing both opposites and their principles. However, in the creation account Atum takes on male form.

Out of the waters of Nun emerged a phallic-shaped hill – the primeval mound. This was the place upon which the first act of creation could occur. On this phallic hill, Atum enfolded his hand around his penis (demonstrating the union of opposites) and masturbated to an explosive orgasm, his seed igniting the birth of the Universe and all life within it. From this fusion point, the Universe expanded, unfolding like a flower through many levels. In the minds of the ancients, this was how the material world became manifest.

The primeval mound, the first 'world mountain', is a metaphor for a vortex of energy – a circular matrix created from its own centre. Some traditions hold to the idea that the waters of Nun surround it. However, it would be more correct to say that the waters (the potential energy) are at the very centre of the mound – like the lava at the centre of a volcano.[2]

It is worth noting that the phallus of Atum-Ra and the primordial mound of creation were both symbolized by the benben obelisk at the temple of the sun at Heliopolis. This pillar marked the site of the mound and, as already mentioned, symbolized the spinal column and was the place where the bennu or phoenix was said to alight.

Atum-Ra's mythical act of creation is similar to the creation of the Universe as explained by modern physicists – the popular Big Bang theory. This holds that the Universe was seeded into life from a point of singularity – the proto-atom of potential energy-information which exploded its contents outwards in all directions.

As the matrix of the Universe expanded, there appeared within it similar points of singularity – centres of the vortices we call atoms and subatomic particles from which all manner of complex patterns of creation are blinking into and out of existence. At another level there are also the black-hole/white-hole vortices – known to our astrophysicists as supermassive black holes – which the galaxies of suns swirl around and from which they are being both created and destroyed.

Ancient Hindu cosmology is very similar. This ancient Egyptian

imagery of the energy rising up through the phallus of Atum-Ra, surrounded by the 'waters' – the matrix of space – is evident in ancient
Hindu lingam-yoni (erect penis-vagina) symbolism. Hindu figures of
the lingam surrounded by the yoni appear to be three-dimensional
versions of the ancient Egyptian sun symbol. It is said that from this
union, the whole universe comes into being. And this would be
correct, as the sexual act reflects the fusion of opposites, the same
mechanistic process that goes on within one's consciousness and also
at the microcosmic levels of reality, the 'seeds' from which all things
are being continually created and recreated.

Atum-Ra and the Ennead

Immediately after the burst of creation from Atum-Ra's phallus, two
beings – the god Shu and the goddess Tefnut – emerge. Shu is the
active force in the universe, the 'male principle' which makes things
happen, and Tefnut is the 'female principle' which limits, regulates,
controls and directs the male energy. She is also known as Ma'at, the
goddess of justice and judgement.

In effect, these interactions between the male and female principles
reflect the same old dual struggle between the yin and yang energies
going on at every level of reality. What they are seeking is balance and
union. On a physical level, this union is the sex act between male and
female. As we will see, it is also expressed in the shaman and
shamaness who journey together to the worlds of spirit.

To return to the Egyptian creation myth, from the sexual union of
Shu and Tefnut emerge the 'Earth god' Geb and the 'sky goddess' Nut
and from their sexual union emerge the four famous deities known as
Osiris, Isis, Set and Nephthys. Osiris takes his sister Isis as his consort
and Set does likewise with Nephthys. These two pairs of deities not
only express the same male–female duality but also the principles of
'light' and 'dark' and 'good' and 'evil'.

Together, this pantheon of nine gods and goddesses is known as the

Ennead, from *ennea*, the Greek for 'nine'. So the Ennead consists of the One (Atum-Ra, represented by the obelisk), plus the eight gods that One generates. Standing in St. Peter's Square in Rome is another obelisk, brought from Egypt in Roman times. Like the dot in the centre of the sun symbol and the lingam that pierces the yoni, this obelisk is at the centre of a circle, in this case an eight-rayed circle design in the paving that radiates out across St. Peter's Square. Although it conveys the same understanding as the Egyptian sun symbol, this eight-rayed design is based on the sun symbol of Shamash *(fig. 26)*, one of the Sumerian Shining Ones *(see Chapter Nine)*, and both designs are themselves based on the early concentric sphere of the shaman.

Figure 26: The Ancient Sumerian Sun Symbol
The eight-rayed symbol of the Sumerian solar god Shamash.

The Shen Ring: Insignia of the Shining Ones

To convey the understanding of cycles in a simple picture, the circle of the sun symbol we saw earlier (the circle with the dot at its centre) developed into the Egyptian *shen*, or *shenu*, ring amulet which symbolized eternity and meant among other things 'all that the sun encircles' or 'all that is'.

In his book *Egyptian Magic*, E. A. Wallis Budge tells us that the *shen* represents the sun's orbit. However, there is a deeper meaning that seems to have evaded the Egyptologists of the late nineteenth to early twentieth centuries.

We note that the *shen* ring is carried by the *ba* – often depicted as a human-headed bird that symbolized the soul of a person both alive and dead *(see fig. 23)*, similar to the 'astral body' of out-of-body experiences, or OBEs. The *shen* ring is a rod and ring bound together, and so we would interpret it as the 'union' or fusion of the male and female opposites. It is interesting to note that the ring and rod are similar to the symbols I and O used in modern-day binary code. In these binary symbols we also see the shaman's stick and the drum, which are brought together on every hypnotic beat so that the shaman can tune into the neutral, hypnagogic trance state to access the other worlds via his astral body.

Again the soul was believed to be neutral, androgynous – neither male nor female, but both – and so at the point of death it was believed

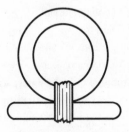

Figure 27: The Ancient Egyptian Shen Ring
The Egyptian symbol of eternity and eternal life (see also fig. 28).

Figure 28: The Cartouche
Dubbed a 'cartouche' (cartridge) by early 19th-century French scholars from its resemblance to a gun cartridge, the ring within which each pharaoh's name was written is in fact a form of the *shen*, the 'ring of eternity', symbolizing eternal life.

that one had to achieve this fusion of opposites within to become the soul that could travel to the higher worlds, and this is the meaning of the insignia of the *shen* ring as held by the *ba*.

The *shen* ring was later used as a symbol of protection and became elongated as the cartouche in which the pharaoh's name was always written *(fig. 28)*. As well as expressing the belief in the pharaoh as king of 'all that is', as Wallis Budge put it, it symbolizes his eternal life and protects him from the chaos that results from the imbalance of opposites. For the ancient Egyptians, fending off the forces of chaos was a key role of the pharaoh. They well understood the inner strength and stability that comes with uniting and binding opposites as One, as demonstrated in the ideal of Upper and Lower Egypt united under one pharaoh, the Lord of the Two Lands.

The *shen* ring, or something like it, is also held by Mesopotamian gods and goddesses as if they had some kind of power and control over this 'fusion of opposites' by which the soul was accessed via out-of-body trance states. Such phenomena were part of their experience, and our theory is that these beings even personified these experiences. After all, they were known as the 'Shining Ones' because they had experienced and possessed the 'Shining' of enlightenment.

No one really knows for certain what object the *shen* physically represents, and hence precisely what meaning it conveys, and no one has examined closely the link between the Mesopotamian and Egyptian versions. There are other connections, too: the Celtic counterpart of the *shen* ring is the torc (neck-ring), as held by the horned figure (perhaps Cernunnos, the Horned God) on the famous Gundestrup Cauldron.

The point at which the opposites are bound together, as sometimes depicted in the *shen* ring and cartouche by what appears to be literally a cord binding, marked the point of fusion, which was also recognized as the most important point in every cycle, as we have seen. This ring was developed further to illustrate these cycles. And because the life

130

force energy that drove these cycles was symbolized by the snake or serpent, the cycle also came to be depicted as a snake swallowing its own tail – the ouroborus *(see fig. 18)*.

*   *   *

In this first section of the book we have looked at the knowledge and belief system of the early shamanistic culture known as the Shining Ones and revealed their profound understanding of cosmic processes. We have also demonstrated how this knowledge has been transmitted over the ages in encoded form in myths and legends, including some as famous and familiar as the stories of the phoenix.

In the next part of the book we will look further at the people responsible for transmitting this knowledge and at the evidence for the guiding presence of the Shining Ones and their spiritual successors in cultures worldwide.

PART TWO

The Shining Ones in History and Myth

The Anunnaki

The Shining Ones of Ancient Mesopotamia

'Oannes is the emblem of priestly, esoteric wisdom; he comes out from the sea, because the "great deep", the water, typifies ... the secret doctrine.'

M. P. Blavatsky, *Isis Unveiled*

The earliest accounts of the Shining Ones can be found in five principal sources:

Sumerian tablets from the library at Nippur, where they are named the Anunnaki (Anannage).

The biblical Book of Genesis, where they are given the name Elohim.

An account in Greek by the Babylonian priest Berossus.

The Book of Enoch, where they are referred to as angels, Watchers and Nephilim.

The Book of Jubilees.

The earliest of these are the Sumerian accounts. The Sumerians invented cuneiform writing and had advanced knowledge of music, poetry, art, mathematics, astronomy and science. 'For the ancient Sumerians music was a tool that helped them describe the cosmos.'[1] They were later conquered by their long-term rivals to the north, the

Akkadians under Sargon I (*c.* 2340 BC). The Akkadians were a Semitic people whose capital city was Babylon. After AD 2000, Sumeria/Akkad declined as a nation and was later absorbed by the expanding empire of Assyria.

According to the Sumerian creation myth, angels known as the Anunnaki or Anannage – Great Sons of Anu – were the founders of their culture. An (Sumerian) or Anu (Akkadian) was the chief sky/sun god and his name means 'Shining'. The Anunnaki therefore are the 'Sons of the Shining One' or 'Sons of Light'.

Christian and Joy O'Brien offer evidence in their books *The Genius of the Few* and *The Shining Ones* that these Anunnaki were 'a culturally and technically advanced people who settled in a mountain valley in the Middle East around 8,200 BC and, as their primary concern, established an agricultural centre [the Garden of Eden] for the teaching and training of the local tribesmen'.[2] They were described as the 'Shining Countenanced Lords of Cultivation' and elevated to gods:

> 'And the leaders of those same Lords became Gods; and the supreme commander of them all – Great Anu to the Sumerians, and the Most High to the Hebrews – vicariously became God.'[3]

Enlil's consort Ninlil or Ninkharsag ruled the Earth. The early Sumerians described themselves as constantly nourished by her milk and called her the 'great mother moon goddess'.

The son of Enlil and Ninlil was the war-god Ninurta, also known as Nimrod, who, like Osiris, became associated with the constellation Orion. Other gods were the moon goddess Nanna and sun god Shamash. There was also Inanna (Sumerian) or Ishtar (Akkadian), Shamash's sister (and consort in some accounts), who was associated with Venus.

The texts that we have on these Sumerian deities vary – in fact they evolve over time, which makes it more and more difficult to see their origins or bring clarity to the tales of Sumerian and other Mesopotamian deities.

We can see, however, that these Shining Ones, who became worshipped as the Sumerian pantheon of gods and goddesses, seem to have been a dynastic ruling family or clan. An, the chief authority, became the universal 'father god', as depicted in a 3000 BC pictograph from the city of Uruk, which he is said to have founded.

The lineages of all these deities are variously described and no clear picture emerges of the relationship and functions among sisters, wives and mothers, fathers, brothers and sons. Considering that many thousands of years must have elapsed between the actual lives of the Shining figures who were to become deified in Mesopotamian lore, the confusion is no surprise.

What is clear is that certain deities do continually stand out – namely An, Enlil, Enki, Ninkharsag, Inanna and Shamash – and that the characters and functions of these deities would go on to form the basis of the Egyptian, Greek and Roman pantheons. For example, like Osiris of ancient Egypt, Enlil was depicted as a bull, and Enlil's brother Enki of the Abzu (abyss and waters) was depicted, like Osiris' brother Set, as a serpent.

Beings from Outer Space or 'Inner Space'?

It is said in the Sumerian accounts that Enlil lived for thousands of years, and some authors have used this as the basis of a theory that the Sumerian Shining Ones were special beings of unearthly origin, coming from 'another world' or even 'another dimension'. However, these authors forget that 'Enlil' was a term used for 'the leader' and was thus passed on, like the term 'king' or 'pharaoh'. It was also the title of the sun, which of course was considered eternal.

The Sumerian texts say that the gods first 'arrived' on Earth at a place 'where Heaven and Earth meet', a mythical sacred mountain, an idea that is perhaps the inspiration behind the mountain-like ziggurat temples where the gods were later worshipped. Again, this has been taken by some researchers as an indication that the Shining Ones 'descended' from beyond the Earth. After giving a convincing interpretation of the relevant cuneiform pictogram in the text, the O'Briens argue that 'arrived' should be replaced with 'descended'. The pictogram in question is a triangular pyramid or mountain-like design with arrows pointing downwards on the apex – hence 'descended'. Although they are not as explicit as, say, Erich von Däniken, it is clear from the orientation of the O'Briens' entire narrative that they also favour the 'ancient astronaut' hypothesis, in other words that the Shining Ones were extraterrestrial beings.

There is another theory regarding the reference to a mountain-like source of the Shining Ones. It could refer perhaps not to a physical location but to the shamanic concept of the 'world mountain' that relates to the enlightenment experience , discussed earlier. In this case, the place 'where Heaven and Earth meet' is also the midpoint, the node between the opposites of sun and moon, day and night, and waking and sleeping, the Eternal Now point of enlightenment. According to this theory, the statement that the Shining Ones arrived at the place 'where Heaven and Earth meet' is best interpreted to mean that they operated from the higher 'source of creation'. They were an extraordinary people with special insights and powers – an elite who had attained the Shining, or enlightened, state.

According to other evidence, the Anunnaki were also seen as a group who arrived from another land across the sea *(see Chapter Ten)*. The term Abzu (abyss and waters), rather than meaning 'outer space', as some would claim, could therefore mean that they 'came from' – in the modern colloquial sense – the astral waters, the spiritual 'inner space'. This is the summit of the world mountain, the top of the world tree, the *axis mundi* and the spinal column. As we have seen, all are associated with the enlightenment experience which formed the foundation of the Shining Ones' beliefs.

The Garden of Eden

There is further evidence for this connection with enlightenment in the Sumerian account. Ninlil or Ninkharsag, 'Lady of Kharsag', the wife of the leader Enlil, asks the Council of Seven to create her an 'Eden' (E-Din). Sumerians referred to E-Din as 'the abode of the righteous ones'.

This is the very same Eden, or plain/plateau, that features in the Bible myth. The tree of life and the tree of knowledge in the biblical garden of Eden allude to the secrets of the Shining Ones. They can be related to the 'tree' of seven chakras, the 'tree' which took the shaman to 'heaven' and which later became the 'tree of life' in the esoteric Qabbalah system. The number seven is of widespread cosmological significance *(see Chapter Three)*. And the Council of Seven is the same as the seven archangels or messengers of the Bible who came down from the heavens or 'the mountain'. (Sumerians built their towers or ziggurats with seven levels; it was said that the Shining deities resided at the top of the ziggurat – the 'Great House', or Ekur.)

We can see therefore that many of the details included in the stories related to the activities of these early Shining Ones are really based on the internal kundalini processes, which they understood to a great degree. We will now look at other myths of the ancient world to see if they can give us further information about the Shining Ones' cosmology.

Fish Beings from the Sea

The Sumerian account states: 'Mankind learned from the Shining Ones; they set things in order.' Why did they feel they had to 'set things in order'? Perhaps this had something to do with the chaotic aftermath of a global, or at least far-reaching, calamity that had destroyed their homeland.

Could the place 'where Heaven and Earth meet' also contain an allusion to the land whence the Shining Ones travelled before arriving in Mesopotamia? An area, perhaps, with impressive mountains, such as the Himalayas? It would be difficult to prove this. In the famous Sumerian 'Kings List' it is stated that the Anunnaki ruled in Sumeria both before and after the Deluge, and that it was after the Deluge that they set kings on the throne to govern in their stead. Other sources state that the Shining Ones first came ashore from a submerged land after a similar catastrophe – an earlier one than the Deluge related in the Bible and other sources.

There is a Sumerian equivalent of the story of Noah, where a man called Ziusudra is warned by Enki to prepare before the event. Did the Shining Ones know when these catastrophic Deluges were going to happen? Did the ancient astronomers of the Shining Ones have a profound knowledge of cosmic cycles, and in particular the precessional cycle? We believe that the Shining Ones linked recurring catastrophes such as the Deluge to the beginning and end point of the 25,800-year precessional cycle.

Berossus and Oannes

One of the principal sources of information about the Mesopotamian Shining Ones comes from a Babylonian priest called Berossus, who lived in the third century BC and wrote a Greek history of Babylonia called *Fragments of Chaldean History*. In it he tells us that during the first year of Babylon a being appeared from the Erythraean Sea who looked like a fish. His name was Oannes – a Greek version of the Babylonian Uan.

Berossus refers to Oannes as 'Lord of the Sacred Eye' and 'God of Wisdom'. The Babylonians gave him the epithet 'Lord of the Waves'. In some accounts he is Adapa, a priest of the Shining One Enki or Ea, though in others he is Enki himself.

The names themselves provide some interesting clues. It is said that Enki would sleep in a freshwater chamber named the Abzu, or Apsu, which was shaped like the ark, i.e. was like a ship or boat. However, we find that Abzu is also the Akkadian name for the underworld. Furthermore, *ab* means, 'father', 'creator', 'the great one' and 'wisdom,' 'snake' and 'serpent', and *zu* or *su* means 'he who knows' or 'the wise one'.

The numerous appellations given to Oannes are also curious and it is possible that he told the people to refer to him by these names. 'Lord of the Sacred Eye', for example, reminds us of the epithets given to Osiris and also of the Eye of Ra or Eye of Horus (see *Chapter Eight*). Also in this regard, 'Lord of the Waves' could apply to waves of energy or wave phenomena as in different frequencies – which isn't as preposterous as it first sounds, considering the shamanic techniques we have already outlined.

Figure 29: 'Fish Beings' of Ancient Mesopotamia
Two images of Oannes/Dagon, after ancient Babylonian depictions. The head of the fish costume shown in the first picture became the mitre worn by Church bishops (including the Pope) and abbots.

Plate 1(above). Gabriel, a Shining angelic being. Kykkos Monastery, Cyprus.

Plate 2(right). Moses with his 'horns' or shining rays, in the church of Santa Maria, Rome.

Plate 3 (above). A Shining angel before the Ark of the Covenant. Southwell Minster, England.

Plate 4 (left). The 'divine self', or God, in balance, with rays of light coming from the 'inner eye'.

Plate 5 (above right). The 'sacred heart' symbol, representing the centre of the illuminated being. Monchique, Portugal.

Plate 6 (right). God the Shining deity, depicted as the radiant, all-seeing 'inner eye' surrounded by angels. Cathedral of St. John Lateran, Rome.

Plate 7 (left). The enlightened avatar depicted at the top of the cross, the summit of the shamanic 'World Tree'. Kykkos Monastery, Cyprus.

Plate 8 (below left). God as the illuminated 'inner eye', also a Masonic symbol. St. Peter's Basilica, Rome.

Plate 9 (below). Masonic symbolism: the set square and dividers, or compasses. St. Peter's Basilica, Rome.

Plate 10 (above right). A Roman mosaic of the swastika, a Shining solar emblem. Paphos, Cyprus.

Plate 11 (below right). The Masonic square and compasses, this time set into the wall of a Protestant church at Llanfairfechan, Wales.

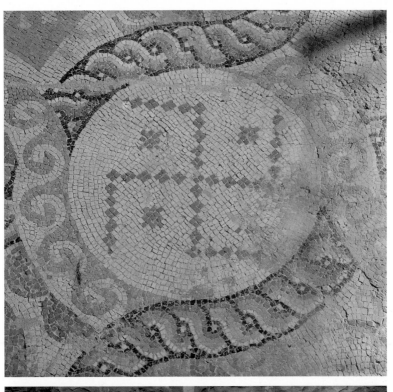

Plate 12 (previous pages). The glory and wealth of Orthodox Christianity is amply displayed in this church in Cyprus.

Plate 13 (above). The Forum, the heart of ancient Rome. The Roman empire was the key factor in spreading the domination of the Christian Church.

Plate 14 (right). Philip Gardiner outside St. Peter's Basilica, Rome, the seat of the papacy and the Catholic church.

The descriptions given by Berossus show that Oannes wore what must have looked like a large fish skin over his body, possibly some kind of costume. It's not difficult to imagine this to be similar to the kind of attire a shaman or member of a cult priesthood would wear. We are told that his language was articulate and human. In brief, he stayed with the people of Mesopotamia four times, for long periods, and tutored them in letters, geometry, the arts and scientific knowledge. He taught them how to build cities and temples and compile just laws. In other words, he civilized the region. Soon afterwards other beings like Oannes appeared.

Oannes: True Avatar and Shining One

Godfrey Higgins, a Rosicrucian, has been described as an initiate who wrote for other initiates. In his two-volume work *Anacalypsis* (1833) he had this to say of these 'fish beings':

> 'With respect to the Oannes, several persons [say there were] two of them, and Berossus says that there were other animals similar to Oannes, of whom he promises to give an account in his second book. These would most likely have been shewn to be renewed incarnations, but the book does not now exist. Has it been purposely destroyed? I suspect the Johns, or Oanneses, are like the Merus, the Buddhas, the Manwantaras, the Soleimans [Solomon] etc. They are renewed incarnations, and the name was given after death, and sometimes during life, to any person whom the priests thought proper to designate as the guardian genius of the age.'[4]

Higgins suggests that 'Oannes' was probably also manifested as John (Johannes) the Baptist[5] This brings us back to the Baphomet cult of the Templars, who were said to have worshipped the two Johns, the Baptist and the Evangelist *(see Appendix)*.

But more importantly, Higgins claims that the ancient and true name of the biblical dove (which, as we have seen is based on the phoenix) is Ionah and Ionas – again Oannes or Iannes. The dove is present during the baptism of Christ by John and in many descriptions hovers above his head, like the phoenix which perches on top of the pillar – the spine.

When we look at the Babylonian image of Oannes we see him holding a cauldron-like vessel in one hand and a sponge or pine cone in the other, as if about to anoint or baptize someone. As Higgins says:

'This is clearly the fish Avatar of India, whether or not it be the Ioannes or Jonas I leave to the reader. I apprehend it is the same as the DAGUN of Pegu and the fish sign of the Zodiac. Very little is known about it, but it exactly answers the description of an Avatar. The extraordinary number of extraordinary circumstances detailed above will compel my reader, I think, to believe that the incarnation of the fishes was once, if it be not yet, among the secret doctrines of the Vatican. I beg those who doubt, to tell me why the fishes tied by the tails are to be seen on the Italian monuments, of the meaning of which none of the priests could or would give me any information.'[6]

It is striking that the mitre worn by the Pope and other bishops is similar to the upward-looking fish headgear worn by Oannes *(see fig. 29)*, as has been noted by many other writers.

Is the conclusion to draw here that Jesus was not the true avatar, the designated 'guardian genius of the age'? This would explain why the Templars were Johannites. Instead, Jesus represents a person who *becomes* initiated (through baptism or anointing) under the guidance of the *true* avatar and great initiator: John, or Oannes, the great Shining One.

Two questions remain: why did the Catholic Church adopt the initiate in place of the great initiator? Was the Church trying to hide the true shamanic origins of its own religion?

The Fish Beings of Sirius

In 1976 Robert Temple published a book entitled *The Sirius Mystery* about the Dogon tribe of Mali and their astronomical knowledge, in particular their belief in a "twin" star of Sirius, the dog star. This twin, the Dogon believe, was the seed of the universe, and its movement around Sirius took about fifty years. Moreover, the 'seed star' was so dense that all the people of the earth could not lift a small part of it. Sirius does indeed have a companion star, Sirius B, which orbits it every fifty years, and is an extremely dense, 'collapsed white dwarf', as astronomers term it. But what is so extraordinary is that Sirius B is tiny, invisible to the naked eye next to the brightness of Sirius, the brightest star, and can be seen only through powerful telescopes. Sirius B was discovered only in 1862, and the Dogon belief was clearly ancient, and central to certain traditional rites, when first recorded in 1930.

So how could the Dogon have acquired their knowledge of Sirius B? The Dogon claim that they were taught it by the Nommos, 'ugly amphibious beings' who fell to earth in a 'fiery' and 'thunderous' ark or ship. The Nommos could live on land but mostly dwelt in the sea, being part-fish, much like the mythical mermen or mermaids.

Again, we are confronted with 'fish beings' – Shining Ones. The Dogon claim that the Nommos came from a planet orbiting a *third* star in the Sirius system. It is possible that the ancestors of the Dogon confused the information they had learned about Sirius with the fish beings' place of origin? We would suggest that the star connection and the idea of 'fish beings' may both have their origin in beliefs about the internal energy phenomenon we refer to as the 'enlightenment experience'.

As we have seen, the shamanic underworld was associated with the 'heavenly realm' reflected in the stars and the night sky. However, for the Egyptians the dog star, Sirius, also represented the dog or jackal god Anubis, the god of embalming who was both guardian of the underworld and guide of the dead. Anubis guarded the 'gateway' into the Underworld, and was watchdog of Sirius, so both Sirius and the gateway into the underworld are the same. And Sirius is also linked to Isis, the 'world mother', whose vagina represented this portal.

The dog is the shaman's guide and as such both the wise guardian and teacher of the shaman (as later personified by Thoth) and the archetypal shamaness (as later personified by Isis), the world mother of wisdom entered by the shaman. As we would perhaps see it today, the shaman's mind becomes like a sperm – a serpent – so as to fuse with the world mother's egg.

As far as the idea of 'fish beings' is concerned, author Manly P. Hall comments:

> 'The early philosophers and scientists, realizing that all life has its origin in water, chose the fish as the symbol of the life germ. The fact that fishes are most prolific makes the simile still more apt. While the early priests may not have possessed the instruments necessary to analyze the spermatozoon, they concluded by deduction that it resembled a fish.'[7]

And also a snake or serpent, we might add. The ancients may have lacked the practical instruments to see into the microcosmic world of cells, molecules and atoms, but looking at the theories put forward by Jeremy Narby, there is again the possibility that through trance, the shaman was able to reduce his point of focus down to these microscopic levels and observe these things subjectively, and in doing so he would *become* the very things he was observing.

This experience in which one 'swims like a fish' within the underworld or higher worlds is also a metaphor for the out of body experience which is obviously the primary experience of the shamanic trance state. One swims in the 'primary waters' of the void – the womb of the world mother.

Perhaps here we have the real reason why the Shining Ones were identified by the symbols of the fish and the serpent: these beings believed that they were able to access the life germ, the cosmic egg of creation, with their minds and initiate a rebirth, not only in themselves but also in the collective consciousness. It is possible that they themselves actually came to exemplify rebirth. Through their knowledge of this process they may also have believed they were able to control the cycles of nature and the patterns of reality itself. Of course such knowledge was for the initiate only.

Our own view is that in their survival of a worldwide catastrophe these people believed that they really had been 'reborn' – as if from the underworld. So it is possible that they told the ancestors of the Dogon that they had come from the underworld; and they said this while pointing up at Sirius. Based on everything we have seen so far, this is a far more feasible explanation than the 'ancient astronaut' theory, in which these 'fish gods' are said to have made a *physical* journey from Sirius.

Furthermore, as we know, the shaman is able to bring back valid knowledge about the nature of reality from his 'visits' to the underworld and so it is possible that this is how knowledge about Sirius B – which cannot be seen by the naked eye – was attained by the Dogon shamans, or the ancestral Nommo Shining Ones who taught them.

Lord of the Waves

The 'fish being' idea also doubtless relates to the Shining Ones arriving out of the waters of the great Deluge, or Deluges recorded in the myths of many different cultures. The Sumerian god Ea was known as 'Lord of the Waves'. He was also known as 'Lord of the Flood', as his arrival in Sumeria is said to have coincided with the cessation of the Flood. Oannes has also been identified with Janus the Etruscan and Roman god of gateways and doorways, and it is said that Janus taught the Chaldeans the arts and sciences and warned them of the Flood. So Ea seems to have come both *after* and *before* the Flood, which again raises the possibility that there were two separate flood events, both perhaps accurately predicted by the Shining Ones, who were thus able to save themselves. This, though, is speculation.

Many commentators have interpreted the 'waters' of the primordial Flood to allude to the vast 'sea' of space, thereby lending support to the extraterrestrial hypothesis. However, as David Ovason has put it:

> 'The fish-man was one of the esoteric symbols of the initi-
> ate in that ancient culture [Babylon]. No doubt *it was
> taught that the man or woman who had so developed them-
> selves as to have free access to the Spiritual world* could be
> regarded as being dual. Such people would be regarded as
> being equally content to walk on the Earthly plane or swim
> in the watery.
>
> 'Such initiates can live on the material plane, with the
> body of the flesh and blood, and they can also live in the
> Spiritual, *in the aqueous world of the Astral for which the fish
> tail is an appropriate symbol*, and where the physical body
> would be an encumbrance. *The initiate's control over the two
> worlds is expressed in the mer-man form*.'[8] [our italics]

Once more we have the initiate swimming like a fish in the other worlds of the shamanic trance state.

Enki was also associated with both the semen and the amniotic fluid (which supports the above) and was therefore a god of fertility. He is also depicted as the half-goat half-fish creature from which the astrological symbol for Capricorn is derived. Sometimes the goat's head is exchanged for the head of a ram. The chief god of the

Heliopolitan cult religion, Atum-Ra, was depicted with a ram's head, as were his son Osiris and the creator-god Khnum. But it is said that the Babylonian god Capricornus was their version of the horned pagan god Pan – meaning 'All'.

Figure 30: Capricornus
The goat-fish Capricornus, after an original Babylonian depiction. Note the resemblance to the fish-tailed representation of Oannes/Dagon in fig. 29.

Enki was also known as 'Lord of the Abyss' – again, reminding us that he was associated with the void or source-centre of creation – the Absolute or Godhead.

The *Ru* Gateway

The symbol of the fish is related to the *mandorla*, the almond shape found in the centre of the *vesica piscis*. The mandorla, which is used as a full-body halo in depictions of sacred beings, is identical to the ancient Egyptian *ru* symbol, which means 'birth passage' and 'uterus' as well as 'mouth'. Its fundamental meaning is 'gateway'. It is the vagina of the world mother – the gateway into and out of the astral under-world used by the shamanic fish beings.

The *ru* is also shaped like an eye, and indeed it symbolizes the third eye, 'the Secret Eye which permits the possessor to see beyond the illusion of the ordinary and the familiar'.[9] The oval *ru* also symbolizes the

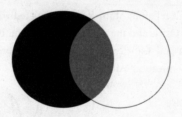

Figure 31: Vesica Piscis
Known to the Egyptians as the *ru*, or 'gateway', the vesica piscis symbol is the almond-shaped figure created by the superimposition of two circles representing the two opposites.

mouth and according to writer Mark Dunn, a self-professed 'urban shaman', the word was essentially associated with speech, and thereby the descended Logos, the utterance of the word which gives birth to reality.[10] Furthermore, Mark tells us that in esoteric symbolism, the circle (derived from the *ru*) and the cross were originally quite inseparable, thus forming the ankh. In this symbol the *ru* oval is the head and the Tau cross the spine. As we can see from its position on top of the ankh, the *ru* symbolized the trance state.

Jesus, the 'anointed' and 'Christed one' symbolized by the fish, is sometimes shown inside the *ru* symbol, the portal between this world and the next, revealing that the shaman is 'the Way' and therefore the door or gateway:

> '...for Ru meant "doorway" or "secret entrance" – and Christ is also "The Way". Christ, like the Ru, is the entrance to the Spiritual world, the guide of the modern initiate.'[11]

As Mark Hedsel comments:

> 'The Egyptian hieroglyphic *Ru* represents the place of birth. It is a vestigial drawing of the Kteis, and of the mouth, from which words are born. By extension, it became the place

148

Figure 32: Christ as 'the Door'
Jesus is really an adaptation of the archetypal 'resurrecting' shaman, the enlightened 'Shining One' later revered as a deity. Here he is shown within the *mandorla* ('almond'), the halo in the form of the vesica piscis (see fig. 31) or *ru* – the psychic 'gateway'. Note the combined halo-and-cross behind the head: this is a solar symbol of ancient origin that resembles the Celtic cross (see fig. 20). Here, the cross is centred precisely on the centre of the head – the thalamus.

where secret knowledge was delivered, from the secret Schools, and the process nowadays known as "rite of passage." Something of this hermetic lore was expressed in the Christian symbolism, which adopted the *Ru* as the Vesica Piscis, which is sometimes used to sheath Christ, Mary and certain saints. In this use, it represents the Spiritual world beyond the "door" of the *Ru*.'[12]

Egyptian Lore and the Seed-Centre

Earlier we looked at the ancient Egyptian sun symbol and noted its connection with the ecliptic centre and the precessional circle traced in the heavens by the tilted axis. This symbol really derives from the concept of Hadit and Nuit, or Nut, which is symbolized in the same way. This in itself may denote a common source of influence.

In brief, Hadit represents consciousness reduced down to an infinitesimal point (the ability of the shaman, as already noted), the zero point within the circle, the source of creation. So it could be seen as the 'seed-drop' of Atum-Ra. Hadit is also a 'point' of view, the True Will, the creative principle within man. It is also symbolized in ancient Egyptian art as the winged orb or globe which really represents one's ability to fly out of one's body (astral travel) as a pinpoint of consciousness – a point of light energy.

The circle enclosing the point of Hadit represents the goddess Nut or Nuit, who is infinite space and the infinite stars. She is the womb or cosmic egg, which receives the seed-drop, the seed of Atum-Ra, which is Hadit.

In the phoenix code, the phoenix rests the egg on top of the pointed pillar or obelisk. The point of the pillar (seed, Hadit) then pierces the egg (Nuit) at its centre, thereby fertilizing it and activating the rebirth of the soul into its new life. In terms of consciousness, and the process utilized by the shaman, this means one's psychic birth or emergence into a new reality.

What the shamanic experience implies is that we all have the ability to take our consciousness back to that first potential point of creation – a belief also held by trance-state artist and magician Austin Osman Spare, who called this ability 'Atavistic Resurgence' and believed he possessed it. Again, one's experience of this point-centre is the enlightenment or illumination phenomenon which has been behind the religious impulse of man throughout history. From this point of zero, one can begin anew; one is able to change oneself and one's experience into something else. All this is wrapped up in the phoenix code.

The Midpoint between the Feet (Omega) and the Head (Alpha)

We mentioned earlier that the archetypal fish-god Ea/Enki/Oannes was sometimes depicted in the form of Capricornus, a creature shown as part-fish and part-ram or goat (fig. 30). To understand fully the symbolism of the 'ram-fish' one needs to bear in mind that in ancient

Mesopotamia correspondences were made between the signs of the zodiac and parts of the human body. The astrological sign Aries, the ram, represents the head and Pisces, the fish, is associated with the two feet, which is why there are two fishes. The reason for these correspondences is that Aries is the 'head' of the astrological year, beginning the annual zodiacal cycle, and Pisces is at the end of the cycle. Thus Capricornus embodies the whole cycle, or rather, the transition point in the cycle, which the shaman seeks to capture.

It is significant that the two fish of Pisces are swimming in opposite directions, similar to the two hands that are drawing each other – or should we say generating each other – in M. C. Escher's famous sketch. This also symbolizes the duality associated with the standing-

Figure 33: Pisces the Fish
The glyph (left) and the two fishes, are widely used symbols for the astrological sign of Pisces. Note the resemblance between the two fishes and the dual ouroborus (see fig. 18).

wave energies we saw earlier – being the two-directional streams given in the shaman's descriptions of his experiences while in the trance state.

Being associated with the two feet, the two fish would symbolize one's existence in physical reality and also the left and right brains – a necessary condition of man's existence in physical reality. And as these quotes from the ancient Sanskrit scriptures the *Upanishads* reveal, the two-directional fish also symbolize the waking and sleeping opposites associated with circadian rhythms and cycles. Does this surprise us?

> 'As a large fish swims alternately to both banks (of a river), eastern and western, even so does this infinite entity move alternately to both these states – those of dreaming and waking.
>
> '…while the Self withdraws itself from all manifestations when it is in deep sleep, it projects itself in waking through the very channels through which it withdrew itself in sleep.'[13]

However, the *ru* reveals just one fish. This is the central oval created by the superimposition of the two circles of the *vesica piscis* – the opposites – which is yet more supporting evidence that this symbol reveals the gateway opened up by the superimposition, or fusion, of both opposites. Through this gateway one leaves the physical world, picks up one's two feet, which become one, as in the tail, and swims like a fish or serpent through the astral waters.

Figure 34: Capricorn Glyph
This glyph incorporates the right-angled lines of the male and the curve of the female.

No wonder then that the archetypal fish-god, Ea, Enki or Oannes is not only associated with Janus, the god of gateways, but also depicted as the goat-fish – or rather ram-headed fish – Capricornus.

Also, like the Celtic god Cernunnos, who holds a ram-headed snake, Enki held a ram-headed sceptre. This seems to be a symbol of the male sperm which 'rams' its way head first through the cell membrane of the ovum.

Oannes and the Chinese Water Beings

Striking parallels are found between the figure of Ea/Enki/Oannes and stories of 'fish gods' as far away as China and the Far East. In ancient Chinese texts we find these 'gods' being referred to as 'water beings'.

According to Chinese folklore Fuxi or Fu Hsi (pronounced 'foo-shee') and his wife Nu Gua or Nu Kua (pronounced 'noo-kooa') were 'fish people' said to be responsible for civilizing the Chinese after the Great Flood, which matches the Sumerian accounts, but which the Chinese date to around 3330 BC.

> 'Fu Hsi is credited, among other things, with domesticating animals, breeding silkworms and teaching the art of fishing. He also invented music and the set-square and compasses to measure the earth. He and his wife Nu Kua restored order to the world after it had almost been destroyed by the monster Kung Kung, not least by their invention of marriage as a means of harmonizing the Yin and Yang of human nature.'[14]

We are told that Fuxi not only invented the set-square and compass – the symbols that were later adopted by Freemasonry – but also gave the Chinese *The Book of Changes*, otherwise known as the oracle *Yi Jing (I Ching)* – a system of trigrams and hexagrams based on the opposites.

Fuxi is male because he holds the *Kan* or set-square in his right hand (connected to his left brain) and also wears the lingam on his head. *Kan* or *can* means 'serpent', so the set-square could translate as the 'serpent's head'.

The set-square, by which the architect draws and measures straight lines and angles, is a male symbol, and the compass or dividers with which one draws a circle is a female-related symbol. Again, what we really have here are the binary symbols one (I) and zero (O).

However, we also find the masonic square along with the fish tail – which is obviously female – in the glyph for the astrological sign of Capricorn *(fig. 34)*. The male-related 'square' is associated with the head of the shaman and the female curve (the fish tail) is associated with the world mother and therefore the underworld in which one 'swims like a fish'.

In representations of Fuxi and Nu Gua, we see the male (archetypal shaman) giving over the *Kan* square to his shamaness (wife or female companion). This reveals that he is entering the world mother. Symbolically, the shaman's head and the underworld become one. This also makes a correspondence with the procreative process, whereby the head of the one sperm breaks away from its tail and becomes the nucleus at the centre of the ovum where it deposits its genetic material to initiate the growth of a new pattern. For the shaman this was a new pattern as regards the internal worlds he experienced, and also his own reality, when he emerged from this experience as if reborn.

This explains why John the Baptist (Oannes) is beheaded after the kundalini goddess Salome dances the Dance of the Seven Veils (seven chakras) and possesses the head. It is said that during the kundalini experience one becomes 'headless' or that one's consciousness is 'bodiless', as one becomes an orb of light.

Looking at all the evidence laid out before us, we realize that the Chinese 'fish beings' were most likely the same people that landed in

154

Mesopotamia and Egypt, bringing their knowledge with them. In our view Fuxi and Nu Gua did not invent the set-square and compass, but brought with them the principles of knowledge these instruments symbolized.

We will now look in more detail at the accounts of the Shining Ones in Egypt.

Neteru, Akhu, Shemsu Hor

The Shining Ones in Egypt

'I have become pure, I have become *Neter*, I have become a spirit.'

From the Egyptian *Chapters of Coming Forth by Day*,
trans. Sir E.A. Wallis Budge

As already noted, according to Ovid the phoenix makes its way from Assyria to Heliopolis, and this tells us that the Shining Ones, or a great number of them, moved from Sumeria to Egypt. Through the symbol of the phoenix of rebirth, we are being told that they were 'reborn' there.

Even today the word 'Egypt' conjures up magical images of pyramids and pharaohs, dry desert mysteries and moonlit Nile scenes from long ago. The history of Egypt reaches back into the mists of time. We are told by Plato (427–347 BC) that the Attic statesman, scholar and philosopher Solon visited the country between 570 and 560 BC. At the city of Sais, the wealthy Solon, who has been described as the 'Onassis of antiquity',[1] was the welcome guest of the priests of the temple of Neith. One of these priests, an old man, told Solon that the Egyptians had a *written* history dating back some 5,000 years. According to Plato, he said, 'Oh, Solon, Solon, you Greeks are all children ... young in mind, you have no belief rooted in old tradition and no knowledge hoary with age.'[2]

Plato was of course insinuating that the additions of the Greek pantheon were taking the nation away from the truths of the ancient beliefs. Those with the eyes to see would know that they had to stay firm to the old ways, the secret ways, for the initiated few only. But Plato was also talking of the fantastic culture of the Egyptians and how the Greeks could be like them. How true is this in our modern technological age? The pyramids of Egypt are still an enigma and we must ask, how did an ancient culture seemingly appear from nowhere and start building with such knowledge and enthusiasm?

Herodotus told part of the tale when he said that Egypt was 'the gift of the Nile'. Without the Nile there would have been no Egypt as we now know it. Location is paramount in creating a civilization, just as developing a business is reliant on the surrounding suppliers and customers, distribution accessibility and centrality. Location is also important with regard to Earth energy. The locations of fissures, volcanoes, tectonic faults, underground streams and areas of large electromagnetic activity also seem to be paramount to the centres of culture. The reason, as previously discussed, is due to the electromagnetic effects created in the mind.

Excavations at Hierakonpolis in 1983 showed quite clearly the early farming development of the Egyptian culture. In 3800 BC there was a habitation of approximately 100 acres known as the 'Amratian' period of the Neolithic.[3] Here we find the first Egyptian tombs. At other Amratian sites along the Nile and at Hierakonpolis itself we can see the burials of the elite class. The imagery here is consistent with the Shining Ones' beliefs.

Around 4,700 years ago, King Djoser constructed the Step Pyramid, the first of the great pyramids, at Saqqara. The kings had become priest-kings, sons of the great Shining One in the sky, and they began to build their own stairway (back?) to heaven.

The rituals of rebirth, the belief in sun gods and moon gods, the spirit of animals and cyclic patterns were all handed down from the shamans of earlier times: the ancient Devas, Anakim, Anunnaki, giants and men of renown. *Egypt was now the creation of the Shining Ones for a specific purpose.*

We are familiar with the accepted chronology of the Egyptian civilization as devised by Egyptologists and archaeologists. We learn at school that the Great Pyramid was commissioned by the Fourth Dynasty pharaoh Khufu (Cheops) as his own tomb and that it was built around 4,500 years ago. However, the myths of the Egyptians, as those of the Sumerians, present us with another picture. Our interest is in the information contained in these myths, the encoded data which reveals something extraordinary about human consciousness – something that seems to have been believed with the utmost conviction, and so we must respect it. Also, if the Great Pyramid were just a tomb that belonged to a pharaoh, then why is the pyramid an emblem of many secret societies, signifying profound secret knowledge, and also a principal symbol of various esoteric mystery schools? Surely there is more to it than a mere tomb? Again we must follow the clues we are being presented with.

Heliopolis: City of the Sun and Shining One

Heliopolis, located just a few miles north-east of Giza but now buried under the sand, is the Greek name for the ancient Egyptian city known by the Egyptians as Iunu or Innu (meaning 'pillar') and by the Hebrews as On (meaning 'light'). The city was also called Annu, and this was also the name of the pillar that was erected there and upon which the city was founded. The name Annu is linguistically linked to Iunu and Innu. However, it is likely to have stemmed from that of the Sumerian god Anu – the highest god of the Anunnaki, the Sumerian Shining Ones.

158

It is no surprise to find that during later dynastic Egypt this pillar is said to have represented the phallus of Atum-Ra, the highest god of the Egyptians. In this instance we can see Anu and Atum-Ra converging as one – the same individual, who may once have been a real living entity and possibly a great king.

We mentioned earlier that one of Oannes' other names was On, the Hebrew name for Heliopolis, and this is interesting because Heliopolis is said to have been the first city ever constructed in Egypt, a pre-dynastic religious centre regarded as the homeland of the gods.

As we have seen, it is highly probable that these 'gods' were an advanced race with shamanic origins. Although we are dealing with fragmentary evidence, it is apparent that they landed in Egypt after or at the same time as arriving in Mesopotamia and possibly other places around the world.

The Neteru or Akeru

According to the 'Building Texts' inscribed on the walls of the Temple of Edfu, located between Luxor and Aswan, the submerged island was the 'homeland of the 'primeval ones', the 'ghosts', the 'ancestors' and the 'Lords of Light', who arrived in Egypt during pre-dynastic times. These divine 'beings', 'gods' or kings, who included the well-known gods Osiris, Set, Horus and Thoth, were known by the Egyptians as the Neter or Neteru (plural), which means 'god', 'spirit' or 'soul' and also 'those who watch, oversee, see'. Some have translated Neter as meaning 'neutral', which is again commensurate with the midpoint or 'neutral point' in consciousness.[4] The fish-like Nommo 'gods' or beings of one Malian tribe, the Dogon – who have been claimed to descend from the pre-dynastic Egyptians – are known as the Monitors, or Watchers (*see Chapter Nine*).[5]

Again according to the Edfu 'Building Texts', a group of 'divine beings,' sometimes known as the 'seven sages' or the 'builder gods' came from an island which had submerged due to a sudden flood, many of its 'divine inhabitants' having drowned. The texts are the only surviving fragments that describe the events surrounding what the Egyptians called Zep Tepi, the 'First Time'.

The Shemsu Hor or Akhu

The historian Diodorus Siculus of Sicily claims to have visited Egypt between 60 and 56 BC, and after consulting Egyptian scribes about their history, was told, 'At first "gods and heroes" ruled Egypt for a little less than 18,000 years ... Mortals have been Kings of their country, they say, for a little less than 5,000 years'[6] – hence the time period given to their own 'written' history, as told to Solon.

The famous Turin Papyrus (1279–1213 BC), also known as the Turin Canon, consists of over 160 fragments of an ancient document now in the museum of Turin, which gives a chronological list of ten Neteru or Akeru 'god-kings' whose reign lasted in total 23,200 years. The last was Horus. After these kings came the age of a ruling priesthood, known as the Shemsu Hor (also rendered as Hru Shemsu), meaning the 'Followers of Horus', Horus having been the last Neter or Neteru god-king. Bauval and Hancock tell us, 'The Egyptians remembered [the Shemsu Hor] as having bridged the gap between the time of the gods and the time of Menes (the supposed first king of the first historical Dynasty *circa* 3000 BC.)'[7]

According to the register, the period of time given to the Shemsu Hor is 13,420 years. Add this to the previous reigns of the 'god-kings' and we are faced with a total of 36,620 years of civilization before the known dynastic ages of Egypt. The papyrus then goes on to list the historical kings known by our conventional Egyptologists, which adds to the likelihood of its authenticity.

The Shemsu Hor were also known as the Akhu, which in Egyptian means 'glorious', 'splendid', 'resplendent', 'shining' – 'the Shining Ones'.

All evidence pointing to the conclusion that these Shemsu Hor were a strange and mysterious shamanic priesthood who carried on the traditions of their predecessor god-kings the Neteru. As American author William Henry points out:

> '*Ak-hu* is the archetypal Cosmic Man of Light, or ideal archetype of humanity found in a host of Hermetic and Gnostic teachings, whether Egyptian, Jewish, Christian or Islamic.'[8]

So we can see that the title of 'Shining Ones' passed on to the Egyptian Akhu. They are the gods of the past, ancients brought to life and worshipped by the masses under a new light, organized and put forward in their various symbolic forms by the élite priesthood. With influence from Sumer, North Africa and Mesopotamia, the Egyptian deities took shape, but behind them were the same beliefs of solar rebirth.

The Edfu texts also tell us that all human knowledge came from the Akhu or 'Followers of Horus' who are said to have come *after* the gods and giants, the Neteru or Akeru, and that it was they who also:

> '...invented the institution of Kingship, and that every Pharaoh from Menes to the Emperor Trajan ruled Egypt in their name. The winged disc was their symbol and a special ceremony, "The Union of the Disc", was held once a year in every temple in the land to symbolize the union of the state with the source of Egyptian civilization.'[9]

The Akhu are based upon real people, priests who passed on their incredible knowledge of the stars, astronomy and astrology within the peculiar stories we today believe to be about real people. They were said to be seven in number – perhaps another allusion to the seven levels associated with the chakra system? Furthermore, the Edfu texts refer to them as 'blacksmiths' or 'metal-makers'. This also relates to the shamanic tradition.

161

The Mansion of the Phoenix

The Edfu texts also tell us that it was the 'ancestor gods' who constructed the temple at Heliopolis – possibly the temple of the sun mentioned by Ovid.

As Heliopolis was once called Iunu, or On, meaning 'light', as well as Annu, it is possible that it had already been founded by the Neteru god-kings, and that these Neteru had much in common with the Anunnaki and the 'fish beings' who either came from Sumeria or landed in Egypt at the same time. We would contend that they are the same culture. This is supported by the fact that the Edfu texts tell us that Heliopolis was the location of their Zep Tepi, the First Time.

As described earlier, at the centre of the temple at Heliopolis there stood a pillar or obelisk[10] called the Mansion of the Phoenix. As we have seen, it was a symbol of the phallus of the central god of Heliopolitan religion, Atum-Ra, from which the universe was 'seeded into being', and was also named Annu, which may mean that Atum-Ra and Anu are one and the same deity. We are told that out of all the creation myths of the ancient Egyptians, the Heliopolitan version was the

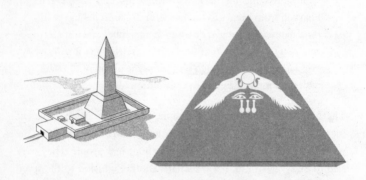

Figure 35: The Benben
An impression of the obelisk-like Benben, the 'pillar of the phoenix' at the sun
temple of ancient Heliopolis.

most popular – possibly because Heliopolis was the original city.

So, the pillar at the centre of the temple symbolized the phallus of Anu or Atum-Ra in that the people who erected it were making a symbolic reference to their 'rebirth' or 'new beginning' in a 'newly created world', after what must have been a worldwide cataclysm if we are to believe the Edfu texts.

The pillar, obelisk or column also symbolized the axis of the sacred mount which arose from the primordial waters like the mountain which emerged after the Deluge, and on which Noah's ark came to rest. Before this happened, the Bible recounts that a dove was set free to find land. This is also symbolic, as the dove is the phoenix, bennu or heron, which sets the egg containing the ashes of its predecessor down on top of the new primordial mound, thereby signifying a spiritual rebirth. In the context of the Flood, *it is the rebirth of mankind*.

More evidence that the phoenix, bennu or heron is related to the 'fish beings' is revealed in the Egyptian hieroglyph for the bennu or heron, as pointed out by William Henry:

> '[It is] possible that it symbolizes the Benben "seed drop" of Atum-Ra (being his "soul" or "spirit" which was believed to reside in everyone of us) and also closely resembles the still popular glyph of the *Ichthys* fish associated with Jesus the Christ, or "Christed one."'[11]

Figure 36: The Egyptian Hieroglyph for 'Bennu'

Figure 37: The Ichthys Fish Glyph

As we know, Jesus is called the 'Son of God' in that, like all of us, he represents the 'seed-drop' of God, but is one who, through the allegory of his 'Passion Play', his crucifixion on a hill, the primordial mound, is a demonstration of the power we all hold within us: we are all creators of the universe and co-creators of our own reality, even though we are not aware of it.

Further evidence that all these pre-dynastic stories are connected to the Grail – the image of a cup or vessel that contains the knowledge of these internal processes – can be found in the Arthurian myth. The sword rising out of the lake in the hand of the Lady of the Lake is the same as the phallus of Atum-Ra rising out of the primordial waters of Nun. It is being presented to one who can use it, who can wield it anew, and therefore symbolizes the potential creation of a new pattern. As we now know, at the individual level, this sword/phallus represents the sushumna channel in the spinal column, the place where the opposite energies unite to initiate the enlightenment experience, which initiates a transformation – a new pattern, a rebirth.

The Winged Disc

We saw earlier that the winged disc was the symbol of the Akhu. We also find these orbs depicted on Mesopotamian cylinder seals, floating above a tree of some kind (the spinal column) flanked by two individuals, who represent the two opposites. In Egypt this disc was known as the *udjat* and it was carved on the side of the pyramidion, or capstone (benben stone), of the pyramids.

This is really an ancient depiction of the pinpoint of consciousness, the orb or point of light which one uses as an 'astral vehicle'. Ancient depictions of winged flying discs or orbs with gods inside them, like the Persian Ahura-Mazda, are really ancient depictions of astral travel. This orb of light is not only said to be released from the body during trance but also at the point of death. Such orbs are possibly the same

Figure 38: The Winged Disc

This drawing, after an ancient Persian relief, shows the winged disc carrying the Persian god of light, Ahura Mazda. The two appendages represent the tails of the two serpents of the caduceus (see fig. 12) – the opposites that have fused together as one at the centre, where the god is positioned.

sort as those captured in recent times on camera, usually at haunted locations.

The winged disc also appears in the form of a winged eye – the all-seeing Eye of Ra or Eye of Horus. We could interpret this as a representation of the third eye, the portal or gateway in consciousness also represented by the eye-shaped symbol *ru*. An important Egyptian funerary ritual was the 'Opening of the Mouth'. In our view, this was akin to the opening of the third eye in that breathing through the *ru* or eye-shaped mouth instead of the two nostrils was like seeing with the third eye instead of the two eyes. We would note that the winged disc is also depicted as a winged eye both in Egypt and Mesopotamia.

Such correspondences may seem absurdly complex, but they were made so as to confuse the masses and keep the secrets of the Shining Ones within a small elite.

Osiris the Shining One

In the Heliopolitan creation account, the first ruler on Earth was Osiris, a son of Atum-Ra. We are told that on his travels to educate the peoples of various lands, the 'good god' Osiris, the 'shepherd of men', won the people over by the playing of songs on various musical instruments and that he invented the two kinds of flute which should accompany ceremonial song. It is possible that one of these was the 'shepherd's flute' as owned by Pan, which may suggest the pagan god Pan and the ancient Egyptian god Osiris are the same deity – one of the Shining Ones.

In their book *The Genius of the Few*, the O'Briens state that Osiris, his family and entourage were Shining Ones whose mission was to teach man about his own spirituality. The traditional knowledge associated with the teachings of Osiris later became the Osirian mysteries related to the ancient Egyptian *Book of the Dead*.

The O'Briens even mention that these Osirian mysteries were associated with the kundalini phenomenon. If so, then it's possible that musical instruments like the flute, or later the lyre or harp, as owned by the Greek god Apollo (the Egyptian Horus), would have been used to demonstrate the different frequency levels associated with the musical scale, information which would later be incorporated in the philosophical system of Pythagoras.

We are reminded of Mozart's opera *The Magic Flute*, which encompasses many masonic ideas and beliefs. Mozart was a Freemason. *The Magic Flute* even features Osiris and Isis, some pyramids and a deadly serpent. In the opera, the flute is used to charm wild beasts. Allegorically, 'wild beasts' means humankind.

We will put an end to the mystery which has perplexed many and state for the first time that the esoteric code of the 'magic flute' is symbolic of the spinal cord and central nervous system, and that the holes or notes of the flute are the seven chakras, which, like the seven reeds of the syrinx and the strings of the lyre or harp, plays the music, i.e. the

Figure 39: Osiris and Horus
The ancient Egyptian pharaoh in the form of the god Osiris (left), stands before Horus (in the form of Ra-Horakhte – 'Ra, Horus in the Horizon'). Ra-Horakhte wears the sun disc of enlightenment encircled by the uraeus serpent, and his staff is the *was* sceptre, signifying power over death. It has the *ankh* of life attached to it, pointing towards Osiris. Through reaching the point of enlightenment consciously, Horus has become the sun god who restores Osiris to life. In Egyptian belief, each pharaoh was the 'Son of Ra' and the incarnation of Horus on earth. After death the pharaoh incarnated in the afterlife as Osiris, father of Horus. Drawing after an ancient Egyptian relief.

chords, frequencies or resonances of one's life.

This would mean that Osiris and other the Shining Ones were able to control man through their knowledge of these processes related to the chakra system.

However, the Osiris story is tragic, and is again allegorical. It is possible that through the death and resurrection of Osiris we are again being given clues as to the 'fall of man' and the catastrophe that may have upended the Earth and caused the Flood.

It is also possible that this catastrophe was the result of the profound knowledge that man had learned from the Shining Ones. The knowledge taught by Osiris was only meant for those initiates who would understand it and preserve it. However, it would seem that it also made its way to the uninitiated, which caused consternation in the Shining Ones' ranks.

There are many theories based on this theme, and not without evidence. This is one reason why the knowledge was encoded for those with eyes to see and ears to hear. To see this we will again return to the phoenix code.

The Phoenix and Internal Alchemy

As we noted earlier, the phoenix is based on the ancient Egyptian *ba*, the soul, depicted as a human-headed bird, which is said to leave the body at the point of death. Looking at everything we have learned about human consciousness so far, we can see that the *kha*, *ka*, *ba* and *akh* of Egyptian cosmology relate to the four psychoanalytical states of consciousness referred to by psychologists:

- The *kha* is the mortal physical body and so we could also associate it with the male-related conscious self which has its focus on the external material world.
- The *ka* is the 'double' that remains with a person throughout life. It is the 'mental body' or 'dreaming body' and so we could

associate it with the female-related subconscious which has its focus on the internal mental realm. In Egyptian cosmology the *ka* is also associated with seven levels, which relate to the seven levels of the subconscious experienced by the shaman as the underworld.

- The *ba* is the union or fusion of the *kha* and *ka* and is therefore the neutral, androgynous soul, the 'third force' and 'third state' of consciousness akin to the shamanic trance state. It is the 'reintegrated ego' and relates more to the unconscious, as man is usually unconscious of it and instead relates to either one thing or the other (the opposites represented by the *kha* and *ka*).

- Finally, the *akh* is the 'source-centre of creation' and would relate to the superconscious. It is the Godhead which the *ba* or 'reintegrated soul' reunites with. In Egyptian cosmology, it belongs to Atum-Ra.

As we have seen, the root name of the mysterious race of 'gods' who were said to have come to Egypt was NTR, 'those who watch, oversee, see'. Neter, also Neteru, was the Egyptian name for the Anunnaki of Sumeria, which means they are the same people. We would say that they personified the *akh* on Earth.

In our view the Neteru gods were perhaps the gods of the Akhu Shining priesthood, the Followers of Horus. They may never have existed and may have been used as archetypes, perfect examples of what the Akhu believed about themselves. It is more than possible that they were the half-animal half-human hybrid creatures and giant snakes seen while in the trance state. In any case there is now no doubt that the attributes given to them reflect the processes associated with the trance state and the kundalini enlightenment experience.

If we want confirmation that these Neteru were seen to personify the *akh* source-centre, all we have to do is look again at the god Aker,

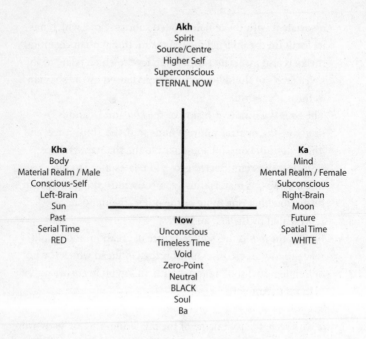

Akh
Spirit
Source/Centre
Higher Self
Superconscious
ETERNAL NOW

Kha		**Ka**
Body		Mind
Material Realm / Male		Mental Realm / Female
Conscious-Self		Subconscious
Left-Brain		Right-Brain
Sun		Moon
Past	**Now**	Future
Serial Time	Unconscious	Spatial Time
RED	Timeless Time	WHITE
	Void	
	Zero-Point	
	Neutral	
	BLACK	
	Soul	
	Ba	

Figure 40: Divided Mind and Consciousness
The cross of divided mind (horizontal) and divided consciousness (vertical), as
related to Egyptian cosmology. Compare also with the shamanic triad (fig. 6).

the guardian of the underworld. In Egyptian mythology Aker is often
depicted as two lions (sphinxes) or two jackals, back to back. It is
evident that these two lions, one looking east to the future and the
other looking west to the past, represent the male and female
opposites. But 'Aker' means 'the present moment' and in all the depictions of the god the *midpoint* between these two lions is emphasized in
that a sun disc is shown rising between them and between two mountains. This image of the sun rising would symbolize 'rebirth' and the
'present moment' or 'Eternal Now'.

And where is this 'Eternal Now' in our triad diagram *(fig. 6)*? It is positioned at the apex. In effect, this would mean that these immortal 'gods' are associated with the vertical division in consciousness – the midpoint, being closer to the source – whereas mere mortals are associated with the horizontal division in consciousness – the mind further divided by the male- and female-related opposites of which our reality is composed.

The Union of the Red and the White

More clues to the same system are given in the esoteric code of 'the red and the white'. 'Phoenix' is a Graeco-Phoenician word which means 'crimson' or 'red'. The phoenix itself comes alive when in union with the 'white stone'.

Here we have the seven levels of consciousness – as in the seven colours of the spectrum – being mixing together to make white light:

- The base colour red was often used to signify all seven colours of the spectrum in the lower material world of the male domain.
- The primary white was often used to signify all seven levels in the higher mental realm of the female domain.

We should bear in mind, too, that red and white are also the colours of the two *nadi* nerve channels in the system of seven chakras *(see Chapter Three)*.

The burning of the red phoenix is another metaphor telling us that the phoenix – or rather the old pattern of its consciousness – is collapsing and reducing down into the stone – the seed-stone – so as to re-emerge as a brand new pattern. The red and the white become the seed-stone, the zero-point centre, the black void when we are unconscious of it, but when we are conscious of it the 'bright white light' of the superconscious.

171

The Followers of Horus and the Naga 'Serpent Beings'

In Indian lore we find stories of the Naga, who are 'serpent deities'. It is possible that the term 'Naga' is akin to the Mexican Nagals, the 'Now shamans' and sorcerers described in the Carlos Castañeda books. (The 'Now' appellation is clearly associated with the mystical concept of the 'Eternal Now'.) While researching this unusual and ancient group we discovered that 'Naga' also means 'seven', 'wisdom' and 'mountain'. In esoteric lore it is a term used for the 'wise ones' – an ancient group like the Shemsu Hor who are spoken of as 'builder gods'.

These 'seven' Indian Nagas are guardians of great treasure and mystical secrets. They bestow 'riches' upon those that are deserving and exist in an underwater realm called Patala, which has been linked by many to the mythical Atlantis. Could they be linked to the 'divine beings' of the Edfu texts?

According to the Edfu texts, these seven wise sages are:

> '…sometimes seemingly divine, sometimes human … always portrayed as the bringers and preservers of knowledge down the ages – as an élite brotherhood dedicated to the transmission of wisdom and to the quest for resurrection and rebirth…'[12]

Resurrection and rebirth from what and to what? Could this have something to do with the Golden Age? This link is interesting because the seven Indian Nagas were regarded as 'the tutelary spirits, gods and guardians of the four points of the compass and the centre'. It was these 'Sages of Wisdom' who appear as the enlightened survivors of a cataclysm that wiped the earth clean, who then set about making a fresh start at the dawn of a new age…'[13]

Most importantly, the Edfu texts tell us that these seven sages and 'other gods' came from an island which had submerged *due to a sudden flood*, many of its 'divine inhabitants' having drowned. As Hancock and Bauval describe it in *Keeper of Genesis*, this island was the 'Homeland of the Primeval Ones' or 'Ancestors', who then arrived in Egypt. It was they, the 'Lords of Light' who became the 'builder gods' of Egypt. Author Andrew Collins suggests that these beings made their home in Giza, the original name for which was Rostau, meaning 'gateway'.

The Nagas also were seen as a semi-divine race of beings known as the Kadru who were said to inhabit the waters or the city of Bhogravati, which was situated under the Earth. But most significant of all, we find that they were also linked with the 'fish beings' of Mesopotamia:

> 'The "fish" is an old and very suggestive symbol in the Mystery-language, as is also "water". Ea or Hea was the god of the sea and Wisdom, and the sea serpent was one of his emblems, his priests being "serpents" or Initiates.'[14]

> 'One sees why occultism places Oannes and the other Annedoti in the group of those ancient "adepts" who were called "marine" or "water dragons" – Nagas.'[15]

The name of these 'fish beings' – or 'water dragons' or serpents – the Annedoti, originates from their progenitor, Annedotus, and is similar to the name given to the Sumerian gods, the Anunnaki: the Shining Ones.

'Specifications of the Mounds of the Early Primeval Age'

Furthermore, the Egyptian texts tell us that these beings constructed several 'sacred mounds' at various points along the Nile. Apparently these mounds were the foundations of temples that were going to be built in the future. It was intended that these sites would bring about 'the resurrection of the former world of the gods – a world that had been utterly and completely destroyed'. For example, the Edfu texts mention that the 'words of the sages':

173

'…were copied down by the wisdom-god Thoth into a book that codified the locations of certain "sacred mounds" along the Nile. The title of this lost book, according to the texts, was *Specifications of the Mounds of the Early Primeval Age*, and it was believed to have contained records not only of all the lesser "Mounds" or temples, but also of the Great Primeval Mound itself, the place where time had supposedly begun.'[16]

We should emphasize that the term 'primordial mound', and all it conveys symbolically, is synonymous with the world mountain of shamanic tradition. This again lends support to our view that these Shemsu Hor, or Shining Ones, were shamanic in origin. It's also possible that the Sem priest-shamans of dynastic Egypt were traditionally, or even ancestrally, linked to the Shemsu Hor.

Graham Hancock and Robert Bauval suggest in their book *Keeper of Genesis* that the people who designed and built the Great Pyramid were again the mysterious Shemsu Hor. According to Reginald Aubrey Fessenden, author of *The Deluged Civilization of the Caucasus Isthmus*, the term 'Rostau', the old name for Giza, is a literal translation of E-kur or Akur, meaning the 'great mountain' or 'great house'.[17] (The O'Briens interpret it as 'mountain house'.) These appellations – also brought to our attention by Zecharia Sitchin – make obvious reference to the Great Pyramid, the shamanic world mountain.

Sitchin tells us that the Sumerians also called their ziggurat temple in Nippur – a truncated stepped pyramid – Ekur, a 'house which is like a mountain', but quotes a poem which exalts the goddess Ninkharsag as the mistress of the 'House with a Pointed Peak' – a perfect pyramid.[18] This is interesting in that the Sumerian goddess Ninkharsag is synonymous with the Egyptian goddess Isis, and according to the Inventory Stele, said to have been written by Khufu, the Great Pyramid was dedicated to Isis.

It is possible, then, that Akur and Akhu both come from the same root word, as does Aker, the god depicted as two lions back to back with the solar disc rising between them. It is also possible that there were once two Sphinxes on the Giza plateau, guarding the entrance to the underworld.

Bauval adds that Akhu can also mean 'astral spirits' as associated with the stars. We would contend that the Akhu or Shining Ones were most probably individuals who believed they had psychic abilities associated with astral travel – akin to today's out of body experiencers and remote viewers – and were able to access the Duat or underworld via the 'astral body', the ancient Egyptian *ba*. There are many ancient Egyptian illustrations showing human figures on the backs of 'feathered serpents' about to ascend to the stars.[19]

This is further supported by the definitions of Akhu provided by Sir E. A. Wallis Budge in his *Hieroglyphic Dictionary*: 'to be bright', 'to be excellent' or 'to be wise' and 'instructed'.[20] And as Bauval says, 'Budge further informs us that the word [Akhu] was frequently associated with "those who recite formulae".[21] These 'formulae' are possibly 'magical formulae' equatable with Hindu mantras and the shamanic 'passwords'.

In brief, the Akhu were an enlightened and highly intelligent group of individuals who seemed to have understood all the sciences associated with mathematics, astronomy, physiology and metaphysics and encoded their knowledge in certain monuments and buildings – the most important of them being the Great Pyramid of Giza.

But what were the 'mounds' that were mapped by the wisdom-god Thoth, or those followers who epitomized him? What did they really represent?

We briefly touched on the subject of ley lines and dragon paths earlier, and it seems that these mounds were believed to be specific locations where the Earth's positive and negative 'lines of force' crossed each other and cancelled out at zero, causing an 'in-welling' or 'up-welling' of energy – a vortex. These places were neutral points in the Earth's magnetic field and could be likened to the chakras in the body. As we suggested earlier, a shaman may have been able to pick up the different vibrations radiating from these anomalous spots through psychic means.

The Nile river, as we know, is serpentine in that it winds back and forth like a snake. The sacred mounds and temples which were built along the river would also correspond to the chakras which align the spinal column. If so, then the Nile Delta would be the crown chakra. It is curious that Behdet, the Delta city that was a regional capital of Egypt in pre-dynastic times and is located on the meridian of the Nile, means 'Crown'.[22]

When we consider that the symbol of the snake or serpent was worshipped in relation to 'resurrection', perhaps we should not be surprised to find that ancient mounds across the world are linked with this very animal and therefore the enlightenment experience associated with it.

From America (for example the famous Serpent Mound of Adams County, Ohio) to Europe (for example the Serpent Temples of Avebury and Stonehenge) and beyond, the artificial mounds of the world can be shown to be related to the creative and life-giving aspects of the serpent.

In 1871, at a meeting of the British Association in Edinburgh, a certain Mr Phene gave an account of his discovery in Argyllshire of a mound 'several hundred feet long, fifteen feet high and thirty feet broad'. The tail tapered away, while the head was surmounted by a circular cairn, which he presumed, probably rightly, to be the solar disc above the head of the Egyptian *uraeus* – a cobra worn on the headdress and exiting from the forehead. This is a symbol of the third eye and therefore the thalamus. The serpent is a symbolic depiction of the 'reptilian' part of the brain upon which the thalamus is located – like an egg in the jaws of a snake or serpent. Indeed, there are many instances of such mounds.

It seems to us that there is overwhelming evidence down the ages, from cultures the world over, that the Earth was once strewn with serpent mounds. In the *Zend Avesta* of Zoroastrianism one of the heroes takes a rest on what he believes to be a bank only to discover that it is a green snake – an obvious allusion to the fact that this was a grassy serpent mound, very much 'alive'. We are reminded here of the alchemical illustration from the book by Abraham the Jew, *Snakes in the Hills* – an extraordinary book once owned by the alchemist Nicolas Flamel. This illustration suggests that the world is literally alive with 'serpent energies'.

Iphicrates related that in Mauritania 'there were dragons of such extent that grass grew up on their backs', thus showing, we believe, that tales of massive dragons in far-off lands could easily be serpent mounds. Strabo relates similar tales of dragons residing in the mountains of India, and Posidonius tells of one in Syria so large that horse riders on either side could not see each other. Bryant claimed these to be Temples to the Ophites (serpent worshippers).

The fact that the serpent was a symbol of new life and immortality points to these mounds being evidence of an ancient and universal belief in some kind of resurrection on a much larger scale and based on the knowledge of the chakra system – which was seen to extend to the body of the Earth itself.

Another point we noted was that in several places these mounds were intended to be entered. Posidonius, for example, said that the mouth of the serpent was so large that a man 'might ride into [it]'. Many legends abound of the 'underworld serpent deities' and so by entering the mouth of the serpent mound could the initiate be ritually entering the underworld? Certainly much of the folklore of Europe and beyond indicates that entering these sacred mounds is to literally enter the 'otherworld'.

In Egypt, the largest 'mound' of all was the Great Pyramid. So what was its purpose? Some interesting conclusions arise from the following word associations:

Akhu = 'Shining Ones'.

Ekur or Akur (Sumerian) = 'Great Mountain' = shamanic
world mountain = 'Great House' = 'House with a Pointed
Peak' = pyramid = *Great Pyramid*.

Akur is also a literal translation of 'Rostau' = Giza = *Gateway*.

Aker = A 'twin-guardian god' (two lions or sphinxes back to
back) who traditionally flank either side of the central
'gateway' – again *the Great Pyramid.*

Conclusion: The Great Pyramid of Giza is the 'gateway' of the
Shining Ones.

An obvious question is: the 'gateway' into what? And, given everything
we have seen so far, the obvious answer is: the Duat, the underworld,
the 'centre of the Earth'. This makes perfect sense in terms of the
shamanic cosmology.

It is said in ancient times Giza was a necropolis, a sacred place of
burial, and that apart from serving as tombs, the pyramids were used
for rituals for the dead. However, the famous Pyramid Texts, considered the oldest known religious texts in the world and found in the
Fifth and Sixth Dynasty pyramids at Saqqara, south-east of Giza, give
ancient descriptions of the out of body experience and even the near-
death experience – a view also related by authors Lynn Picknett and
Clive Prince:

'It is generally accepted as fact that the Pyramid Texts
describe the afterlife journey of the King, but there is much
internal evidence that this is simply not so – or rather that
they do not exclusively describe an afterlife journey at all.

'We believe that they actually describe the classic out-of-
the-body flight of the shaman, who is, significantly, often

regarded as physically dead while in his trance, in which he visits the world of the dead. The gods and monsters encountered in the Pyramid Texts are strikingly similar to those described across the world by tribal shamans.'[24]

This view was also embraced by W. M. Fix, who published these OBE/shamanic connections in his book *Star Maps*.

In the myths and legends associated with Giza, it is often mentioned that Thoth was associated with the three pyramids in some way and particularly with the Great Pyramid. Professor I. E. S. Edwards identifies the 'Great Primeval Mound' to be the natural mound or outcropping of rock which lies underneath the Great Pyramid of Giza and suggests that it was used specifically for the location of the Great Pyramid, which was built over it. This is supported by the Edfu texts, which also inform us that it was the 'Seven Sages' who initiated the construction work at this 'Great Primeval Mound':

> 'This work, in which Thoth also participated, involved the setting out and erection of the original "mythical" temple of the "First Time"...
>
> 'Also constructed under the direction of the "Seven Sages" was an edifice specified as *hwt-ntr*, "the mansion of the god": "Speedy of construction", men called it by name. The sanctuary is within it, "Great Seat" by name, and all its chapels are according to the norm.'[25]

In our view, the *hwt-ntr,* or 'mansion of the god', can only be the Great Pyramid, and this is also the view of Bauval, Hancock and various Egyptologists. But what is this 'sanctuary', this 'Great Seat' within it?

The 'Great Seat' is interesting in view of the ancient Egyptian depictions of the goddess Isis. The name 'Isis' actually means 'seat' or 'throne', and she wears the *stone* seat or throne as part of her headdress, *on top of her head.*

If this is the same 'Great Seat' which is being referred to in connection with the Great Pyramid, then it can only be symbolic, as so far no seat or throne has been found inside the pyramid. There is of course an empty sarcophagus in the so-called King's Chamber. For what it's worth, we might add that some have also compared this 'seat' or 'throne of Isis' with the empty throne of Osiris, her dead husband, and also the 'mercy seat' located on the lid of the Ark of the Covenant. And it is said that the dimensions of the sarcophagus are identical to the dimensions of the Ark of the Covenant given in the Bible.

But what does the head, or something inside the head, have to do with the Great Pyramid?

What is really interesting about this is that the seat of Isis, or seat of Osiris, was also depicted in ancient times resting on the top of pyramids in place of the capstone. This has led some researchers to suggest that maybe some of the pyramids were capped with stone seats. In cosmological terms, the capstone tip of the pyramid represents all of creation converging on the original point of the universe. This 'Great Seat' therefore represents the 'throne of God' – the source-centre of creation from which God looks down on the Earth.

However, we also find this seat or throne resting on top of the head. This can only mean that the pyramid also represents the human head or skull and that this source-centre of creation is located above the head. This brings us back to the bindu of the Hindu mystical tradition, the 'seed-drop' centre of the highest chakra, which is located above the head.

We were intrigued by these subtle references to this pyramid/head connection. Some also bear some relation to the alchemical Philosopher's Stone. And there are more clues which link the pyramids to this 'stone which isn't a stone'...

In view of what we had discovered about the phoenix of transformation, rebirth and immortality, as well as the ancient city of Heliopolis and its link with the central Mesopotamian 'fish deity'

180

Oannes, we found the following quote from Bauval and Hancock's book *Keeper of Genesis* of interest:

> 'Moreover it can hardly be an accident that the capstone or Pyramidion placed on top of all pyramids was known in the ancient Egyptian language as the Benben and was considered to be a symbol of the Bennu bird (and thus also of rebirth and immortality.) These capstones were replicas of the original ... which was kept in Heliopolis, perched atop a pillar in a temple called the "Mansion of the Phoenix."

> 'Is it not apparent, therefore, that we are confronted here by a tightly knit complex of interwoven ideas, all additionally complicated by masses of Egyptian dualism, in which stone stands for bird, and bird for stone, and both together speak of rebirth and of the "eternal return"?'[26]

Being confronted by a 'tightly knit complex of interwoven ideas' is an understatement – and we are only now beginning to fully understand the pattern which is fast emerging.

The holistic method of information transference whereby one can use the same principle to gather all the necessary information together actually corresponds to the enlightenment experience itself, whereby one accesses all information at once. However, without the same level of enlightened consciousness to get us by, for many of us our 'divided' mind, trapped in space and time, is limited and fails to even see the 'bigger picture', so we can only piece it together a bit at a time. This is why for us the research in which we have been engaged has been such a rollercoaster ride through so many diverse themes. We first set out to provide evidence for just one of our insights, but the more deeply we dug, the more connections we discovered, and all related to that initial insight.

With all the above in mind, let's return again to the phoenix code and see if we can unearth more clues.

Unravelling the Phoenix Code: Part 2

Unravelling this 'tightly knit complex of interwoven ideas', we find that the phoenix code is also linked to the Grail code. To see this one only has to study the symbology behind the dove.

The dove, which was first revered in Sumeria, also makes its appearance in the Flood story of Noah and during Christ's baptism as recorded in the New Testament, as noted earlier.

We also noted that, in Wolfram von Eschenbach's Grail romance *Parzifal*, on every Good Friday the dove descends from heaven to Earth and arrives at the Grail castle, bringing with it the 'communion host' which it lays down on the 'stone' – and we are told that this 'stone' is the Grail.

As most Christians would know, the 'communion host' is the 'crossed bread' or 'wafer' offered to the congregation during Holy Communion of Eucharist and said to represent the body of Christ.

It is apparent to many now that the story of Jesus was really based on the worldwide shamanic or pagan 'resurrection god' and so it is natural that the story of the phoenix itself would be resurrected as the 'dove' of Christianity. If so, then this would mean that Christ's body is synonymous with the 'egg' that contains the dead body belonging to the predecessor of the reborn phoenix – hence the reason why Christ's resurrection is celebrated with the traditional 'Easter egg'.

Obviously we are again dealing with a reincarnation theme here, which would mean that Jesus was himself a reincarnation of a former avatar or god-king – even if this reincarnation was only metaphorical in the fact that his story was a retelling of an older tale.

We should remind ourselves that, as stated by scholars, the biblical dove or the phoenix of the classical world is really a mythical rendition of the Egyptian concept of the soul, the *ba*.

The delivery of the egg which contains the body (memories) of the former self and the divine spark, the soul of Atum-Ra, is obviously significant here, and it is possible that we are being told that the 'reincarnated one' whose soul the phoenix of rebirth actually personifies is someone who reincarnates consciously and is aware of his own immortality, remembers his former lives and, most importantly, understands his mission in this life.

However, on another level, as already mentioned, the phoenix, and therefore the Grail, also symbolizes the rebirthing process of every individual who goes through the life-death-rebirth cycle and the 'rebirth' of the human race as a whole after a worldwide catastrophe which is possibly part of the cycle.

As regards the Deluge, the egg is also Noah's vessel carrying the survivors through this disaster. Remember that the egg is placed on top of the world pillar and the ark rested on a mountain (Ararat) – the world mountain – and that Noah had earlier sent out a dove to fly to land – the mountain.

And on yet another level, using the metaphor of the bird that flies from one place to another, the phoenix also symbolizes the migration of the survivors from one place to another.

According to the Grail romances, this collective rebirth is also symbolized in the reincarnation of a particular individual – the 'Shining One', the archetypal god of an advanced shamanic-based culture.

The Phoenix and the Equinoxes

The above connections are all the more significant when we remember that the dove brings the 'communion host' to the Grail castle every Good Friday – and Good Friday is associated with the death-rebirth of Jesus, who is himself based on the ancient 'resurrection god' associated with the spring equinox.

Furthermore, we find that the phoenix, too, is active around this time. In Pliny's account of it, based on the words of the Roman senator Manilius, we are told that:

'...the period of the Great Year coincides with the life of this bird, and that the same indications of the seasons and stars return again, and that this begins about noon on the day on which the sun enters the sign of the Ram.'[27]

There are a couple of clues here which are significant.

First of all we will deal with Manilius' mention of the 'Great Year' being the life span of the phoenix. Different classical writers have suggested different life spans here. Herodotus and Ovid say 500 years; Pliny and Solinus 540 years; Suidas and Syncellus 654 years; Martial and Lactantius 1,000 years; and Chaeremon 7,006 years. However, the Greek poet Hesiod (c.700 BC) said that the phoenix lived for 972 human generations and we find that of all these references, his is the most ancient. Now if we allocate 26–27 years for each generation, we find that Hesiod's figure comes closest to the cycle of precession, which is 25,920 years! In fact the precessional cycle is the 'Great Year' mentioned by Manilius.

The precession of the equinoxes is measured by the huge circle traced in the northern hemisphere by the tilted axis of the Earth. This fact that the phoenix's life span is related to one rotation of the cycle means that it dies and is reborn again at the point where one precessional cycle ends and another begins.

As we know, the phoenix as the dove also makes an appearance at the point where the 'yearly cycle' ends and begins again, and this is emphasized in the second significant clue given in the account by Pliny. At the end of the verse quoted above, we are told that the death/rebirth of the phoenix is also associated with the sun entering the zodiac sign of Aries the ram on 21 March – again, the spring equinox. This date is on the cusp between Pisces the fish and Aries the ram.

As mentioned earlier, in the magical correspondences made between the 12 zodiac signs and the different parts of the human body, Pisces is related to the feet and therefore the end of the cycle and Aries is associated with the head and therefore the beginning of the cycle. In other words, the date of the spring equinox represents the Alpha-Omega – the end and beginning point of a cycle.[28]

The equinoxes have always been times for celebration and are still deemed sacred in the neo-pagan traditions. It is said that the reason why is because, like the 'resurrection god', the sun was seen to 'die' and 'rise' again at this time in the year.

To return to the Great Pyramid, its 51.84° angled sides and 30° latitude (29 degrees, 58 minutes, 51.06 seconds north latitude, to be exact) mean that the sun is directly overhead and casts absolutely no shadow at noon during the equinoxes – the two 'neutral points' in the cycle.[29]

Once again we are being referred to that crucial end-beginning point in the cycle – the Eternal Now.

Conclusion

Ancient Egyptian texts reveal that the Shining Ones emigrated from Sumeria to Heliopolis, bringing with them the knowledge of cycles which they presented in their building of the world tree – the pillar or obelisk that stood inside the 'Mansion of the Phoenix'. This monument symbolized their 'rebirth' after the catastrophe that had claimed their homeland.

From Heliopolis it is possible that they then moved on to Giza and built the Great Pyramid, the world mountain, another symbol based on the shamanic world tree and incorporating the same principles of knowledge. However, the Great Pyramid had a purpose, as not only did it incorporate all of their metaphysical and scientific knowledge concerning the geophysics of the Earth, but it was also a gateway to the underworld. We will conclude this chapter with an ancient account that was believed to be the words of Thoth himself:

> I raised high over the entrance, a doorway, a gateway
>
> leading down to Amenti.

There would be few with courage to dare it,
few pass the portal to dark Amenti.
I raised over the passage a mighty pyramid,
using the power that overcomes Earth force,
Deep and yet deeper I placed a force-house or chamber;
from it I carved a circular passage reaching almost to
the great summit.

Tablet 1 of *The Emerald Tablets of Thoth*, translated by Doreal

(adapted)

Angels, Nephilim, Watchers, Dreamers

The Shining Ones in the Bible and
The Book of Enoch

'I speak about the Elect Ones and concerning them.'

The First Book of Enoch, 1:2

In our investigations we have looked at various cultures descended from the Shining Ones, and the links between them. We do not have a clear-cut picture and there are a lot of grey areas. However, one example of such links is the biblical Flood story. This Hebrew myth is very close to one found in the Sumerian *Epic of Gilgamesh*; furthermore, the Genesis account ends with the Tower of Babel (Babylon), set in a region which was part of the Sumerian empire. The Bible story suggests that the secret knowledge associated with the Shining Ones was brought initially to Babylon and then moved on from there.

In all these cultures there are records of special groups that, in our view, represent the Shining priestly elite – a small and powerful group who had experienced enlightenment. In Sumeria we found the *egregor*, or 'Watchers', and the numerous epithets given to them tell us that they too were Shining Ones. Shining Ones are also found in the Bible, where they are thought to be the angels of the Lord. The

Egyptian Neteru can also be translated as 'Watchers' and this is also the meaning of the name 'Essene'. The Essenes were the Jewish sect said to be behind the writing of the Dead Sea Scrolls *(see Chapter Thirteen).*[1] Furthermore, according to Ewald, the name 'Essenes' or 'Essees' is derived from a Hebrew character meaning 'preserver' or 'guardian', and they called themselves 'Guardians', 'Sons of Light' and 'Servants of God' as well as 'Watchers'.[2]

One piece of etymology struck us as important and pointed again to Sumeria being the home of the Shining Ones, perhaps after the destruction of their homeland. The name 'Sumer' comes from 'Shumer' and means literally 'the Land of the Watchers'. It was none other than the ancient biblical land of Shin'ar, which means 'the place of the shining ones'.

Shining Ones in the Bible

The Sumerian word *el* is usually translated as 'God', and in the Bible the word *elohim* is usually translated incorrectly as 'Lord', but it is actually the plural of *el*. The O'Briens point out that *el* means 'brightness' and 'shining'. Indeed, the Semitic word *el* is found in many ancient languages. For instance, the Anglo-Saxon *aelf* ('elf', or supernatural being) means 'shining being' and so *el* needs to be translated not as 'God' but as 'the Shining One', and *elohim*, being plural, should be 'the Shining Ones'. This is the most commonly used term for 'God' in the Old Testament. If you read the Bible and replace the term 'Lord' with 'Shining Ones', you will see a remarkable difference – the Bible how it was meant to be.

Angels

Something that may be surprising is that in the Bible we find that angels, which are often thought of as shining beings, are simply earthly men. The word 'angel' (*malakh* in Hebrew, *aggelos* in Greek, *angelos* in

Latin and *engel* in Anglo-Saxon) means 'messenger'.[3] In the Bible, we do not find angels with wings; there are no original stories of them being supernatural. They are, in fact, quite ordinary mortals. It is frequently Gabriel (meaning 'man of God' or 'man of the Shining One') who informs the people of a future birth. Was he a shaman? A doctor? Michael is the warrior and protector, who is accompanied by angels wielding swords. Each of the angels has his own specific duty, an *earthly* duty. They were people with titles, angelic titles, messengers and ambassadors of 'God', just like the early shamans.

One of the angelic titles, 'Cherubim', means 'exiles' and could be an indication of the origins of the angels. Maybe they were ordered to leave somewhere, perhaps for not conforming. In Genesis 4:16, the Land of Nod is symbolic of the people of Israel, as Nod means 'wandering'. It is not much of an extrapolation therefore to assume that the priesthood (Cherubim, angels) were also wanderers.

Another example of a symbolic title is that of 'Enoch', which means 'consecrated'. There are two Enochs in the Book of Genesis. When Cain and his wife bore the first Enoch and built a city of the same name, the scripture is actually telling us that the people of Cain were consecrated before God. A second Enoch – another consecrated one – would later write up the history of these 'fallen wanderers' who spread across the globe as the great Shining Ones, teaching, measuring and building the world's most mysterious ancient monuments.

Other angelic beings in the Bible are called Seraphim (Numbers 21:6 and elsewhere). These are not mystical beings – they have hands, a face, legs – but they do have powers from God, because they are 'in the light' and they have the symbolic wings of the early shaman, referring to the bird flight, the trance-state ability to fly. Their name means 'Shining Ones' or 'fiery serpents' – they are enlightened beings via the power of the kundalini serpent. Mystical Jewish literature tells us that the angels can fly, tell the future and shapeshift and are *emanations of the divine shining light*.[4]

In the New Testament, the angels are messengers and are also prophesied to take part in the Judgment at the end times.

Enoch and the Watchers

A group called 'Nephilim' or Watchers seems to have been appointed to guard the Garden of Eden. But, as related in *The Book of Enoch*, they then began to mix with the indigenous peoples of the surrounding area:

> 'And it came to pass when the children of men had multiplied that in those days were born unto them beautiful and comely daughters. And the angels, the children of the heaven, saw and lusted after them, and said to one another: "Come, let us choose us wives from among the children of men and beget us children." And Semjaza, who was their leader, said unto them: "I fear ye will not indeed agree to do this deed, and I alone shall have to pay the penalty of a great sin." And they all answered him and said: "Let us all swear an oath, and all bind ourselves by mutual imprecations not to abandon this plan but to do this thing." Then sware they all together and bound themselves by mutual imprecations upon it.'[5]

From this union a hybrid race was produced, a race of 'giants':

> 'And all the others together with them took unto themselves wives, and each chose for himself one, and they began to go in unto them and to defile themselves with them, and they taught them charms and enchantments, and the cutting of roots, and made them acquainted with plants. And they became pregnant, and they bare great giants, whose height was three thousand ells: Who consumed all the acquisitions of men. And when men could no longer sustain them, the

giants turned against them and devoured mankind. And they began to sin against birds, and beasts, and reptiles, and fish, and to devour one another's flesh, and drink the blood. Then the earth laid accusation against the lawless ones.'[6]

'And then Michael, Uriel, Raphael, and Gabriel looked down from heaven and saw much blood being shed upon the earth, and all lawlessness being wrought upon the earth.'[7]

These insurgents also passed on knowledge and taught men combat and how to make weapons:

'And Azazel taught men to make swords, and knives, and shields, and breastplates, and made known to them the metals of the earth and the art of working them, and bracelets, and ornaments, and the use of antimony, and the beautifying of the eyelids, and all kinds of costly stones, and all colouring tinctures. And there arose much godlessness, and they committed fornication, and they were led astray, and became corrupt in all their ways. Semjaza taught enchantments, and root-cuttings, Armaros the resolving of enchantments, Baraqijal astrology, Kokabel the constellations, Ezeqeel the knowledge of the clouds, Araqiel the signs of the earth, Shamsiel the signs of the sun, and Sariel the course of the moon. And as men perished, they cried, and their cry went up to heaven…'[8]

All this was seen as a violation of the laws laid down by the Shining Ones who were possessive of their knowledge:

'Thou seest what Azazel hath done, who hath taught all unrighteousness on earth and revealed the eternal secrets which were (preserved) in heaven, which men were striving

> to learn: And Semjaza, to whom Thou hast given authority
> to bear rule over his associates. And they have gone to the
> daughters of men upon the earth, and have slept with the
> women, and have defiled themselves, and revealed to them
> all kinds of sins. And the women have borne giants, and
> the whole earth has thereby been filled with blood and
> unrighteousness.'[9]

Enoch, a scribe who was taught by the Shining Ones, was then employed as a messenger or intermediary between the Shining Ones and these 'fallen ones' who had decided to abandon their 'divinity' to live amongst mankind. He was sent to tell the insurgents that a severe sentence had been passed on them and that they were soon to be punished.

In brief, the punishment was the Flood. It is as if the Shining Ones wanted to wash away the sins of the Earth that had been created by their own kind – the 'fallen ones'.

But how did they do it? *What awesome power did they possess?*

Leviathan

In *The Book of Enoch* we read: 'Afterwards the judgement shall take place according to His mercy and His patience. And on that day were two monsters parted, [one] a female monster named Leviathan, to dwell in the abysses of the ocean over the fountains of the waters.'[10] We shall remind the reader of the words from the Book of Job 3:8: 'Let them curse it that curse the day, who are skilful to rouse Leviathan.'

When we read these words from the Bible, we sense a reality behind them, even though the name 'Leviathan' suggests a mythical beast of some kind. Leviathan was actually the Hebrew name for the celestial 'dragon of the deep' or the 'dragon of the Abyss', which was believed to reside deep inside the bowels of the Earth in the underworld or the Abzu.

In Sumeria and Babylonia this dragon or serpent was known as

Tiamat. Other names given to this creature are Behemoth, Asp and Rehab. Of late, Tiamat has been the subject of many catastrophe theories. For instance, Zechariah Sitchin believes that Tiamat was a planet that orbited the sun where the Asteroid Belt is today and that the planet Marduk and its satellites, which Sitchin says are on a 3,600-year orbit around the sun in our solar system, collided with it, breaking the planet in two and sending both parts into an orbit closer to the sun. One part then became the Earth and the other became the moon. As overly dramatic and unlikely as this may sound, there are many supporters of this theory. However, a moving celestial body is hardly something that one would describe as having been 'roused' – awakened or stirred up.

In his book *The Day Behemoth and Leviathan Died* David Allen Deal writes that Leviathan (Tiamat) was a planetoid (that he also calls Tristan) that impacted the Earth, burying itself so deep that it became the Earth's inner core. Others have added that this may explain the Cathar belief in Rex Mundi, 'the Lord of the Earth' who rules the world from its central core.

These theories are interesting in view of everything we have seen so far. However, in his book *Middle Eastern Mythology* Professor S. H. Hooke informs us that an ancient cult or scattering of individuals once existed who worshipped the dragon or 'serpent of the sea' and that these people may have even *conjured up* this 'Serpent of the Abyss'. He says this creature was Tiamat. Having cross-referenced the emerging data, we found the individuals referred to by Professor Hooke could only be the Shining Ones.

This monster is known worldwide, but views on it differ. In China the dragon is worshipped and is not considered 'evil' or something that should be destroyed, as in the West with its dragon-slayer saints and heroes, but rather something that should be cultivated. It is again said to reside somewhere beneath the Earth and according to the editors of *The Necronomicon*:

'...it is a powerful force, a magickal force, which is identified with mastery over the created world; it is also a power that can be summoned by the few and not the many.'[11]

So it is more than possible that we are not talking about a creature as such, but a force of some kind – and a rather terrifying force at that. According to Job 3:8, then, Leviathan is really a 'spiritual power' awakened by an adept individual or group whose business it was to stir up this power, perhaps for malevolent purposes.

What this force is exactly seems to have something to do with the Earth's telluric currents – the positive and negative magnetic lines of force that radiate outwards from the core and compose the Earth's underlying energy grid. In China, as already mentioned, these meridians are known as 'dragon paths' and in the West they are called 'ley lines'. The ancient and mystical knowledge associated with these 'Earth energies' has recently re-emerged in Rupert Sheldrake's morphogenetic field theory, which has led many to refer to this underlying system as the morphogenetic grid.

It has also been suggested that the ancients had some control over the grid and could manipulate it through ritual magick. We are told that ancient pagans would raise a 'cone of power' through 'circle dancing' and that this is associated with 'rousing Leviathan'. The same method is used by dervishes in the Middle East and by Native Americans as well as by the Venda tribe in Africa, who engage in the sacred 'Python Dance'. The Gnostics too would utilize the 'round dance', as did the Christians, who would walk the Labyrinth every year inside Chartres Cathedral. We are also reminded of the Biblical story of the fall of the city of Jericho – the result of Joshua and his army marching around the city seven times. On the seventh time the city shook and was destroyed. Obviously these stories are metaphorical, but may contain some truth in that such rituals were tried and may have been seen to be successful.

To see exactly where all this data about Leviathan is really leading us, we will again consult the editors of *The Necronomicon*:

> 'For the Orgone of Wilhelm Reich is just as much Leviathan as the Kundalini of Tantrick adepts, and the Power raised by the Witches. It has always, at least in the past two thousand years, been associated with occultism and essentially with Rites of Evil Magick, or the Forbidden Magick, of the Enemy, and of Satan ... and the twisting, sacred Spiral formed by the Serpent of the Caduceus, and by the spinning of the galaxies, is also the same Leviathan as the Spiral of the biologists' Code of Life: DNA.'[12]

Kundalini no less – a phenomenon we are always being forced to consider and the very force that lies behind the experience in which man's consciousness is able to engage directly with the most powerful force in the Universe – the *synergetic* energy of the void. Indeed, Leviathan has been recognized as the coiled energy of the kundalini serpent.

Were the Shining Ones able to tap into this force – a force that is also inside the Earth? It's a question we must ask, having looked at all the clues we have been given. We would agree it is a fantastic scenario, and could all be fantasy, but we should also keep in mind that we are being led to acknowledge the processes that underlie our very existence – at least that much is true.

We are being told that there were two catastrophes or floods: one that destroyed the former homeland of the Shining Ones and one that was deliberately engineered by these people to punish those insurgents and their offspring who had spoiled their agenda in the East.

As for the offspring – the giants – who were supposed to have been destroyed by this 'act of wrath', some of them survived and we will look at the stories surrounding them later *(see Chapter Thirteen)*. For now, let us return to the Bible and look at one of its most important – and misunderstood – stories: that of Mary's miraculous conception of Christ.

The Original Meaning behind the Conception of Christ

The Catholic doctrine of the Immaculate Conception refers to the inpregnation of the Virgin Mary, mother of Jesus – the idea being that she conceived in the normal human way but without the taint of Original Sin.

One popular Christian tradition has it that she conceived Jesus when a lizard crawled into her ear and came out through her mouth as the 'Word'. Indeed, Pope Felix believed this and in Seville Cathedral there is the figure of a lizard above a doorway, an indication of this belief. The idea seems absurd to us, until we realize that it is a shamanic metaphor in origin.

The 'Word' is associated with the vibratory 'sound of creation' in that the 'Word' that God uttered within the 'void' is the primary frequency which produces all creation – the whole spectrum of frequencies. In the East, especially in India, it is believed that this primary vibration or frequency is encapsulated in the word 'Om' or 'Aum'. The ancient Egyptian heron or bennu bird also symbolized the Word, as it was the first creature to utter the first call at the break of dawn, announcing the new day in the cycle.

The lizard entering Mary through the ear and exiting through the mouth represents energy – in the form of the lizard or serpent – as a continual, in-flowing and out-flowing process. Physically this process originally takes place in the head or brain, and it is self-perpetuating, self-referencing and self-organizing. So what you put in, you get out – 'as ye sow, so shall ye reap.' In our language, 'What you think, or focus on, you will experience.'

This process is symbolized by the *ouroborus*, the lizard or snake swallowing its own tail, an allusion to the fact that the patterns of reality we experience will tend to repeat themselves in cycles, and mostly because we are unconscious throughout the process.

The suggestion is, however, that instead of creating the patterns of reality unconsciously, Mary, like the shaman, became conscious at the

196

crucial point in the process and became enlightened, and so was touched by the 'Holy Ghost' (the neutral life-force) and so she *conceived consciously*. The consensus pattern of reality that we all create unconsciously was changed, transformed. This transformation was also conveyed metaphorically in that she then bore the 'shaman-god-saviour' – a lizard-wizard, a 'serpent being', an 'anointed' 'Christed One' – who was 'reborn' back into the world so as to bring wisdom, again transforming reality in the process.

Jesus was also known as 'the Word'. So Mary gives birth to the 'Word' through her mouth, the *ru*, the third eye, the gateway to the underworld and the world mother. In fact she herself *becomes* the world mother.

Again, the most important thing is that this conception takes place in the head. The lizard enters through the ear – which symbolizes the inward path of spiralling energy as in a vortex – and fertilizes the 'egg' in the head – the thalamus – and exits the mouth, which, as we have seen, symbolizes the vagina and therefore rebirth. So this allegory also conveys the idea that this creative process in consciousness is really a *recreative* process similar to what we find in the toroidal vortex model.

The Magi

A striking feature of Matthew's account of the birth of Jesus is the appearance of the three 'wise men of the east' or 'kings'. They belonged to a group known in Greco-Roman times as *Magi* (singular *Magus*), members of an esoteric elite with roots in ancient Persia – a land adjacent to the Shining Ones' Mesopotamian heartlands. Persia – Iran – appears to have been a region where many Shining Ones taught and passed on their skills.

The Magi were originally the priestly caste of the ancient Persians and are thought by some to have been followers of Zoroastrianism, the religion founded by the prophet Zoroaster. (He is said to have been born of a virgin and is expected by believers to return *three* times in the future). Magi rituals were very similar to the later rituals of alchemy and are probably directly related. They certainly had a strongly astronomical and astrological element, as indicated by the account of the three Magi in Matthew's gospel (Matthew 2:2).

The Magi appear to have had no temples, and by the time of Jesus (1st century) they seem to have been nomadic, wandering from place to place like the original Shining Ones (and indeed like the wise men in the Nativity story), practising esoteric arts, for their skill in which they were widely famous. Their secret rituals were carried out 'in heaven', on mountaintops, the places that were 'near the gods'. (The priests of Egypt, Mesoamerica and the Far East carried out their secret rituals on man-made mountains: ziggurats and pyramids.)

The Magi also worshipped the sun and, like their shamanic antecedents, believed in reincarnation. The biblical wise men who venerated Jesus were probably seeking the reborn sun god, and their gifts to Jesus were the same as those that the Magi offered to their sun god. Gold was the symbol of royalty and immortality; frankincense symbolized divinity; and myrrh represented death, rebirth and reincarnation. As mentioned earlier, at a deeper level, these three gifts symbolize the three organs of the brain. Frankincense and myrrh are made from the 'oils of the tree' and relate to the pineal and pituitary; the gold is the thalamus.

When we understand the meaning of the names traditionally given to the 'three kings' (the names do not occur in the New Testament), the Shining connection is even clearer: Melchior is 'King of Light' or 'Shining One'; Caspar is 'the White One'; Balthazar, the 'Lord of the Treasures'. The secret treasures of the Shining Ones can only be found when we accept the light and adorn ourselves with 'white' clothes.

If these particular Magi existed, they would have received their training from the shamanic tradition. The Classical author Ammianus Marcellinus tells us that the Magi obtained their knowledge from the

Brahmins of India, and Arianus refers to the Brahmins as Magi. The Brahmins got their knowledge from the shamanic and serpentine Shining Ones.

It seems most likely that the Magi were the 'new shamans'. They were found in several localities and known as astrologers. Astrology was also popular in contemporary Judaism – as demonstrated by the prominence of the star in the Nativity story of the Jewish-Christian evangelist Matthew. The Magi also practised the study and divination of dreams (oneiromancy) and the hidden ways of ancient science – shamanic Shining ways, handed down from generation to generation. And indeed the three wise men of Matthew's account receive a divine message in a dream (Matthew. 2:12).

Dream interpretation is a prominent feature in the Old and New Testaments. The most famous episodes in the Hebrew Bible (Old Testament) include Jacob's dream of the ladder reaching to heaven, with angels ascending and descending upon it (Genesis 28:11–22), and the prophetic dreaming of Jacob's son, Joseph, in Genesis 37: 5–10. Joseph is also a renowned dream-interpreter, successfully explaining the dreams of pharaoh and others during his captivity in Egypt (Genesis 40, 41). His skills in this regard are superior even to 'all the magicians and wise men of Egypt' (Genesis 41:8). Jacob and Joseph were descendants of Abraham – a Shining One that we will discuss further in chapters thirteen and fourteen.

Another prophetic dreamer is Joseph, the putative father of Jesus, who receives prophecies from angels (Matthew 1:20–23; 2:13; 2:19).

There is further evidence, even in the official scriptures, linking the shamanic Shining tradition, exemplified by the Magi, to these key figures of Judaism and Christianity, and Jesus himself. In Luke's genealogy of Christ (Luke 3:23–38), his ancestry is traced back through Joseph – the Shining shaman to Mary's shamaness – to the house of Levi, the Israelite priestly elite, and beyond through Judah (brother of Joseph the dreamer and another son of Jacob), Abraham and beyond to Adam. It is no wonder then that the Magi should have taken an interest in the prophesied birth of Jesus – they saw it as the arrival of a great Shining priest-shaman for the new age.

We will come back to the subject of the Shining Ones and Judaism. In the meantime, let us return to the Watchers and look at what became of their hybrid offspring, the giants.

1 2

Giants

Memories of the Watchers?

'And it came to pass, when men began to multiply on the
face of the earth, and daughters were born unto them, that
the sons of God [Watchers] saw the daughters of men that
they were fair; and they took them wives of all which they
chose ... There were giants in the earth in those days; and
also after that, when the sons of God came in unto the
daughters of men, that they bare children to them, the same
became mighty men which were of old, men of renown.'

The Book of Genesis 6:1–4

In the Bible and elsewhere we encounter the enigmatic figures
referred to as 'giants' or 'men of renown'. Does this mean that man
has degenerated and actually reduced in stature since those ancient
days? Our view was that if we were right about the universal spread of
the Shining Ones then we would find stories of giants around the
world in myth and folklore – the folklore memories of the Watchers.
We believed that if we could find the giants of old, then we would find
the remnant of the Watchers.

Giants in the Bible

We had already discovered that a race of giants was mentioned in the Bible – the Nephilim (Genesis 6:4, Deuteronomy 1:28, Numbers 13:32), the Rephaim (Joshua 12:4) and the Anakim (Joshua 14:15). These ancient giants were known as Shining Ones.

Much of the biblical writing concerning these giants speaks of antediluvian times – the time before the great Deluge, which tales from Mesopotamia and *The Book of Enoch* tell us was the result of a war in 'heaven' caused by a union between the Watchers or giants and the women of Earth.

As well as being called Nephilim – 'fallen ones', like the fallen Watchers of *The Book of Enoch* – these giants are also known as Anakim, after Anak, who may very well have had a father called Arba who was the original builder of Hebron *(see* Genesis 35:27). Here we have a subtle link with architecture and structure.

In Deuteronomy we also have: 'The Emims dwelt therein in times past, a people great, and many, and tall, as the Anakims; which also were accounted giants, as the Anakims.'[1] The word used here for 'giant' is Raphah, which simply means 'giant'. So there were yet more giants existing after the Flood spoken of by Moses and in a different area from that of the Canaanites.

The Bible tells us after the time of Noah the children of Israel were sent as spies into Canaan to prepare for the invasion. These spies discovered giants in the land and said to Moses:

> 'Nevertheless the people be strong that dwell in the land, and the cities are walled, and very great: and moreover we saw the children of Anak there. … We be not able to go up against the people; for they are stronger than we. And they brought up an evil report of the land which they had searched unto the children of Israel, saying, The land, through which we have gone to search it, is a land that eateth up the inhabitants thereof; and all the people that we

saw in it are men of great stature. And there we saw the giants, the sons of Anak, which come of the giants: and we were in our own sight as grasshoppers, and so were we in their sight.'[2]

The word used for giants – Nephilim – is the same as that used in Genesis 6:4, and so we are being told that indeed the giants survived the Flood. It seems that afterwards there was a second irruption of these fallen angels, evidently smaller in number and more limited in area, for they were confined in Canaan, and were in fact known as the 'nations of Canaan'. It was for the destruction of these that the sword of Israel was necessary.

We also find that Moab was 'also accounted a land of giants; giants dwelt therein in old time; and the Ammonites call them Zamzummims; a people great, and many, and tall, as the Anakims; but the Lord destroyed them.'[3] One of the giants is even named and crops up in this story several times. His name is Og and he was the king of Bashan:

'For only Og king of Bashan remained of the remnant of giants; behold, his bedstead was a bedstead of iron; is it not in Rabbath of the children of Ammon? Nine cubits was the length thereof, and four cubits the breadth of it, after the cubit of a man.'[4]

Indeed, Bashan was said to be of huge stature, 'the land of giants'.[5] King Og himself was supposed to have lived for 3,000 years.

Joshua also mentions giants or 'Rephaim'. These were thought to have lived in the region near Sodom and Gomorrah in the time of Abraham.[6]

Other Giants

It seems that it was long before Christian times that giants began to take on the evil and demonic aspect familiar from folk and fairytales (such as Jack and the Beanstalk). *The Book of Enoch* says:

> 'But now the giants who are born from the [union of] the spirits and the flesh shall be called evil spirits upon the earth, because their dwelling shall be upon the earth and inside the earth. Evil spirits have come out of their bodies. Because from the day that they were created from the holy ones they became the Watchers: their first origin is the spiritual foundation. They will become evil upon the earth and shall be called evil spirits. The dwelling of the spiritual beings of heaven is heaven; but the dwelling of the spirits of the earth, which are born upon the earth, is in the earth.'[7]

Enoch tells us that the Watchers were going out far and wide in order to measure, specifically north. This would have a significant bearing upon European stories of giants who were said to have built the ancient monuments such as Stonehenge.

Phonetically similar to 'Og', as in King Og of Bashan, is the Sumerian Ogma or Ugmash (also related to Shamash the sun god), who has been linked with Ogma of Irish myth and legend, one the Tuatha dé Danaan *(see below)*, known as Ogma *grian-aineach* or 'He with the countenance of the sun' – the Shining One. In Irish mythology, the giants were actual gods who had fallen from heaven, like stars falling to Earth, and in Nordic and Greek legend the giants fought against the gods.

Most giants are said to live below the ground, which is symbolically a cave or underworld, the dwelling of the shaman, and are said to possess the powers of the Earth goddess. The modern image of the slow and stupid giant is at odds with ancient symbolism; it is very likely that this may have been an attempt by the Christian Church to dispel the worship or reverence of the old ways.

Most giants were also bearded. A beard was primarily an ancient symbol of manhood and power. Eventually it became the symbol for wisdom, authority and even divinity. We find in old literature that many insults against rivals derived from the lack of a beard. This is why Egyptian rulers always wore beards, whether real or false. Queen Hatshepsut is known to have worn a false beard on Egyptian state occasions as a symbol of her divinity and power. The tomb masks of pharaohs display long beards, which show their divinity after human death. Baal, the Canaanite and pre-Judaic sun god, was bearded, and this may be one of the reasons why today we imagine God to have a white beard. Another reason for this is that El, the Canaanite high god who later became the Hebrew creator-god Yahweh, also wore a beard.

The giants were also renowned as great builders. At Les Pierres Plates in France, the *allée coudée* passageway offers indications of the skills of those buried there. In his book *Megalithic Mysteries*, Michael Balfour puts it like this:

> 'The place is like a deserted teaching hospital; the reception area is on the left, and prehistoric medical illustrations have been left on the walls – ribs, hearts, lungs, livers, stomachs, below collar bones and neck recesses, with spinal cords, channels of life.'[8]

Those who used such places and were buried in them were medicine men, and quite practical ones by the sound of it. Across the globe the Shining Ones were described as serpent physicians, serpent healers, medicine men, and so on.

The Wheel of Giants

Now we will take a brief look at the site of one of Israel's greatest mysteries, which is relatively unknown in the Western world: the Circle of Rephaim.

Known by several names, such as Rugum/Rogem Hiri ('Wheel of Giants'), or Rujm al-Hiri, which is Arabic for 'stone heap of the wild cat', Gilgal Rephaim, a massive circular construction, is to be found in the Golan Heights, 10 miles (16 km) east of the Sea of Galilee at an altitude of 150 feet (500 metres) above sea level. This Stonehenge-like monument is one of the world's least-known wonders and looks remarkably like the Atlantis of Plato's description.

Believed to have been built *c.*3000 BC, it is not a burial ground, nor a standard stone circle. Nor is it a dwelling. In fact nobody knows what this peculiar place is for sure. But considering everything we have looked at already, we can identify this concentric-ring design as a symbol of the entrance into the enlightened state.

The diameter of the site is 508 ft (155 metres) with a wall 6.5 ft (2 metres) high and 10 ft (3.3 metres) thick. The total weight of the stones used in the construction has been estimated at between 37,000 and 42,000 tons. In the centre of the rings is a cairn with a tumulus on top measuring 65 ft (20 metres) across from a later date (about 1,000 years later).

Some scholars link the Near Eastern gods Ashteroth and Tammuz (descendants of An, the supreme Shining One of Sumer) to the site as fertility gods. Apparently, according to work carried out by Professor Anthony Aveni and Dr Yoni Mizrachi, the precise measurements of the site are in proportion exactly the same as those used in Egypt and ancient Mesopotamia, proportions which were based on the human body. This 5,000-year-old link in time to Egypt and Mesopotamia is very interesting.

Apart from this evidence and some minor jewellery, little else has been discovered about the site. What is known is that for some reason it is linked with giants, specifically the giants mentioned in the biblical stories. Significantly, it stands in the biblical region known as Bashan.

As with various other mysterious sites around the world, the full extent of Gilgal Rephaim can only be viewed from above. There are no mountains overlooking the site and it is built upon a flat plateau or Eden, and so it defies the sight of man on Earth and mirrors the Edin of the skies. It has been suggested that it was therefore a message to the gods in the sky, and we should not rule out this possibility, although it also could have been seen as a message *from* the gods.

Around the region of Gilgal Rephaim there are thousands of dolmens. Moshe Hartel, the chief archaeologist of the Golan, has said that they have identified 8,500 dolmens of 20 separate styles, with each tribe having their own style. Some of the biggest dolmens weigh over 50 tons and are some 23 ft (7 metres) in height, with not all of them, for some unknown reason, including a burial. This massive complex of dolmens surrounding the Gilgal Rephaim in fact covers a larger area than the whole Giza pyramid complex.

One more peculiar fact now needs throwing into the cauldron – the building of circles was not a common practice amongst the herdsmen of the area at the time, and so we are left to conclude that this site may be of outside origin.

Incidentally, the Hebrew name 'Gilgal' means 'stone circle', as in Gilgal Rephaim, 'stone circle of Rephaim'. There are Gilgals all over the Middle East. Take 'Gilgal' apart and we have *ag il ag al*, which means 'the mighty god'. Gilgals are mentioned several times in the Bible. Saul was made king at Gilgal or at a stone circle. The captain of the Lord of Hosts told Joshua that the place was holy.[9] Bullocks, sheep and oxen were sacrificed at Gilgal.[10] Angels of the Lord came from Gilgal – again a stone circle.[11] Samuel travelled year on year between Bethel (house of God), Gilgal (stone circle) and Mizpah (watchtower) and judged the people.

The circle is also linked to the cycle, and as we now know these ancient concentric-ringed designs are symbolically associated with the cycle of life-death-rebirth and reincarnation. The emphasis is on the centre, of course, but also the gateway into the centre – the crucial point in all periodic systems and cyclical phenomena, symbolized by the mouth-tail point in the *ouroboros* snake.

We must ask, are all these references just symbolic pointers to a wandering priesthood who once used the powers of the Earth's energies? As we discovered, the circle, spiral-circle and concentric-ring symbolism all relate to the vortex also. So the only logical conclusion we can come to is that these stone circles were built to mark the vortices in the Earth's magnetic field, the places where the positive and negative lines of force cross and converge. As we noted earlier, these were believed to be gateways between dimensions, places that could trigger the kundalini awakening associated with spiritual rebirth.

Who built the Circle of Rephaim? The answer has to be the Watchers. There is a further clue here. Sirius is the star that is symbolic of the underworld, where the giants, Watchers and fallen angels are supposed to reside. It is said to be the home of the 'fish beings' who visited the Dogon tribe *(see Chapter Nine)*. It is associated with Isis, but is also the dog star of Anubis and/or Thoth and therefore the shaman-accompanying dog. There are two large openings in the Circle of Rephaim, facing north-east and south-east, the north-east one allowing the first rays of the sun on the day of the summer solstice – now 21 June – to enter the geometric centre. The south-east opening did not point to the rising sun on the winter solstice – now 21 December – as expected. It points, some say, directly to Sirius.

We wondered how this linked with the biblical Watchers. In Genesis 14:5 we are informed that the giants or Watchers inhabited Ashtherot-Karnaim. This has been identified with the Canaanite city of Ashtarot just 10 miles from the Gilgal Rephaim. Ashtherot was in fact the Canaanite goddess of love and war, who was depicted as pillars

208

in the Temple of Jerusalem (Asherah poles) in later years and linked in entirety to the serpent and the Shining Ones of Mesopotamia. The link? Ashtherot was the Canaanite name for Sirius. And to add to this, in line with the circle and Ashteroth is Mount Hermon, which Deuteronomy tells us the Sidonians called Sirion.

Another link is the theory of some scholars, especially Christian scholars, that Gilgal Rephaim is the burial place of the king of Bashan, the very same Og we mentioned earlier. In fact Jewish oral tradition states that the reason these giants survived the Flood was because King Og stowed away on the ark – indicating again that the giants were both ante- and post-diluvian.

Dr Mattanyah Zohar of the University of Jerusalem has suggested that the circle may have been a ceremonial centre, much like Stonehenge, where thousands of nomads gathered at certain times of the year for religious and tribal purposes. If this is the case, then it clearly backs our hypothesis that the Shining Ones had a central religious core and were wandering the world spreading their belief system, knowledge and control. Indeed, the very size and weight of the whole complex indicates a highly organized and efficient system of administration, like the pyramids of Egypt in later years.

We wondered about the surrounding area and whether there were any further clues to be gathered there.

The area is known as the Golan and the rough period we were interested in – about the fourth–third millennia BC – was called the Chalcolithic. Currently only about 25 sites have been found in Golan and minimal archaeology has been carried out in comparison to the sites of Egypt. Most of these sites are situated east and north-east of the Sea of Galilee in an area of basaltic rock and high rainfall, thus allowing for excellent herding but not so good crop farming, i.e. a nomadic existence.

During the period we were interested in we found that the various villages consisted of between 20 and 40 dwellings built on terraces in rows and sharing a common wall. The houses were lower than ground level, with thick walls, and were reached by steps, thus keeping the heat at a minimum. Finds from the domestic element of this period have shown, like elsewhere in the world, the pottery was decorated with zigzags and spirals – features we already knew to be indicative of the serpent and enlightenment aspects of ancient history.

In the household finds with a more religious purpose the archaeologists discovered figurines measuring approximately 10 inches (25 cm) in height. The form was of a round pillar with a shallow bowl on top, thought to be for offerings. The pillars were fashioned with features such as eyes and ears, mouths and a protruding nose – a symbol of the breath of life or Word. Several of the figures even had horns and beards and we knew already that these were symbols used by the Shining shaman. The horns signified illumination and the beard wisdom.

The Asherah poles of the Temple in Jerusalem spoken of in the Bible were also said to have been anthropomorphic, and this again links the culture in the area to the Sirius connection. We also noted that the 'offering' bowls were placed on the 'heads' of the figures. These figures from the period contemporaneous with the Gilgal Rephaim must be related, and if so, are additional archaeological evidence for the existence of the Shining culture in the area. In fact they also show just how old the concepts clearly outlined in the Bible really are. The tradition of King Og having stowed away in the ark and then inhabiting or even building his new nation in Golan are now not so ridiculous. It may be that the Shining Ones survived the flood that they are said to have caused and then spread into more temperate climes, where the bloodline of the original Watchers, giants or Shining Ones continued, and with them the folklore.

What does indeed seem peculiar with this story of giants is the almost worldwide idea of an ancient bloodline that goes back thousands of years to the fallen angels or Watchers.

Greek Giants

According to Greek mythology, the giants were the 'sons of the earth' (Greek, *Ge genis*), which would link them with the Hebrew 'sons of God' and the switch between matriarchy and patriarchy.

In Greek myth the giants were generated from the blood of Uranus, which resulted from his castration by Chronus (time). The sons of Uranus and Gaea, the mother goddess, fell to Earth in much the same manner as the angels of the Hebrews. So, *Ur* (possibly the Mesopotamian city where Abraham learned his trade etc.), *An* (Shining One), *us* (descriptive) was castrated and therefore nearly destroyed by time, and his bloodline continued into the Greek pantheon of giants.

The Greek giants even became powerful enough to try to unseat the father-god Zeus and the other Olympian gods early in their rule, thus showing their link with the battling and fallen Watchers of Sumeria, who did the same thing. In fact, this must be a memory of the same story.

When the gods were victorious, they were said to have imprisoned the giants in Tartarus, the deepest part of the underworld, or alternatively under the Earth, in much the same way that the Watchers were cast down in Sumerian and biblical stories.

These giants had long hair – a trait we noted also with the Shining Ones, Templars and hundreds of others involved in this story.

Interestingly, in sculpture they were represented with the tails of serpents, and as Cyclops or Cyclopes, they show the one-eyed definition which is also seen in Sumerian 'one-eyed serpent' Shining Ones.

European Giants

Across Europe there are monuments such as standing stones, burial mounds, barrows and cairns and even natural formations like rocks and crags in the shapes of chairs, desks and tables that were considered to be the relics of a race of giants who were thought to have lived in certain localities. Of course this relates back to the Watchers of Enoch who went north to measure and build.

There are also literally hundreds of tales of giants, mostly similar and therefore showing a common origin. In England some myths have giants as the descendants of the 33 daughters of the Emperor Diocletian, a great builder. They murdered their husbands and were set adrift in a ship that eventually reached England. We had to laugh at the obvious masonic allusions within this tale. Was this the influence of the giants of old acting upon modern secret societies?

According to Geoffrey of Monmouth, these giants were the only inhabitants of England when Brutus arrived from Troy. Geoffrey also wrote that the last giant was eliminated by Corineus of Cornwall, who enjoyed wrestling with the giants, and when Brutus was attacked by a group of them at Totnes, he defeated them all except for a monster called Gogmagog. This one remaining giant Brutus offered to Corineus as a wrestling partner. Gogmagog, of course, is a biblical name, encompassing the name of Og, the giant king of Bashan, and the root of the ancient Ogma language and of Ogmius, the ancient Celtic giant deity. The story of Gogmagog has many parallels in other mythologies.

In Scotland giants were reputed to eat human flesh – a method of explaining the sacrificial aspect of these ancient peoples. There were various groups of giants across Scotland. One group was the Fomorians, who lived in the Highlands, and some believe they were a remnant of the Fomorians of Ireland who came to Scotland, bringing their tales of giants with them.

The Fomorians of Ireland were a race of giants who occupied the island in ancient times – the dates are unspecific. They were not the first people there, however, and had to do battle with the inhabitants, the followers of Partholon, to claim the land. Following the Fomorians came the Nemeds (Nimrods?) who were easily beaten and enslaved by the Fomorians.

Next came the Fir Bolg, who were more successful and subdued the Fomorians, going on eventually to live peacefully with them. According to the Irish source, the Fir Bolg and the people known as the Tuatha dé Danann or 'People of Danu', i.e. 'People of the Shining Ones' (Danu is the feminine version of the Mesopotamian god Anu), were both descendants of the same people, the Nemedians, who were said to have come to Ireland from Greece. The Nemedians had been all but destroyed by the Fomorians, and the remnant fled abroad: some back to Greece, from where they later returned as the Fir Bolg, and some to the 'northern islands of the world', where they acquired great supernatural knowledge and skill in all the arts. The latter returned as the Tuatha dé Danann, who defeated and made peace with the Fir Bolg.

The chief male god of the Tuatha dé Danann was the Dagda (Good God), also called 'the Mighty One of Great Knowledge'. His son was none other than Ogma, or Oghma, the giant whom we mentioned earlier. Both were famed for superhuman strength and knowledge, and the Dagda had a giant cauldron that brought back to life anyone immersed in it.

These people of the tribe of Danu can in fact be linked with the Bible and serpent worship. Walker tells us:

'Writers of the Old Testament disliked the Danites, whom they called serpents (Genesis 49:17). Nevertheless, they adopted Dan-El or Daniel, a Phoenician god of divination, and transformed him into a Hebrew prophet. His magic powers were like those of the Danites emanating from the Goddess Dana and her sacred serpents. He served as a court astrologer and dream-interpreter for both the Persian king Cyrus, and the Babylonian king Nebuchadnezzar (Daniel 1:21, 2:1), indicating that "Daniel" was not a personal name but a title, like the Celtic one: "a person of the Goddess Danu".'[12]

We see from this, and other references, that the Tuatha dé Danann were people who came from the Middle East and left their holy rituals along the way. These holy ways included astrology and dream interpretation. This method of divination is highly related to the waking-sleeping hypnagogic state.

The Tuatha dé Danann themselves were finally defeated by the Celts (Gaels) and the land was divided – the Tuatha dé Danann ruled the unseen underworld or otherworld, the Celts the upper world. It is possible that this whole mythological story is based around a common astro-theological theme that has spread over the course of thousands of years into all manner of cultures.

*   *   *

Let us now return to the connections between the shamanic Shining tradition and the great world religion which underlies much of the Western cultural heritage: Judaism.

Israel in Egypt

The Shining Roots of Judaism

'And I will give this people favour in the sight of the Egyptians.'

Genesis 3:21 (King James Version)

We have seen how the Jewish and Christian scriptures contain many references to the Shining Ones and their practices, from the accounts of the Elohim, angels and giants to stories of shamanistic dream-prophecy, and of course the accounts of Jesus and John the Baptist – among countless other references. Christianity, which produced the New Testament, began as a sect of Judaism, but where did Judaism itself come from? We believe that the roots of Judaism are to be found in the most unexpected places – not solely with the Canaanites, as has been suggested. Neither are they purely the amalgamation of the collected beliefs of a nomadic tribe or group of tribes. In our belief, the true roots of Judaism are to found in the traditions of the Shining Ones, as transmitted through ancient Egypt.

The term 'Jews' is relatively recent, dating as it does to post-Old Testament times. It arose *c.* 63 BC when the Romans incorporated the eastern shores of the Mediterranean into their empire and gave the land between Syria and Egypt desert the name of Judea, after the old land of Judah.[1] The people of the Hebrew Bible – the Christian Old Testament – are usually termed 'Israel', 'Israelites' or 'Hebrews'. Their leaders and prophets are often tellingly symbolic figures. For instance, the name of Samson derives from the Hebrew *shemesh*, 'sun', which is identical to Shamash, the Sumerian sun god (Hebrew and Sumerian are related Semitic languages). He loses his hair – a woman cuts it off – and therefore his power. Hair is symbolic of the rays of the sun and when the sun's rays are cut off, its power is shortened. But more than this, the sun is symbolic of the enlightenment experience of the Shining Ones and therefore by having his hair cut off, Samson also had his mental power reduced.

The story of Samson may be based on a real person, but at this distance in time finding proof of the existence of most biblical characters is difficult. Some of the Israelite kings are named in inscriptions, but earlier figures such as Moses, Abraham, Jacob and Isaac are extremely difficult to locate outside the Bible. The reason is simple: many of them were just characters created to mirror the celestial equivalents. Others are priests of the 'celestial twins' (sun and moon) and take on their name, which becomes a title. This title then passes on with each generation: in the Bible, this is what we should understand when we read of such figures as Enoch and Noah apparently living for several centuries.

There is much which is accurate within the Hebrew Bible, and we should take this into account when refuting some of the evidence it gives, although, as with any history written by a people about themselves, it is heavily biased. Many of the biblical stories come from the surrounding areas, such as Canaan, Babylon and Egypt. There is evidence to suggest that many of the stories and themes it contains actually came from as far away as Central Asia.[2] This would explain some of the more shamanistic ideas in the scriptures.

The Egyptian Connection

There is an idea that some of the Israelite tribes were made up of the 'Hyksos', Semitic seafaring people from the eastern Mediterranean who took power for a time in ancient Egypt. This may have been when the Israelites lived in Egypt. Later the Hyksos were expelled, which may account for the Israelites leaving to find their own 'Promised Land'. All this is conjecture, and we do not actually have very much hard evidence about the 'Hebrews' outside the Bible. There are some references to them in Egyptian inscriptions as the *Hapiru* (Hebrews), and temple records and other cultures also mention them.

The strongest possibility is that the Israelites were an amalgamated group of nomadic tribes. They probably came together for strength in the world of ever-increasing empires and kingdoms. It may be that this grouping sided with the Hyksos or were employed by them to help take control of Egypt. While they were in Egypt, possibly under Ramses II (13th century BC), some were perhaps slaves. This same collection of tribes subsequently left Egypt and either integrated with the Canaanites or invaded their land and took control of them. The powerful knowledge of Egypt, added to their already vast knowledge of shamanic rituals, made them a small but spiritually powerful force.

Founders and Patriarchs

The Bible has it that the sons of Noah, Shem, Ham and Japheth, populated the Earth, and were the founders of the major regions known at that time:

Shem: Hebrews, Chaldeans, Assyrians, Persians

Ham: Egyptians, Philistines, Hittites, Amorites

Japheth: Greeks, Thracians, Scythians, Syrians

It is from Shem that the modern word Semite is derived, which in an ancient context refers to Babylonians, Assyrians, Arameans, Canaanites, Edomites, Moabites, Israelites, Arabs and Ethiopians. The Israelites were part of all of these, the saviours or religious guides of them all.

According to the Bible, the father figure of the Jews is Abraham, the first of the patriarchs of Israel. He is supposed to have lived c. 2200 BC, about the time of many megalithic building projects around the globe, including the Great Pyramid. He was by tradition the son of Terah, a descendant of Shem, and was thought to be a contemporary of Hammurabi, king of Babylon.

Abraham was born and lived in 'Ur of the Chaldees' in Mesopotamia. The area was farmed as early as approximately 10000 BC. It was occupied properly as early as the fourth millennium BC. The great ziggurat of Nanna the moon god and his moon goddess wife Ningal was built here and the city was known as the city of the moon god. The ziggurat represented the great cosmic mountain of the gods and undoubtedly Abraham would have visited the site – if he was an actual individual, that is.

Elaborate religious objects have been found in graves at Ur, some of which show the 'ram in the thicket', an image similar to that in the biblical account of Abraham's abortive sacrifice of his son Isaac.

It is assumed that the archetypal Abraham would have attended the priest school, then left the city to move around with the nomads of Canaan, and later still moved to Egypt. That Abraham was given the title of 'father' implies that he wielded great authority over the people, and this became the subsequent meaning of the title. One of the first instances of the application of this title is to be found in Judges 18:18, c.742 BC, when the priest of Micah is made 'a father and a priest to us … and he took the ephod [priest's robe], the household idols, and the carved image, and took his place among the people'. This is a prime example of the title being bestowed by the people, with all the idols, carved images and robes relating to the Shining Ones' office.

In Muslim tradition, Abraham is called Ibrahim and his surname is Khalil Allah, or 'friend of God'. His father was a *wazir* to Nimrod, the great-grandson of Noah, who was a warrior, king of Babylon and founder of Nineveh and, reputedly, the builder of the Tower of Babel. When Ibrahim's mother was due to give birth to him she was led secretly away by angels to a concealed cave near Damascus, referred to by the local community as 'Bethlehem', which is the title given to a sacred grove dedicated to Adonis or Tammuz – a solar deity. These angelic ministrants made the birth painless and the newborn babe was placed into the hands of 'Shining Ones' to bring him up in the secret ways.

Again we have an angel and a cave involved in the birth of a child, although this time not in the Bible.[3] The cave signifies the womb of Mother Earth, the angel a messenger. The pain was taken away by the drugs and medicinal knowledge of the 'ministrant angels'. The boy was then 'chosen' by these angels to be instructed in special knowledge. This was the child's birthright, the result of the high position and ability of his father. This was a cult ritual of initiation.

The cave 'near Damascus' is close to Qumran, where the Essene legacy lies *(see below)* and where the Gnostic traditions were taught to the ascetic followers of the light, and to the 'Bethlehem' birthplace of Christ.

The process of initiation continues. Later in the story, when Ibrahim could speak, he went outside the cave, saw a bright star and said, 'Surely this is my Lord,' but the star disappeared and he changed his mind. The same happened with the moon and the sun, until eventually he cried out to God and asked him to reveal himself. So the Archangel Gabriel came and instructed the young man in the truth. This indicated that he was not to put his trust in the stars he could see in the sky but the ones on Earth who bore the same names.

To return to the Hebraic Abraham, he is said to have dealt with the Egyptian Pharaoh and even practised magic in order to bring plagues on the Egyptians. His name changed from Abram (A-brahm) to

Abraham, following the priestly tradition of giving new titles and names. In Genesis 14, Abraham, as the 'father', gave the king of Salem the title of Melchizedek, which meant 'King of Righteousness'. Throughout history there has been only one kind of person who could give names to kings: a religious pontiff. Was Abraham some kind of great religious leader, respected even by other nations? Or was 'Abraham' the *title* of such a pontiff? Does this mean that the Israelites were not so much a nomadic nation as a nomadic religious group of special priests, like the Shining Ones?

It may be that the king of Salem was actually a member of the priesthood himself, of the order of Zadok, and was given the title Michael (meaning 'He who is shining' or 'He who is like God'), the title of the chief angel or archangel.[4] We know that priests both within and outside the Jewish community actually took on the names of the angels, in the same way that the Dalai Lama takes on his name when he is reincarnated. This, if true, would make the king of Salem a high priest in the order of Zadok and, in the official function of Michael, the chief messenger of the people.

Ancient Hebrew Worship

The priestly system had by now developed into an intricate esoteric cult which was highly related to the Shining ways and beliefs inherited by the ancient Egyptians *(see Chapter Ten)*, especially regarding solar worship and astrology. The Hebrews had a lunar calendar, and feast-days based around heavenly cyclical patterns, with new moon festivals and full moon feasts celebrating the waxing and waning of the mother moon goddess:

> 'At the height of your months you shall present a burnt offering to the Lord, two young bulls, one ram, and seven lambs in their first year…'[5]

'And he built altars for all the host of heaven [angels or stars] in the two courts… Also he made his son pass through fire, practised soothsaying, used witchcraft [or old ways] and consulted spirits and mediums.'[6]

'The children gather wood, the fathers kindle the fire, and the women knead dough, to make cakes for the Queen of Heaven.'[7]

The 'Queen of Heaven' is the name of Ishtar, the Mesopotamian goddess associated with Venus. In Egypt in the fifth century BC there is evidence of Jews worshipping this Queen of Heaven, and throughout Jewish history the Queen of Heaven in one form or another has been ever present.[8]

It would certainly make sense for a group of nomadic tribesmen to have within their priesthood the knowledge of the stars, if only for use in navigation. This would make the priests seem more powerful to the group and almost 'magical' in their understanding of the gods of the sky. It seems that the Hebrews believed that God made and controlled the stars for our destiny. Both Hebrews and other nations of the time worshipped the stars, as we can see throughout the Bible:

'Lest you lift your eyes to heaven, and when you see the sun, the moon, and the stars, all the host of heaven, you feel driven to worship them and serve them…'[9]

This was a warning against this rapidly growing belief, whilst behind the scenes the priests themselves were involved in the practice. In 2 Kings 17 there is a reproach from the priests and to the priests for moving towards the worship of the 'host of Heaven' and Baal, the old Canaanite god who shared so much with Yahweh, the god of the Israelites. In 2 Kings 21:3,5 and Isaiah 45:6, Psalm 50:1, there are references to a sundial and the fact that the directions of the sun and moon are greatly important to the Jews.

In summary, there are numerous passages throughout the Hebrew Bible and other writings of the time which show us that the Hebrews were involved in the worship of the sun, a moon or Earth goddess, the stars as the 'host of heaven' and various other animal-faced gods.[10]

Yahweh

Yahweh, the Israelite deity, was an amalgamation of many divine aspects, and there is evidence in the Bible that the early Israelites may have had not just one god but several, of which Yahweh (Jehovah) was the greatest. Not until the later books of the Old Testament (such as Ezra and Nehemiah), composed during or after the Bablylonian exile in the sixth century BC, is Yahweh seen as the *only* god, and a god for all humanity. Earlier, the Israelites seem to have regarded Yahweh as their particular supreme national god, just as other peoples had national gods of their own. They were obviously less mighty than Yahweh, but their existence was acknowledged.

One such god was Baal, worshipped by the Canaanites and the Phoenicians. Baal simply meant 'lord', as in Baal-berith, 'the lord of the covenant', and Baalzebub, 'the lord of the flies'. Among the northern Israelites, Baal was widely venerated alongside Yahweh. The shrines of the Baal were stone altars, with sacred pillars nearby, very similar to, and from the same period as, the huge megalithic structures of the northern shamans.

The 'Shining prophet' Elijah or Elias (ninth century BC) fought the Baal cult and engaged in a contest of shamanic magic with the priests of the cult – a battle between sorcerers that ended with Elijah having the Baal prophets put to death. Later, Elijah is said in the Bible to have risen to heaven in a flaming chariot, but was expected to return and herald the Messiah – in the New Testament, John the Baptist was asked if he was the returned Elijah. It is likely that the Shining Ones actually trained many Elijahs in their ways as magicians, fathers or, later, Popes – all being given the title 'El', for 'strong' or 'Shining', to show where their origins lie.

Yahweh and the Shining Goddess

From about the sixth century BC, and most likely well before, the Israelite god was part of a duality, certain aspects of the deity being feminized, as for example Sophia, Divine Wisdom. It was well understood that for there to be creation there had to be intercourse between the gods (a union of opposites). This belief can be traced back to the early shamanic beliefs.

This dual nature of God, male and female, was nothing new. It was widespread then and survives today in Gnostic and Kabbalistic traditions. It even survives in the cult of the Virgin Mary in Catholicism – subtle evidence that no matter what we see on the face of a religion, there is always a continuation of the old ways below the surface.

Ashtoreth, Asherah, Ashteroth, Astarte, Ishtar or Inanna are all names of the mother goddess – in fact, as Sir James Frazer pointed out, she was given so many names that she was eventually believed to be different deities. The names were given to her different aspects, as happened with Yahweh and Ra the Egyptian sun god, who has so many similarities to Yahweh. In *From Fetish to God* , E. A. Wallis Budge writes about Ra: '…there was no god before him … His unity is absolute. He was a Trinity, i.e. he had three persons or characters.'[11]

The mother goddess's images are usually the horns of bulls or the crescent moon, showing the union between the sun (bull) and moon (horn). One of her names, Ashteroth, can mean 'grove' or 'single standing stone' or 'pole within a grove'.

When we consider that the image of the great goddess was a simple white shining cone, pole or even pyramid with her head at the top, we can begin to see the universal usage. Megaliths, pyramids and various other temples display evidence of having been whitewashed. In Golgi in Cyprus, conical stones are raised to the mother goddess, as in the temples of Malta and in the Sinai, and in the great open sanctuary of Astarte at Byblos in Syria (the city sacred to Adonis) there is the tall obelisk or standing stone. In the moonlight all these stones shine a remarkable blue colour. They almost come to life. The stones of many of the megaliths of northern Europe shine blue in rain (the gift of Yahweh or the male god) and by moonlight, therefore being a union of physical opposites and thus enabling a transition to a 'third state'.

Ishtar, the great mother goddess, was married to Adonis. Adonis is used throughout the Bible, in the Hebrew form 'Adonai', as a title for the Lord, where pillars or standing stones are erected in his honour. The worship of Adonis was widespread from Egypt to Babylonia, and the Greeks were using the name 700 years before Christ. Versions of 'Adonis' were Tammuz, or Thammuz, and the Babylonian Marduk. In Babylonian stories, Tammuz appears as the lover of Ishtar and the natural world is the fertile result. As already mentioned, the symbol of Tammuz is the *tau* cross (T). This ancient symbol was used for many purposes, including divination, as a staff of the Magi and as a guide to the stars, and may have been used as a sundial. The triple *tau* is also related to the idea of hidden treasure.

In summary, the tribal Jewish god has a dual nature. He is referred to in the Bible as Adonai and as such can be traced back to the solar Tammuz, an idol-god who died every year and then came back to life again in spring.[12] The cyclic patterns of existence are at the root of one of the world's largest faiths.

Stories of these 'nature' gods are reminiscent of the Hindu Agni, god of fire and shining. Abraham and Moses see Yahweh as shining, bright fire or light. The burning, but cool, bush, the bush of light, recalls the Druid god striking the mistletoe bush and lighting it up. The ram in the thicket is symbolic of the fire of Ra (depicted as a ram) in the tree. In Egyptian, the phrase *Amun-u-El* means 'Amun is God' or 'the Shining One'. The Hebrew equivalent is *Emmanuel*, 'the Shining One [or god] is with us' – the name of the predicted Messiah.

Moses the Wise

So who put all this together? Who crafted such a marvellous and symbolic collection of writings that is the Hebrew Bible, or Old Testament? One figure is said to have written the first five books, the Pentateuch or Books of the Law, which contain the legal, moral and ethical foundation of Judaism: Moses.

Jewish tradition and folklore claim Moses as the first Great Magician: the Bible itself tells us that 'Moses was trained in all the wisdom of the Egyptians.'[13] The name Moses is itself Egyptian and means 'Son', as in the pharaonic names Rameses (Son of Ra) and Amenmesse (Son of Amun). He is thought to have lived *c.* 1400 BC. Miriam (Mary), his sister, is said to have founded alchemy. Tradition has it that during his stay in Egypt, Moses was an initiate in the mysteries of Osiris and helped to build the pyramids, with the help of non-slave Semites. Moses also carried a staff or rod, as did Isaac. Some have claimed that he was actually the Pharaoh Akhenaten, who also carried the royal sceptre, which was topped with the caduceus-like coil of a snake.[14] Magical powers are attributed to the rod and it is a sign of authority. Symbolic of the world tree, it was wielded only by the powerful father of the Shining Ones.

The snake also has symbolic meaning. It was always involved in the worship of the sun god and was often the symbol of the sun. The link with the snake is paramount in our research on the Shining Ones, the reason being quite simply that the kundalini awakening that was central to their Shining status was seen as the power of the serpent. In the Bible, Moses was seen to have exercised his power over this serpent, first with the staff of Aaron and secondly with the brazen serpent which was held up in the wilderness.

The first-century Jewish historian Josephus claimed that Moses was a Heliopolitan priest and an initiate at the temple of On, the Egyptian centre of the sun cults. It was here that he was credited with building an open-air prayer house or stone circle to the sun god. This was also the place where Joseph married Asenath, the daughter of Potipherah; a priest of On.[15]

In Exodus 34, he came down from Mount Sinai with a face that 'sent forth beams'. A mistranslation in the Latin Bible rendered this as 'sent forth horns', and so Moses was often depicted in the Middle Ages with horns. Interestingly, one thing we do notice about the serpent, especially in Gnostic literature but also in ancient hieroglyphs and pictoglyphs, is horns. This must be purely symbolic, like the horn of the unicorn, but the mistranslation was perhaps a deliberate one by a Shining initiate for those 'in the know'.

Moses is also credited with having led an Egyptian army as their general. Although some are sceptical of this, it would quite easily fit with the fact that Druids and shamans were responsible for leading men into battle, as indeed was Abraham, the Shining priest-king of Salem.

To sum up, all the ancient Shining beliefs were brought to life in the beliefs and scriptures of the Israelites. Divination, star, sun and moon worship, blood rituals, sacred mountains, bulls, crosses – all the familiar Shining elements are to be found there.

The Essenes

In the last centuries BC, there arose within Judaism a sect known as the 'Hasidim' or 'Pious Ones', who saw themselves as the guardians of the pure Shining tradition. It appears that a group of Hasidim left Jerusalem because they were opposed to the high priesthood of the Jerusalem Temple and objected to the increasing Hellenization of Judaea at the time. The Hasidim lived away from the city, where they practised their own brand of Judaism in communities such as that at Qumran in the Judaean Desert near the Dead Sea. It was near here that the famous Dead Sea Scrolls, hidden in caves as the Romans advanced, were discovered in 1947. According to the scrolls, the community called themselves 'Children of the Light' or 'Shining Ones'. They are better known to us as the Essenes.

The scrolls also tell us that the Essene 'Way' was one of asceticism and communal living. The many strict rules of the community included washing in cold water and wearing white garments. The Essenes were apparently against slavery and perhaps bought slaves to set them free. The community was also tightly controlled and hierarchical: the 'governor' was called the 'crown' – an allusion no doubt to his Shining, enlightened status – and under him were a 'council' and the 'multitude'. They venerated a founder called the Teacher of Righteousness, and it seems that in the early first century they were biding their time, awaiting their moment in history. Much has been written on the Essenes elsewhere and we would refer the reader to the mass of literature on the subject. Qumran was abandoned during the Jewish Revolt against the Romans (66–70 AD), and no one ever returned to retrieve the scrolls that had been so carefully hidden. Where did the Essenes go? Were Essenes among the creators of the cult of Jesus that was to become the Christian Church, which was later co-opted by the Roman Empire? It is speculation, and perhaps further research will uncover any such links in detail.

Druids and the 'Lost Tribes' of Israel

When we look at the European traditions of the period we also see a highly organized system with essentially the same beliefs. The ancient ideas of the world tree, reincarnation and rebirth, worship of the sky with all the host of heaven and the great father and mother deities are all there. The gods may differ slightly in title, but their names still mean 'to shine' or 'be bright'. Were these beliefs taken to Europe by a branch of the ancient Israelites?

This may not be as fanciful as it may sound. For, early in the first millennium BC, the northern tribes of Israel were forcibly deported from their homeland by the Assyrians, much as the Israelites of Judaea were later deported en masse to Babylon. However, while the Judaeans eventually returned from their Babylonian exile, the northern Israelites did not. Where they went is highly uncertain. However, among these 'lost' tribes were the people of King Omri. Israel was called 'Omri's Land' by the Assyrians, and King Omri traded far and wide, especially with the Phoenicians, who are known to have traded in turn with the tin-mining communities of southern England.

By tradition, the priests of Celtic Europe – an area that stretched at that time from Spain and Britain eastward into the Balkans and Anatolia – were called Druids. They practised divination, astrology and tree worship in much the same way as the earlier peoples of the area. The name 'Druid' may mean 'truth' or possibly 'oak', but we do know that these priests were called 'asps' or 'adders', almost certainly because they had experienced the kundalini enlightenment.

According to modern Druid tradition, the supposed founder of the third temple on the site of Stonehenge was Hu Gadarn Hyscion (or Isaac's son). He was an Egyptian Hebrew and the man who supposedly led the people of King Omri, the K'Omri, the people of the covenant, to Britain. It was he, the present Druids claim, who founded the 'people of truth' or Druids. Ancient burial mounds and barrow mounds were called S'iuns by the Druids, which means 'mounds of stone'; the similar Hebrew term Zion means 'mountain of stone'. The genuine antiquity of modern Druid traditions is open to debate, but perhaps at least some of the ancient barrows of Europe – which are often aligned to the midwinter sun – were memorials for a lost home-land erected by exiled holders of the Shining tradition.

14

Shining Ones of the East

Hinduism, Buddhism and Jainism

'You whose face resembles a hundred shining autumn full
moons;

Blazing with resplendent rays of light like a gathering of a
thousand stars.'

From a Tibetan Buddhist scripture in praise of the bodhisattva *Tara*

The same shamanic ideas spread and became an integral part of the
culture wherever the Shining Ones journeyed, as is well docu-
mented by archaeological finds.[1] The priestly Shining Ones élite were
powerful figures who were subsequently mythologized and apotheo-
sized as gods or demi-gods, great and mighty figures of ancient times.
The shamans who were the inheritors of the Shining Ones' secrets
made use of their connection to these now mythical predecessors in
order to legitimize their own claim for power within their respective
social or religious groups.

We have seen how Shining beliefs have manifested in the ancient cultures of the Near and Middle East and Egypt, and subsequently in
Judaism and Christianity, which arose in this crucible of culture. We
have shown too how Shining Ones left their mark on the ancient traditions of Europe. In this chapter, we travel eastward from the Shining
heartlands of western Asia and examine the Shining tradition as it
evolved in the belief systems that arose in ancient India.

The Shining Ones of Hinduism

Hinduism, with its many Devas – which, incidentally, is Sanskrit for 'Shining One' – has its roots in India dating back several millennia BC. In Hinduism, Devas are groups of exalted beings, gods or angels. In Buddhist cosmology they are similar, living in their own realm, but regarded as mortals.

There are three kinds of Hindu Deva: enlightened mortals, spiritually superior mortals and Brahman (the first of the great divine triad of Vishnu, Shiva and Brahman). According to modern Hindu mystics, the Devas arrived on Earth before humans but remained dormant until humankind reached the appropriate level of evolution. Accounts like this have led some authors to advocate the 'alien' hypothesis – the idea that 'alien reptiles' or serpents spawned human civilization. But it can be shown that the use of the term 'serpent' in this context is simply *symbolic* and the associated stories are simply hiding a true and very rational history.

In the Sanskrit *Mahabharat*, the great epic of India, we find much in common with Egyptian and Sumerian cults. The Celtic cross with the winding snake is also extremely similar, if not identical, to emblems on Hindu votive tablets and later Persian seals, and is reminiscent of the caduceus, which appeared in Mesopotamian cultures *c.* 2600 BC and later in the wider world. It consists, as do the Hindu and Celtic images, of two serpents twisting around a rod or staff. In Roman times it became the wand of the god Mercury, who was associated with Hermes and Thoth. In medieval times, we see this image repeated in the Kabbalists' Tree of Life. It is a universal image and is directly related to the ancient serpent cult.

With Hinduism, as with other religions, we also see the shamanic ideas being added to by various leaders and priests to control the masses. The core elements of the Shining Ones' ways have always remained, however, and it is this hidden belief system for which we are searching.

In the Hindu tradition we find some of the old beliefs that are now so familiar to us from other religions and cults – concepts of goddess and god, animism, trees, purification by water, fire sacrifice, shamanistic trances induced by *soma* (a plant believed to heighten spiritual awareness, also used later by Zoroastrians), a trinity and marking the date of a person's birth so that a horoscope may be drawn up.

A priestly elite, the Brahmans, evolved from within the Shining One culture and went on to compose the Hindu scriptures. According to Simon Weightman in *The Handbook of Living Religions*, Brahmans were 'unrepresentative of the beliefs and practices of the great majority of Hindus at any given time'.[2] Therefore the scriptures and teachings were not commonly practised but were kept within a small elite. The *Chandogya Upanishad* 'Instruction concerning Brahma' tells us, 'That, indeed, is below. It is above... It indeed is the whole world... The Soul, indeed, is below. The Soul is above.' This parallels the Hermetic 'As above, so below.' *Upanishads*, it is worth noting, means 'secret teachings'.

In the *Rig Veda* (*Sacred Songs*), we find the Hindu Agni as a sage, priest, king, protector and father. He is commissioned by men to convey messages to god by going up to heaven. He is in essence a shaman and Shining One. No surprise when we find out that Agni means 'the Shining One', so that 'he may illuminate the nights'. Agni inhabits the mist between human and god, he is the historical blurring of the point at which man ceases to be man and moves through the magical powers of the pen and the mind into that holy place of Godhead. He is an example of how a Shining One, an actual person, takes on the likeness of a 'god'.

In the *Bhagavad Gita* (4:5–11) we also have some striking similarities with the beliefs we have already seen:

'I have been born many times, Arjuna, and many times hast thou been born. But I remember my past lives, and thou has forgotten thine.

231

'Although I am unborn, everlasting, and I am the Lord of all, I come to my realm of nature and through my wondrous power I am born.

'When righteousness is weak and faints and unrighteousness exults in pride, then my spirit arises on earth.

'For the salvation of those who are good, for the destruction of evil in man, for the fulfilment of the kingdom of righteousness, I come to this world in the ages that pass.'

Buddhism

Some of these beliefs were carried into Buddhism, which arose in India in the fifth century BC. In Buddhist tradition, the Buddha, an enlightened or Shining being, was only the latest of many Buddhas stretching back into the distant past. There are also many *bodhisattvas*, Shining beings who refuse to enter *nirvana* but instead choose to help out humankind or set things in order, an idea reminiscent of the Elohim of Sumeria. One of these *bodhisattvas* is Maitreya, who is regarded as the Buddha of the future, a coming saviour like that also expected by Christianity, Islam, Judaism and many other faiths.[3]

There is much to link Christ to the Buddha – most importantly, both attained enlightenment around the age of 30. Buddha said, 'Who sees *dhamma* sees me. Who sees me sees *dhamma*.' Christ said, 'If you had known Me, you would have known My Father also; and from now on you know Him and have seen Him.'[4]

Buddha sent his followers on the path to the truth with his 'eightfold path' to enlightenment. This can only be achieved through the Three Trainings: *morality*, *concentration* and *wisdom*. All these focus the mind on the path. To do this we must practise yoga, or 'yoke' ourselves to the path and obtain the help of the *siddhis*, or powers. 'Yoke' again means to unite the male and female or positive and negative opposites within us. The siddhis (the result of this union, or fusion in consciousness, which grants us extra energy) are what we now call 'paranormal' abilities – telepathy, feats of memory and magical powers, all of which are related to and used in many, if not all, of the other faiths, and all of which are directly related to the phenomena that surround the enlightenment experience which gave rise to the term 'Shining'.

While he did not encourage his followers to employ magical powers, the Buddha is said to have fought many magical battles, as did Moses and others in the Bible.

The idea that Buddha is not one man but one of many is an indication that there are, or were, many other enlightened or Shining Ones. As the Buddha said, there are more to come – from the same sacred and elite priesthood from which he and his predecessors arose: the Shining Ones.

Jainism

The early Shining belief system also influenced other religions in the East. There was a remarkable cross-fertilization of ideas. For example, there is much evidence to suggest that the Essenes and other ascetics, and the early Gnostics, visited Tibet and the surrounding area. The Hindu and Buddhist mandala, or circle, the symbol of the universal cycle, was later shared with Chinese and Japanese traditions and European Gnosticism and alchemy.

In Jainism, which arose at the same time as Buddhism and in roughly the same area of India, we see the same forces at work. The available Sanskrit sources describe the practice of lifecycle rituals, which are also carried out in all the other early traditions. Jains conceive time in vast cycles, as do Hindus and Buddhists (and those of ancient Central America). Jain tradition calims that in each half-cycle there will appear 24 great teachers (Jinas or Tirthankaras). The word

'Jinas' is phonetically similar to the Assyro-Babylonian *jinni*, plural *jinn*. The *jinn* were superhuman and serpentine guardians or saviours who later became the *jinn* of the Islamic world, a class of spirits formed by fire and living on the sacred mountains (heaven) of Kaf, which encircle the world. In other words, their home was the heavenly zodiac. Their forms are sometimes those of enormous men or giants, which leads to the idea that these ancient people or priests take on larger forms as time goes by and giant imagery therefore indicates a more ancient and superior spiritual people (and not, as some authors assert, large 'reptilian aliens').

The last Jinas in this cycle was Vardhamma Jnatrputra, and he was given the title Mahavira, which means 'Great Hero' – a term related to the sun. At 30, he abandoned his life as a warrior and took up the role he was born to. In other words, at the 30° point he moved from one zodiacal point to another. He died at the equally significant age of 72 – yet another zodiacal number, as there are 72 decans or portions to the zodiac.

The leadership of Jainism was taken over by the disciples and the religion then spread throughout India. The disciples, when they wore anything at all, wore simple white garments, which we will see as characterising Shining groups down the ages. They were a nomadic priesthood, and it is probable that they simply traveled from one Shining lodge or monastery to the next, wandering the roads and byways of the Earth, passing on their knowledge so as to escape into the enlightened realm. As with all other faiths, the Jains are in search of absolute knowledge to release them from the cycle of rebirth – the road to enlightenment or Shining.

Another familiar aspect of the religion is the renaming of the priesthood. Each new priest is given his official title, after which his old name is rarely used. Jains also go through ritual deaths and rebirths via fasting. This is a ritual to enable them to experience the Shining effects internally.

In temple rituals, the Tirthankara is shown standing with arms and hands held out at the side in the symbol of the cross. This is strangely reminiscent of the cross of Christ. Crosses are deeply rooted in Jainist beliefs, especially the ancient Indian solar emblem, the swastika. Its ancient significance is peaceful, perhaps 'peace under the sun', that is, in the whole world. Jains are noted for their commitment to avoiding harm to any life form – they will even wear gauze over their mouths to avoid inhaling tiny flies.

*   *   *

It seems that the Shining Ones spread their worship eastward and westward across the world. For thousands of years they worshipped the light within themselves as if it were the sun god, and took this idea of illumination wherever they went. We will now look at some of the most powerful groups with a Shining heritage that have influenced civilization: secret societies.

PART THREE:

The Shining Ones Today

15

Secret Societies

A Modern Link to the Shining Ones

'All secret societies have almost analogous initiations, from
the Egyptian to the Illuminati, and most of them form a
chain and give rise to others.'

Le Couteulx de Canteleu, *Les Sectes et Sociétés Secretes*, 1863

The secret societies that we will look at in this chapter are on the
whole spiritually based and have in common the idea of illumination, which links them to the tradition and beliefs of the 'Shining
Ones'. First, though, let us consider what a secret society actually is. At
the most basic level, it is a group of individuals who come together for
a shared purpose, but who restrict the membership of their group. The
details of a society's beliefs, purpose, and practices are generally
revealed only to those within the society, who may in turn be graded
in a hierarchy: the extent of a member's knowledge of the inner workings of the society generally depends on their position within that
hierarchy. We may compare this to an 'open' or 'public' specialist
society, such as a birdwatching society or a golf club, to which any
interested member of the public may apply on their own initiative,
and whose purpose, rules, organization and calendar of events are
freely available to all.

Initiation

Membership is usually by selection, not application, and those chosen as candidates for membership often undergo a form of initiation. The process of initiation into a secret society may begin before the prospective member is even aware of it, with individuals being noted by existing members as potential future candidates for initiation. In fact, studies of societies have shown that this process is almost random, the true selection coming much later. Initiation rituals make the initiate feel more important when accepted – even though very few are actually turned down at this stage. This is a universal practice – it is also found in other organizations that allow everybody in, but at different levels. The idea of there being different levels ensures that the new initiate strives to become an adherent or full member by learning the ways of the club or society – and thus becomes fully engulfed in the world of the society.

Secret societies take membership a step further by including certain practices and information that the initiate must learn. These include secret handshakes and words, special days of the year known only to the few, and privileged insights into standard texts. Comradeship is fostered through regular meetings that allow the member to feel part of a wider 'family'. Serving military personnel will tell you that one of the major factors in the success of their unit is camaraderie. The sense of 'belonging' can be such that to leave would feel like 'losing a family'.

Generally, initiation involves a ritual built around an apparently obscure or abstruse myth. In the first stages the new member is 'cleansed' or in simple terms cleared of any thinking that would not benefit the society. There are also tests to determine whether the initiate has the ability to move on further. The Knights Templar allegedly tested initiates with spitting on the cross. If the initiate failed to spit upon the cross as requested, he was rewarded for his true faith with membership. But if he *did* spit upon the cross then he had shown true discipline and unquestioing obedience to the master. He would also be accepted as a member, but on a 'fast track' that would see him rise higher up a hierarchy that would be closed to the first, 'ordinary' member.

> 'As soon as the proselyte arrived at the ninth degree he was ripe to serve as blind instrument to all passions, and above all to a limitless ambition for domination … We thus see those who should have been protectors of humanity abandoned to an insatiable ambition, buried under the ruins of thrones and altars in the midst of the horrors of anarchy, after having brought misfortune upon nations, and deserving the curse of mankind.'[1]

In all instances, in the 'illuminated' societies we are focussing on, the ultimate enlightenment experience seems to be kept back for the very highest levels of initiation. Lower levels of illumination are permitted and used for the lower degrees.

Secret Societies in the Outer World

Secret societies are initially the preserve of the select few, but they can eventually become opened to, and accepted by, the wider population. Take, for instance, Christianity. In the early years of its existence it was classed as a dangerous cult or secret organization due to having to remain underground for fear of persecution. (The pagan Roman state religion believed itself far removed from the Christian cult creeds, though in reality they embraced the same solar beliefs.) Christianity had secret signs, secret gestures, special myths and rituals, just as any secret organization. Eventually this 'underground' religion grew to the extent that members in positions of state authority joined it. This in turn made it more and more acceptable, and eventually, in the fourth century, Christianity was embraced by the Roman state and became the official religion of the empire. Subsequently all other religions were banned; from this point the imperial Church fought its own 'underground streams', such as Gnosticism, which retained the secret knowledge of the original shamanic religion.

Today we have secret societies across the world in every country, all with their own agendas and all being carefully watched by the state. History has shown that these societies, with their elite memberships, can alter the political power balance of the world. The eighteenth-century revolt of the American states against the British was backed, led and inspired by the secret society of the Freemasons. The French and Russian revolutions were similarly created by secret organizations.

Another interesting point to note, and something that relates entirely to our understanding of the Shining Ones, is that many great minds were members of secret organizations. Mozart was a Freemason and Plato was an initiate into the mysteries of Eleusis – he even tells us how he was initiated. He claims that he was placed in a pyramid for three days, died symbolically, was reborn and was then given the secrets of the mysteries. The Great Pyramid of Giza has often been claimed as the very pinnacle of the mysteries and the names given to it by the Egyptians – Ikhet and Khuti – mean 'glorious light' or 'Shining One'.

The Search for Enlightenment

The number of closed societies with spiritual basis reflects the number of people who are searching for some form of enlightenment. Something within each of us calls out for a higher state of being or consciousness. Some psychologists believe that this is evolutionary, that within us there is a constant urge to 'improve'. However, we are all searching in different ways.

Enlightenment to many is something similar to the Christian 'born again' concept. This perception is incorrect and we need to look to the enlightenment of the Shining Ones for the truth. Although kundalini is widely written about in the East, especially in India, and forms the basis of many Eastern beliefs, a study of the secret societies of the globe will show that aspects of the kundalini enlightenment experience have been used in every spiritual society worldwide to draw people in and keep them, while often denying them full knowledge of its processes.

In 1922 G. G., also known as Dargon (a name created to hide his real identity), wrote:

'For centuries there have existed certain esoteric schools of mystical philosophy originating apparently in several Oriental currents of thought meeting in the Levant, Egypt, and the nearer East. We find in these schools elements of Buddhism, Zoroastrianism and Egyptian occultism mingled with Grecian mysteries, Jewish Kabalism, and fragments of ancient Syrian cults. Out of the hotchpotch of Oriental philosophy, magic, and mythology arose in the earlier centuries of the Christian era numerous Gnostic sects, and after the rise of Mohammedanism, several heretical sects among the followers of Islam – such as the Ismaelites, Druses, and Assassins – which found their inspiration in the House of Wisdom in Cairo.

'To the same sources may be traced the ideas that inspired such political-religious movements of the Middle Ages as those of the Illuminati, Albigenses, Cathari, Waldenses, Troubadours, Anabaptists, and Lollards. To the same inspirations must be assigned the rise of the early secret societies. The Templars are said to have been initiated by the Assassins into anti-Christian and subversive mysteries, and we find similar traces of an old and occult origin in the Alchemists, the Rosicrucians, and the later mystical cults of the Swedenborgian...'[2]

The Ismaelites, Druses, Assassins and Templars are all directly linked to the enlightened Shining tradition. Let us look at the latter two in more detail.

The Assassins and Templars

The enigmatic group known as the Assassins was based in Persia at least as far back as the eleventh century. They take their name from *Hashishim*, 'hashish takers', hashish being a trance-inducing drug thought by many to help the leaders control the minds of the followers. In one famous legend, Hasan, son of Sabah, the Sheikh of the Mountains (the Assassin leader), said to an official of an emperor's court, 'You see that devotee standing guard on that turret-top? Watch!' He made a signal and immediately the devotee threw himself off the turret to his death. 'I have 70,000 men and women throughout Asia,' he went on, 'each one of them ready to do my bidding.'

In the first instance this illustrates a remarkable control over the mind of another individual. It also implies that the Assassins were much older than the Middle Ages, since no elite society can acquire 70,000 devotees overnight.

The Assassins went through a cycle of initiation based upon seven levels. This relates to the seven chakras in the nearby Hindu tradition – a tradition based around the energy of the serpent and linked to the Shining Ones via Persia.

At the seventh level the Assassins attained the great 'secret' that all of creation was one. The experience of being at one with the cosmos involved the use of hashish and clever rituals, and an understanding of the universe's creative and destructive elements. The Assassin initiate could therefore make use of the great power held within him. The Assassins firmly believed, and in our opinion rightly, that the rest of humankind, with the exception of other initiates, knew nothing of this power.

Contrary to popular belief, the Assassins were not originally

Muslims. It was only later in their history that they had to turn to Islam as a means of survival. On the other hand, they have always been linked to an ostensibly Christian order, the Knights Templar, founded in the Near East during the early Crusades. The two groups had dealings with each other and regarded each other with mutual respect. Could it be that the Templars understood the Assassins' greatest secret and brought this 'Holy Grail' back to Europe with them?

At the time of their second grand master, Buzurg-Umid (Great Promise), the Assassins were situated at Alamut, otherwise known as the Viper's Nest. Buzurg-Umid made a deal with the Christian King Baldwin II of Jerusalem, a man closely connected to the Templars. Indeed, in 1129 the Templars and other crusaders allied with the Assassins to take Damascus. This is an indication that the Assassins were not in any way Muslim: they were even said to be prepared to take on the cloak of Christianity, should it bring them further power. This is a good illustration of the workings of secret societies that arose from the Shining tradition: they worked together because they held the same beliefs. There is a masonic tradition that Guillaume de Montard, a Templar, was initiated by the 'Old Man of the Mountain', the Assassin spiritual leader, in a cave in Lebanon and that the Assassins held beliefs related to serpent worship.

The question has to be asked, did the Templars use the same mind-control techniques as the Assassins? There is evidence to suggest that they did understand the use of drugs, especially for the relief of pain. Robert Anton Wilson, in his book *Sex and Drugs*, indicated his belief that the Templars used hashish and in fact learned of it from the Assassins. This is not an unreasonable assumption.

Templar rituals and beliefs also have links with many Middle Eastern religions. The Golden Head of the Sufis, for example, may be related to the Baphomet of the Templars. The Sufis, as Idries Shah points out, were involved in the 'worship of a mysterious head [which] could well be a reference to the great work of transhumanization that takes place in the aspirant's own head'.[3] This was the idea that one's own humanity was transmuted through the enlightenment experience, which was the deeper meaning of the alchemist's quest to turn base matter into gold.

Also, the initiation ritual of the Sufis involved passing through a doorway of two pillars, symbolizing the neutral-point gateway between two opposites. This was the portal into a world of illumination, knowledge and enlightenment. If it is true that the Freemasons emerged from a fount of Templar knowledge, this could be one of the origins of the masonic twin pillars, named Jachin and Boaz. These pillars are also similar to the twin pillars that pilgrims to Mecca must pass through (Safa and Marwa).

It seems that the enlightenment secrets of the Shining Ones were very much alive and being passed on from century to century. The Templars were officially disbanded in the early fourteenth century, but the occultist Eliphas Lévi (1810–1875) stated that they were still very much alive in the eighteenth century and were known as Johannites. Their secret aim, Lévi claimed, was to 'rebuild the Temple of Solomon' (an allusion to the internal enlightenment process). Albert Pike, the Masonic historian, states the following:

> 'The Order ... lived under other names and was governed by Unknown Chiefs, revealing itself only to those who in passing through a series of degrees had proven themselves worthy to be entrusted with the dangerous secret. The secret movers of the French Revolution had sworn to overturn the Throne and Altar upon the tomb of Jacques de Molai.'[4]

The Templar Grand Master Jacques de Molay was exectued in 1314 at the command of King Philip the Fair of France. It is said that he vowed revenge upon the king of France and the Pope who had authorized Philip's persecution of the Templars, Clement V: both went on to die within the year.

As we can see, there is a thread running through the heart of all these organizations – the thread of illumination, or Shining.

Methods of Induction

Much of this ancient esoteric teaching passed into what is known as Gnosticism, which in the early centuries AD had seriously contended with two other Shining cults, Christianity and the worship of Isis, for popularity. The Gnostics cannot be generalized, but they share a central concern theme – that of illumination and enlightenment. The methods are familiar. Many Gnostics believed that they could achieve enlightenment by achieving altered states, others by fasting and meditation.

In the Greek mystery rites of Eleusis, the initiate would also undergo a prolonged period of fasting followed by a period of 'waiting'. Eventually, the initiate was led into the temple and enjoyed a ritualistic meal, thus producing increased levels of sugar in the blood and putting the mind almost into a trance state. Then initiates took part in a whirling dance, coupled with sleep-inducing drinks and witnessing ritual performances by the priests. By this point, when the initiate was at the peak of a heightened state, sacred objects and words would be revealed to him or her.

Similar initiations are believed to have evolved in India, although they came originally from Sumeria. Strangely, these rituals involved a sevenfold cord that marked the success of the initiate – and which, according to some scholars, was symbolic of the snake. The results were the same – initiates reached a deeper understanding of themselves and believed that they were in touch with the divine. Their desire to regain this state ensured their continued loyalty to the Eleusinian mystery cult.

Aristotle wrote that 'Those who are being initiated do not so much learn anything, as experience certain emotions, and are thrown into a

246

special state of mind.'[5] This 'special state of mind' was a plasticity that the priests could bend and manipulate to their own ends – just as the Old Man of the Mountain manipulated the Assassins.

All these methods and means to manipulation were passed on through time into all manner of modern secret societies. In the 'High Priesthood of Thebes', a society first known in Germany in the eighteenth century, it was written:

> '[The initiate] was led to two high pillars between which stood a griffin driving a wheel before him. The pillars symbolized east and west, the griffin the sun and the wheel the four spokes of the four seasons. [The initiate] was taught the use of the level and instructed in geometry and architecture. He received a rod, entwined by serpents and the password Heve [female serpent], and was told the story of the fall of man.'[6]

The symbols within this initiation clearly are of Shining origin.

Similar themes are found in the initiations and rituals of witches. Whirling, dancing and a general build-up to a state of frenzy or ecstasy would bring the participant into a trance state, aided by drugs, such as the 'ointment' used by the witches to help them fly, which contained hyoscine. The coven leader would then guide the coven through ritual words and incantations leading to complete mind control. Such control, indeed, that the participant would often give up his family and friends, as in groups that we would nowadays call 'cults'.

Manipulation and Control

The awakening of the mind through ecstasy is, on the one hand, a release from the norm and a breakthrough into a state of freedom, but, on the other, a dangerous tool used by many secret societies, cults, and even mainstream religions to control and manipulate for their own ends. It may be that some have nothing but good intentions at heart, but history has shown repeatedly that greed is all-powerful and can take over the soul of many initially well-meaning groups.

Has there been a group watching, monitoring and manipulating us through time, a close-knit elite which began as a group of enlightened shamans who came to enjoy power so much that they now exercise control over many aspects of our lives through secret societies and other organizations? In our view, there are too many resemblances among the beliefs and practices of religions, sects, societies and 'cults' worldwide for the similarities to be mere chance. Throughout history the masses have never known the truth. We believe, for example, that only now is the true history of Jesus Christ coming out – that, in our view, he was not 'real' in the sense that people claim, that he did not literally die on the cross and come back to life, but was in fact a solar, serpentine Shining One who attained enlightenment. In our view, the Church – specifically the mighty Roman Catholic Church – has known this truth, but has misled its congregations in order simply to hold on to power – at the expense of its own original Shining ideals.

In the final chapter we shall look further at the evidence linking the Shining Ones to the Catholic Church, perhaps the most powerful organization in the history of humankind. While researching this book, we spoke at length with a very senior lecturer from within the education system in Cambridge, England. He did not wish to be named for the obvious reason that he is in the 'religious' department. After we had told him about some of the things we were going to include in this book he said quite calmly and with a quaint old-fashioned English air of authority: 'Oh dear, you're going to let the cat out of the bag.'

16

The Present Day

Where are the Shining Ones Now?

'A great part of Europe – the whole of Italy and France, and a great portion of Germany, to say nothing of other countries – are covered with a network of these secret societies, just as the superficies of the earth is now being covered with railroads. And what are their objectives? They do not attempt to conceal themselves. They do not want constitutional government. They do not want ameliorated institutions; they do not want provincial councils nor the recording of votes.'

Benjamin Disraeli, future Prime Minister of Great Britain,
Hansard's Parliamentary Debates

We have found the Shining Ones in every culture of the world over a period that reaches back into the days of ancient Sumeria and Egypt.

During the course of our research we have come across recurring themes within the ritual and language employed by the various cults, societies and religious organizations that all seemed on the surface to be disparate groups. As we moved down the centuries we kept finding the same keys that had aided us in unlocking the door of mystery. And yet, one thing was eluding us – what about now?

We were more than a little afraid to go down this route. Philip had already had some strange experiences and threats that were unnerving for family men such as us. Nevertheless, our intention from the start was to discover the truth about the Shining Ones and the question of whether they are still manipulating the people of the world had to be answered.

We had plenty of places to start. Should we begin with the Templars and trace their masonic descent, as others have done? Should we look at Adam Weishaupt and the Illuminati? Is the Skull and Crossbones Society of Yale in the USA the breeding ground for future presidents? And what about the Bilderberg group and the royal families of Europe? Some if not all of these groups will be familiar to the reader. But what is the truth?

We decided that we should go back to what we had learned. We had discovered that down the ages many organizations, however seemingly diverse and contradictory, had all been various fronts or derivatives of the Shining Ones. It was as if they were all part of a wheel. The outer rim is the face of the group or society. One side of the rim cannot see what the other side is doing, or even that it exists. The centre can see what is happening in all directions but is distanced from it, while still holding all the spokes in its grasp.

The same is true in the world of secret or exclusive societies. The world sees the groups that form the rim, but that is all. But we are just like those who are on the rim – we cannot see the centre of the wheel from our perspective. So, we decided, the only way to work out what was at the centre of the wheel today would be to see the whole rim and try to deduce what the centre must be.

The first thing we did was to write down a few of the candidates for 'outer rim secret society or 'suspicious' organization. These included the Freemasons, Rosicrucians, Illuminati, Knights of Malta and Opus Dei. Now all we needed to do was to see if all these positions on the rim revolved around the same centre.

The Freemasons

First we looked at the Freemasons. Their history is not simple. In fact it is virtually impossible to decipher the truth from the myriad histories in hundreds of books on the subject. We are going to keep the subject to a minimum.

Many masonic historians claim that their lineage stretches back to the biblical Temple of Solomon and its builder Hiram of Tyre – they are even told this in their ceremonies. Others claim descent from Roman and Greek stonemasons and the Roman augurs, who we know had 'special knowledge' of the land and the energies related to it. The general consensus, though, has the Freemasons emerging from medieval stonecutters, the skilled craftsmen who built the great cathedrals and churches of Europe and included many mysterious images and secrets within their masterly carvings. This version of the history of the masons claims that their 'lodges' evolved from the huts the medieval masons erected on site. According to the theory, as time progressed, the masons grew in power, owing to the demand for their services, and formed groups that became known as lodges.

However, there is also evidence to show that in the fourteenth century the masons were already a well-established group and included – or had been developed by – Knights Templar who had escaped Catholic suppression and fled to Scotland. The first official documentation we have is from 1356. It is from England and describes the formation of the London Masons' Company and the ordinances governing the lodge that was already established at York Minster. The term 'Freemason' itself first occurs in 1376.

Evidence from before this period comes in the form of the symbolism being employed in the great building works of Europe from the eleventh century onwards, following the First Crusade and the setting up of such organizations as the Knights Templar and the Cistercians. The Templars and the non-warrior Cistercian monks were more than incidental in bringing back from the crusades both the seed of alchemical enlightenment and the building skills of the Islamic world. This is seen in the Gothic arch and the octagonal designs incorporated into most Templar and Cistercian buildings, as well as other building works carried out under their tutelage.

Also built into these structures are many numerological symbols and 'mystical' metaphors that we have discussed elsewhere in this book. These methods were understood and carried on by the Freemasons, who today ritualize these ancient ways, though most do not understand their correct purpose. These building metaphors are as ancient as Stonehenge and the Great Pyramids, even if the term 'Freemason' is not.

By the 1600s the lodges began admitting men who were not operative masons and were termed 'gentlemen masons; the minutes survive from 1599 from two Edinburgh lodges, Aichison's Haven and St Mary's. By the mid-seventeenth century there is clear evidence of the existence of large lodges. Elias Ashmole, creator of the Ashmolean Museum in Oxford, recorded in his diary for 1646 that he was made a mason in the lodge at his father-in-law's house. 1717 saw the formation of the first Grand Lodge of London, and the first American lodge opened in 1733.

In the following decades the Freemasons exerted influence by instigating, at least in part, the revolutions in America and France, and later still, that in Russia.[1]

The Masons and the Catholic Church

Popular opinion has it that there is friction between the Catholic Church and the Freemasons. But in fact the two organizations are closely linked. The Freemasons can clearly be shown to have evolved from esoteric groups, such as the Templars, that were themselves established by papal authority.

So what influence do Freemasons have today? Freemasonry is now a global phenomenon with members from across the business community, religious establishment and politics. The masons also have links with many other 'orders', such as the Sovereign Order of the Knights of Malta. As businessmen ourselves, we have met a very large number of businesspeople who use the masonic handshake – even if they do not realize that we know. Many of them are small business-men, but others are far bigger players. Masonic influence reaches right around the world. Most presidents of America, most British prime ministers, in fact most world leaders tend to be connected to the Freemasons, as do European royal families (who are masonic patrons).

One particular masonic group achieved particular notoriety: P2, or *Propaganda Due*.

P2

The lodge P2 was set up in the nineteenth century by the Grande Orient Lodge of Italy. It claimed descent from the nationalistic society of the Carbonari (Charcoal Burners), who from the 1820s were agitat-ing for Italian unity. The origins of the Carbonari are strikingly similar to that of the masons in that they claim to have begun in Scotland, the resting-place of the Templars. The idea of the Carbonari being mystics from Scotland strongly suggests that their true origin lies within the masonic order and therefore with the Templars. It also suggests that they believe their origins to be with mystics – individuals who experi-ence part of the enlightenment process.

In 1976 the Freemasons closed P2 down, but it continued under its own authority. It came to the forefront in the scandal of the Banco Ambrosiano of Milan, one of Italy's principal banks, which collapsed in 1982 with debts of between US$700 million and $1.5 billion. This was followed soon after by the death of its president, Roberto Calvi, who was found hanging in a manner in accordance with masonic ritual under Blackfriars Bridge in London. When the initial British inquest returned a verdict of suicide, there was disbelief in Italy. P2 were known as *I Fratelli Neri* – the Black Friars.

It has been claimed that the Banco Ambrosiano's money had been siphoned 'offshore' to the Institute of Religious Works – the Vatican's own bank – and that the 80 million *lire* that the Catholic Church claimed to have lost through the collapse of the Milan bank had in fact gone right back *into* the Catholic Church. Calvi and various senior Vatican officials were implicated in the affair and Calvi was later revealed to be a member of the previously secret P2 lodge run by Licio Gelli, an ex-member of the SS.

A second inquest on Calvi reached an open verdict, leaving the murder option open. Investigations continued in Italy, where a murder trial began 2003. Pippo Calo was among the accused; he was a member of the Sicilian Mafia, one of the world's most secretive criminal organizations, which had dealings with the Banco Ambrosiano and has been linked to the scarcely less secretive masons.

Two former members of P2 have revealed some information which relates to our story. They say there is a villa in Tuscany where, hidden in the courtyard, there is a ritual fountain shaped like a rearing cobra with an inflated hood and a single eye. Inside this all-seeing eye is a camera that keeps check on visitors. This is the striking cobra we have seen as far back as Sumeria and Egypt – the great 'one-eyed' Shining One at the very centre of a modern-day secret society which has been claimed to have links to the heart of Catholicism. According to some writers, P2 was also implicated in the death of the short-lived Pope John Paul I, who some believe was assassinated.[2]

Following the revelations of the doings of P2, the Italian government collapsed – an example of masonic political influence?

The Rosicrucians

The earliest real documentation for the Rosicrucians dates from 1597. It is said that a certain alchemist travelled across Europe seeking to begin a society to carry out his newly discovered alchemical ideals. In

1614 the Rosicrucian 'manifestos', the *Fama Fraternitas* and the *General Reformation of the World*, appeared. They claimed as their founder one 'Christian Rosenkreuz', clearly a pseudonym – it means the 'rosy cross of the Christians'. Rosenkreuz is said to have travelled across Arabia, studied at Fez in Egypt and returned to Europe with a message – one that was decidedly ancient and was originally created by the Shining Ones.

If the supposed founder of this enigmatic group is a fiction, who did begin it? What other clues do we have? There are also parallels with Arabic Illuminati schools, such as those of Abdelkadir Gilani, who was known as the 'shining rose'. However, when we look at the origins, rituals and beliefs of Rosicrucianism we find something very similar to Freemasonry.

Just like the Freemasons, Rosicrucian methods required the deepest of concentration upon the 'master' and absolute adherence to the 'way'. It was another method of control, and a way of maintaining it at a time half of Western Europe had broken from Catholicism and firmly adhered to the new Protestant Christianity in its various forms.

Today the Rosicrucians are a worldwide order with thousands of members, but their influence is minimal. There is a hint, however, in one of their books, published in 1910, that the influence of the person or soul they call 'Ego' will keep returning to influence the development of humankind:

> 'Many centuries have rolled by since the birth, as Christian Rosenkreuz, of the individual who we know and honor by the name – the founder of the Most Holy Order of the Rosy Cross.
>
> 'Though by many outsiders his existence is regarded as a myth, it is nevertheless true that his birth marked the beginning of a new epoch in the spiritual life of the western World. That particular Ego has also been in continuous incarnation ever since, in one or another of the European

countries, taking a new body as his successive vehicles out-lived their usefulness, or circumstances rendered it expedient that he change the scene of his activities. Moreover, he is incarnate today, an initiate of high degree; an active and potent factor in all affairs of the West – although unknown to the world.

'As are all such individuals, he is a representative of the Central Conclave of the Elder Brothers of humanity. His mission was and is to show the spiritual significance of all scientific discoveries, thus counteracting as far as possible the deadening influence of materialistic science, which, for reasons previously given, the Elder Brothers dread more than any other manifestation of human activity.

'To this end he labored with the Alchemists centuries before the advent of modern science.'[3]

In this extract we are told that there is one source (Ego) from which all 'spiritual illumination' has derived, and which has been manifesting itself throughout time – and we would agree. However, we would claim that this source is none other than the Shining influence, oper-ating over time as evolution has moved humankind forward. Rosicrucians call this influence 'the Central Conclave of the Elder Brothers'; we call it 'the Shining priesthood'.

The text continues and tells us who can 'see' the secret of Rosicrucianism:

'It hides from the profane, but reveals to the Initiate the more clearly how he is to labor day by day to make for himself that choicest of all gems, the Philosopher's Stone – more precious than the Kohinoor; nay, than the sum of all earthly wealth!

'Apparently Christ himself wrought this "marvelous Stone" while incarnate in the body of Jesus…[It has been called] "an Elixir of Life. It is all, and much more than has ever been claimed for it. Moreover, most people have had it in their hands often, but know it not!" How absolutely and unqualifiedly true that is, yet at the same time how thoroughly misleading, none can guess save those who know the secret, but even the eavesdropping traitor who had listened and overheard the words spoken among the brethren could have profited thereby.

'To those who are entitled to the knowledge, many a mystery will reveal itself "between the lines" in this work, suggested but not spoken, for to reveal them, save from the lip to ear to worthy persons and under proper circumstances, would be a grievous breach of faith not to be contemplated.'[4]

The secret 'knowledge' referred to here is clear – it is the enlightenment experience.

We are even told that in order to become initiates we cannot simply apply. As with many secret societies, we will be watched from the wings and our merits counted to see whether we are worthy of being offered the 'golden key to the temple'.

Today we find this once influential secret society offering courses with credit card payments. The Rosicrucians still claim, however, to be teachers of the mysteries and custodians of the sacred teachings of a spiritual power more 'potent in the life of the Western World than any of the visible Governments; though they may not interfere with humanity so as to deprive them of their free will'.[5]

If we also read 'between the lines' this implies that they are indeed an *invisible* government, a secret group taking the form of seven 'brothers' who 'go out into the World whenever occasion requires; appearing as men among other men or working in their invisible vehicles with or upon others as needed; yet it must be strictly kept in mind that they never influence anyone against their will or contrary to their desires; but only strengthen good wherever found'.[6]

A person's 'will' is, of course, dependent upon what has already influenced him or her; and the concept of 'good' is also relative.

The Illuminati

In *Essai sur la secte des Illuminés*, published in 1789, the mason De Luchet wrote:

> 'There are a certain number of people who have arrived at the highest degree of imposture. They have conceived the project of reigning over opinions, and of conquering, not kingdoms, nor provinces, but the human mind. This project is gigantic, and has something of madness in it, which causes neither alarm nor uneasiness; but when we descend to details, when we regard what passes before our eyes of the hidden principles, when we perceive a sudden revolution in favour of ignorance and incapacity, we must look for the cause of it; *and if we find that a revealed and known system explains all the phenomena which succeed each other with terrifying rapidity, how can we not believe it?*'

The Illuminati are for many the 'Men in Black', the silent masters in the background who plot our futures. To others they are a fable, a 'boys' club' created by frustrated Freemasons in the eighteenth century. There is, as ever, truth in all, but we must understand that most of the time we end up believing exactly what we are led to believe by the marketing and propaganda.

Standard history tells us that the Order of the Illuminati was started by Jean Adam Weishaupt, who was born in Bavaria in 1748. His father, Baron Ickstatt, was a professor at the University of Ingolstadt, having married the niece of the curator. The baron secured a scholarship at the Jesuit College for Adam, who went on to become a law student at the age of 15. In Jesuit-run Ingolstadt dissent was not permitted, even though the Jesuits had been partially suppressed in 1773 by Pope Clement XIV. It was in their world that Weishaupt was brought up.

By 1775 Weishaupt was professor of canon law at Ingolstadt and it was in this year that he chose (or somebody chose on his behalf) to plan an association that he would head. This association would 'oppose the forces of superstition and lies' and many commentators think that Weishaupt so hated the Jesuits that he intended to do away with them once and for all. But others believe that he was trained by the Jesuits for the purpose of raising a worldwide army of spies who would constantly be feeding back information – information that the Jesuits could no longer get through their confessions. In fact, the Illuminati even set up their own confessions. They introduced an 'obligation of unconditional obedience', similar to Ignatius Loyola's *Constitutions*. The members were expected to engage in 'mutual surveillance' and there was a form of confession that every member had to make to his superior.

All of the information thereby gained would then be fed back to the Jesuits by the very people who were supposed to be against them. How better to find out what is in the mind of the opposition than to *pretend to join* the opposition? This is a standard double ploy utilized for centuries by the secret services of all religions and states.

Weishaupt and his close friend Zwack were banished for creating the Illuminati and never seen again. Some believe they simply went to Saxe-Coburg and the Netherlands to start the whole organization again. Just how much influence the Illuminati finally had (or continue to have) is unknown. That is the idea of secrecy. But what can be seen is that following their creation by Weishaupt there were several worldwide *revolutions* and the balance of power shifted as never before. Here too, we can perceive a link with the masons.

259

The Knights of Malta

This order can be traced back to the Crusades in one long uninterrupted historical line. Some modern orders have similar names, but they are mimicking the true order, which is now based in Rome, having been expelled from Rhodes and Malta by successive invading armies. The Knights of Malta, more formally known as the Knights of the Hospital of St John of Jerusalem (Knights Hospitaller), did not suffer the same fate as the Templars. When the Templars were disbanded in the fourteenth century many of them joined the Knights of St John and took with them their mystical ways and knowledge.

The Knights of Malta now has connections across the world and is a sovereign order directly responsible to the Pope, which means it has ambassadors and holds political sway as well as diplomatic immunity. The order maintains diplomatic relations with Europe, North America, South America and Asia, with the authority of the Holy See. It has specialized agencies in the United Nations and other international organizations. The St John's Ambulance service is one branch of this worldwide order.

The Knights, or at least individual members of the order, have allegedly been linked to various scandals. For instance, in the 1980s when Colonel Oliver North authorized the Iran-Contra scandal, he needed connections in the underworld, and got involved with various shady organizations and individuals. One of these was Al Carone, a fellow colonel in the US Army – and a member of the Sovereign Military Order of the Knights of Malta.

In an interview with the author John Travis, Fra. Andrew W. N. Bertie said:

"'There's nothing secret about the order, but a lot of people think there is." Bertie added 'The fact that five of the six US ambassadors to the Vatican have been members of the Knights of Malta is "sheer coincidence".'[7]

We might wonder about how probable this 'coincidence' really is.

Opus Dei

Opus Dei are a relatively recent Catholic order with close links to the Pope. They are not huge, but are secretive and have great influence. They have centres strategically positioned in or outside colleges and universities across America, where they gather information, money and recruits for their 'good works'. They recruit their members from among the brightest students, which encourages a sense of elitism and belonging. They do not deny accusations that they target the rich. They are said to have lost over US$50 million when the Banco Ambrosiano of Roberto Calvi collapsed *(see page 253)*, even though the money was allegedly siphoned off indirectly back into the Vatican's own bank.

The Opus Dei are open about their secrecy. In their own magazine, *Cronica*, they tell their members to keep their slates clean:

> 'Dirty clothes are washed at home. The first manifestation
> of your dedication is not being so cowardly as to go outside
> the Work to wash dirty clothes. That is, if you want to be
> saints. If not, you are not needed here.'[8]

A Jesuit priest told ABC News: 'I think they really fly under everybody's radar screen and they're a lot more powerful than a lot of people think.'[9]

During the late 1950s and the 1960s, Opus Dei members came to control the economic ministries of Spain as well as other important cabinet posts. This was in keeping with the organization's aim of influencing the development of society indirectly.

During the research of this book we contacted many people. One of them was Dianne DiNicola of the pressure group Opus Dei Awareness Network (ODAN). Some of their material implicates Opus Dei in the Franco regime in Spain.[10] We also found through our own research that Opus Dei's role was more than incidental in the Franco regime and helped with its financial organization. Opus Dei members were in charge of the Ministries of Finance to such an extent that some Spanish writers called them the 'Spanish Mafia'. Today, others have termed them the 'Holy Mafia'.

Father Gonzalo Munoz, a Melbourne Catholic priest, believes people should be wary of the group:

> 'The more we expose them the better ... My concern is really that they are trying to influence the church with values that are contrary to the Gospels. It's about elitism, it's about wealth and prestige ... My concern is that they are going to infiltrate universities.'[11]

It seems to us that Opus Dei is not only almost a secret society, but also highly influential in the world today.

The Bilderberg Group

> 'The Bilderberg Group, an informal secretive transatlantic council of key decision makers, developed between 1952 and 1954... It brought leading European and American personalities together once a year for informal discussions of their differences... The formation of the American wing of Bilderberg was entrusted to (Gen.) Eisenhower's psychological warfare co-ordinator, C.D. Jackson, and the funding for the first meeting, held at the Hotel de Bilderberg in Holland in 1954, was provided by the Central Intelligence Agency. Thereafter much of its funding came from the Ford Foundation... The subjects over which the annual meetings ranged were wide ... but it is clear that the [1957] Treaty of Rome was nurtured by discussions at Bilderberg the previous year.'[12]

This modern-day group of the powerful elite has been accused of being the brains behind a new world order. On the other hand, they themselves claim that they simply meet to discuss, in a free and easy way, the concerns of world leaders:

'In short, Bilderberg is a recognized, flexible and informal international leadership forum in which different viewpoints can be expressed and mutual understanding enhanced.'[13]

The origins of this group rest with one man, Joseph Retinger, a Catholic with links to the Jesuit order. At one time he even recommended the turning of Hungary, Austria and Poland into a tripartite state under the guidance of the Jesuits. This never happened, of course, but Retinger was certainly influential. As Sir Edward Bedington-Behrens, a former British civil servant, recalls:

'I remember Retinger in the United States picking up the telephone and immediately making an appointment with the President, and in Europe he had complete entrée in every political circle as a kind of right acquired through the trust, devotion and loyalty he inspired.'

Retinger was involved in secret and underground activities, even parachuting into Nazi Germany at the age of 58. He founded the European Movement, which gave rise to the Council of Europe in 1949. They set up in Strasbourg, where Retinger worked.

Retinger believed in unity and that it did not really matter how that unity was brought about. He certainly liked to involve big business and use its influence on the general public. We are, after all, tied to our television screens and led by marketing men (like us). Retinger believed that the political and religious differences which created the disunity between certain states could be brought together through a corporate ideal – if everybody wanted the same thing, they would all *be* the same.

Strangely, a market-led revolution has indeed been taking place.

The former USSR is now part of the capitalist economy and in the process of commercialization; the same will be true of China. Commercialization is creeping across the world like an invading force.

In 1952 Retinger proposed that there should be an open and frank discussion between the different organizations and individuals that controlled the world. This should be in secret to allow those taking part to air their views without the worry of it appearing in the newspapers the next day. This was the birth of the Bilderberg Group, which was named after the hotel in Oosterbeek where the first meeting was held in May 1954.

What influence the Bilderberg Group has had on world events is uncertain, but what does appear to have come out of the meetings is at least one other group that has also been scrutinized by conspiracy theorists: the Trilateral Commission.

The Trilateral Commission

'The Trilateral Commission was formed in 1973 by private citizens of Japan, Europe [Common Market countries], and North America [United States and Canada] to foster closer cooperation among these core democratic industrialized areas of the world with shared leadership responsibilities in the wider international system. Originally established for three years, our work has been renewed for successive triennia (three-year periods), most recently for a triennium to be completed in 2006.'[14]

The Trilateral Commission is a private organization, founded at the initiative of David Rockefeller. It consists of over 300 private citizens from Europe, Japan and North America and is there 'to promote closer cooperation between these three areas'.

The Trilateral Commission has come under a lot of scrutiny and has been implicated strongly in many conspiracy theories – however, with as many members as it has, it is no surprise that some of them are connected to other organizations such as the Knights of Malta, Jesuits and Freemasons. Not least of these is David Rockefeller himself, former president of the Chase Manhattan Bank.

The Rockefeller dynasty made its forutne running the United States Steel Corporation. By subsequently setting up the Rockefeller Foundation, the family established a firm basis for helping the people of America, and later still the world, with charitable contributions. The Rockefellers are often linked with the Rothschilds in the conspiracy world. We will leave it up to readers to do their own further research on these two families.

Conclusion

Much of what we have outlined about these groups is familiar to those who study alternative views of history. But what is new is thinking of all of them − and many other smaller groups − as part of the rim of the same wheel, branches of just one tree. They have all essentially arisen from the same hub or stem: The Catholic Church, which in turn, in our view, can be traced back to ancient Sumeria and the Shining Ones.

The secret doctrines of the Shining Ones have steered the development of humankind for possibly 50,000 years, and continue to do so today. No matter what form the Shining elites developed in order to direct their followers, the old Shining ways have always been there. The priestly elite of Hinduism and the wise teachers of Buddhism and Jainism continue to emphasize the pursuit of enlightenment, a path in which the deepest Shining secrets will gradually be revealed to the committed individual. Eastern paths of Shining wisdom also stress compassion: the universe is seen as one, and all beings are connected and nothing happens independently of anything else.

However, the Catholic Church, the biggest and most influential of the present-day Shining groups, offers a different path for its follow-ers. The compassionate command to 'love your neighbour as yourself' is there, certainly, but the path of the Church is centred less on the pursuit of enlightenment and more on personal responsibility for 'sin' and obedience to Church doctrines. The Pope may no longer wear the triple-crowned white and gold papal tiara (a headdress replete with Shining symbolism), and the true Shining understanding of the story of Jesus, the great Shining One, may have been deliberately obscured, but in the Church, power has remained in the hands of an elite, and the old Shining habits of keeping secret knowledge among a tight-knit group of the initiated have been retained. In the Catholic Church, some of the ancient Shining ways are as strong today as they have ever been.

But what of the future? Some say that we are turning away from traditional religion, particularly in the West. And yet we still *believe*. While we are certainly less happy, today, being told what to think from the pulpit, there still exists a great desire to follow some sort of 'higher path'. According to Wade Clark Roof in his book *A Generation of Seekers*, we now have no qualms about 'inventing' our own religions. We happily piece together elements from a range of spiritual paths and traditions – from Gnosticism to Hinduism to Celtic paganism – to suit our individual personalities and lifestyles, in much the same way that the larger, older faiths fitted in with the masses (as an example, con-sider the way the Church adapted its festivals, such as Christmas, to existing popular pagan feasts[15]).

This tendency towards what has been called 'do-it-yourself' spiri-tuality has benefits for some of the inheritors of the Shining way, but poses a potential challenge to others. On the one hand, Buddhism, Hinduism and a revived Celtic paganism – none of which in any case have a centralized worldwide organization – can be said to have bene-fited from the growing Western interest in alternative paths. On the other hand, the Catholic Church has clearly lost out as attendances decline and people turn away from priestly control of their lives. It remains to be seen whether the keepers of the Shining flame at the heart of the Catholic Church will allow the decline in their power to continue.

Appendix

Threes and Sevens in World Myth, Religion and Folklore

Divine Triads

The best known example of the triad is the Father (Godhead), Son and Holy Ghost of Christianity. But there was also the ancient Egyptian divine triad of Osiris, Isis and Horus, and the ancient Druid holy triad of Beli, Taran and Esus, not to mention the three great gods of Greece – Zeus (the sky), Poseidon (god of the sea and the power of the earth) and Hades (the underworld), mirrored in the Roman Jupiter, Neptune and Pluto. Hinduism has the triad of Brahma the creator, Vishnu the preserver and Shiva the destroyer.

The Egyptian trinity of Isis, Osiris and Horus is linked with the Knights Templar and the figure of John the Baptist. The Templars were accused of worshipping the 'evil' image of a human head – a carved head reliquary – which they called *Baphomet*. This head has been described as having two faces back to back, or perhaps three heads or faces – two faces back to back with a third placed centrally (like the three-headed Celtic god Bran, another Shining One). Some say that Baphomet had the face of a man or a woman or both. But if it had two faces, then in our view it was most probably a head with a male and a female face back to back, in which case it is more than likely that it was modelled on the two-faced Roman god Janus, the god of new beginnings and/or endings, of spiritual portals and gateways. (Janus was

also the god of change, transition or transformation from one condition to another and one 'world' to another, which relates to the
midpoint between the opposites being a gateway.)

Our theory is that the two or three faces or heads of the Baphomet
head were those of John the Baptist and John the Evangelist with Jesus
in the centre. It is known that the Templars worshipped John the
Baptist. They also preferred St John's Gospel to the other three, and so
it is possible that they also worshipped St John the Evangelist (St John
the Divine), who is often depicted as clean-shaven and effeminate
looking. Images of heads, both male and female, abound in Templar
literature and art.

The Baphomet figure is based on the ancient Egyptian triad of
Osiris, Isis and Horus and other triads. These tricephalic (three-
headed) images symbolize the three forces in consciousness – positive,
negative and neutral – whether or not the midpoint is clearly indicated
by a third face or not.

Our reasoning behind this is based on the alchemical symbolism of
the androgyne, the union of male and female opposites. As we have
seen, the chief male god is almost always associated with the sun or sky
and the chief female goddess with the moon or Earth. From the union
of these deities comes forth the 'son of the sun': a trinity is created.
'One becomes two, the threefold appears.'[1]

The Three Jewels

The triad is also, and ultimately, based on the three organs in the brain.
In Jainism's *Sacred Book of the Jains*, which holds all the secret teachings for those with the eyes to see and minds open enough to
understand, we read the following: 'One should ever make his own self
radiant by the light of the three jewels.' That is, truly to understand, to
see the light – to be 'enlightened' – we must utilize the 'three jewels'.
Having now gathered enough evidence, we are confident that these

three jewels really represent the three organs in the brain: the pineal and pituitary glands and the central thalamus.

These three jewels are also the three golden apples located at the top of the tree in the Greek myth of the Garden of the Hesperides – the tree guarded by a serpent named Ladon. The tree is the same seven-levelled tree or ladder representing the spinal column. For the Druids this same triad was symbolized by three white berries from the mistle-toe of the oak – the gods of the tree of life, the spirits within the tree. Buddhist belief also has three jewels which release us from the clutches of rebirth on the material plane. The initiate will say, 'I go for refuge to the Buddha [the initiator], to the Dharma [the teachings, the word of the Buddha], and to the Sangha [the initiated as a body].' They are the path to enlightenment: the father, the son and the spirit. The three jewels, apples, or berries correspond with everything we have men-tioned so far as regards the male (pineal) and female (pituitary) opposites and, more importantly, the neutral point (thalamus), where the two are united as one.

There are many more correspondences. It is possible that the concept of the trinity and everything related to it emerged from the collective unconscious. However, for the idea to occur on such a global scale shows more than just a dissolution theory – it shows a well thought out plan, a plan which is subtle and almost hidden, but not from those with the eyes to see.

Sevens

Seven is the symbolic number of the universe, or macrocosm, with the human as the microcosm, so it was therefore also connected in numerology to the perfect man. It is also the number attributed to Mother Earth, safety, perfection, plenty and fecundity. But most importantly, seven was deemed important in the process towards the enlightenment experience. Three signified the heavenly part of the seven, and four the Earth and human part. Only together would they unite as seven. In other words, one climbed the tree or ladder – the four lower chakras associated with the external material realm – to reach the three organs or glands (power centres) in the head associated with the internal psychical realm. There were seven in all. The chakra system is the ultimate source of the significance of sevens in myth, legend and mystical and spiritual systems the world over. Here are just a few of the correspondences:

Seven chakras ('wheel' vortices), reflecting the seven levels of consciousness and existence. The reality limit of these seven levels is demonstrated in the piece of paper that cannot be folded more than seven times.

Seven elementary hues to the spectrum, blending to form white. This has correspondence with the climactic phase of the kundalini awakening, the explosion of 'bright white light' at the centre of the head.

Seven notes on a scale.

Seven electron orbits, levels or 'shells' of the atom.

Seven days in a week.

Seven days of Creation.

Seven Sacraments of the Catholic Church.

Seven Deadly Sins and **Seven Virtues**.

Seven Last Words of Jesus. The gospels record seven 'words' or utterances of Christ from the cross before his 'death' and 'resurrection'. The cross is the shamanic world tree or *axis mundi* and therefore also the human spinal column. Speaking seven times from the cross/spine symbolizes the seven chakras, and the culmination of all seven is the 'feigning death' experience that leads to the 'resurrection' of enlightenment.

Seven Joys and **Seven Sorrows** of Mary.

Joshua walked around Jericho **seven times** before the walls fell down. (Jericho was the first civilization, according to some, and was home to a large group of shamans.)

Seven heavens (Qur'an, Bible, Book of Enoch, shamanic and Druid belief).

The **'seventh son of the seventh son'** in several traditions is believed to have great healing and psychic powers. Native Americans determined actions based on its effects 'unto the seventh generation'.

Seven steps to heaven – a popular belief, as featured on ziggurats, pyramids and other artificial mounds based on the shamanic world mountain or primordial mound of creation.

Seven Sages or **Wise Men** of Greece.

Seven Ages of Man.

Seven senses, according to the ancients. These are under the influence of the seven planets of classical times. Fire moves, earth brings sense of feeling, water gives speech, air taste, mist sight, flowers hearing and the south wind smell.

Seven Wonders of the ancient world.

Seven Pillars of Wisdom in Islam.

Seven Sages or **Shining Ones** of ancient Sumeria and elsewhere. The seven sages of different cultures symbolized the seven chakra levels, and their final deification as a pantheon of seven refers to the human becoming divine through ascending each level and reaching the source of enlightenment and illumination.

Seven Japanese gods of luck.

The **Seven Champions** of English legend.

Notes

Unless otherwise stated in the text, all biblical quotes are from the New King James Bible, Tyndale.

Introduction

1. Giorgio de Santillana and Hertha von Dechend, *Hamlet's Mill: An Essay Investigating the Origins of Human Knowledge and its Transmission through Myth*, David R. Godine Publisher Inc., 1969, p.1

2. This statement is supported by Christopher Knight and Robert Lomas in *Uriel's Machine: The Ancient Origins of Science* (Arrow Books, 2000). On p.32 they write: 'Our analysis of the failings of prehistoric theory seemed to be pointing towards the pre-existence of knowledge.'

3. To give one example we can look at the famous Greek myth of Ariadne's thread leading Theseus out of the Minotaur's dark labyrinth into the light. This could be compared to the 'underground stream' of esoteric lore that leads to the sea (fount of knowledge) and it could also be likened to the sushumna nerve channel of Hindu chakra theory *(see Chapter 3)*, up which the kundalini energy ascends in the enlightenment experience, leading to the centre of the skull and the godhead – again the fount of knowledge.

4. For the original text of Enoch, *see The Book of Enoch*, R. H. Charles, W. O. E. Oesterley (eds), Book Tree, 1998, *also* http://www.reluctant-messenger.com/enoch.htm and http://www.reluctant-messenger.com/1enoch01-60.htm

Chapter 1: The Prehistoric Link

1. Baigent, Michael, *Ancient Traces*, Viking, 1998, p.110

2. Such anachronistic artefacts include a 10 inch (25 cm) long 8-carat gold chain found in a lump of coal, a metallic vase composed of a zinc and silver alloy and decorated with flowers in bouquet arrangements which had been dynamited out of solid rock 100,000 years old, a nail found

embedded in a fist-sized lump of one-million-year-old auriferous quartz and a gold thread found embedded in rock.

These finds, if authentic, are astonishingly early but still within the accepted timescale: it is believed that humans have been around for between one and two million years. However, between 1991 and 1993 gold prospectors on the Narada river on the eastern side of the Ural mountains in Russia discovered some unusual tiny spiral-shaped objects, the smallest measuring about one ten-thousandth of an inch. Tests showed that the objects were composed of copper and the rare metals tungsten and molybdenum and were between 20,000 and 318,000 years old. If this find is authentic then it suggests that there was once an ancient 'nanotechnology'.

In 1926, a lump of coal with a fossilized human tooth on it was reportedly found in a coal mine in Bearcreek, Montana. The tooth was so old that the enamel had turned to carbon and the roots to iron. The coal deposits that yielded the coal with the tooth are estimated to be 10 million years old. In another case, a 2 inch (5 cm) long machine-made metal screw was reportedly found inside a piece of feldspar calculated to be 21 million years old.

Most spectacularly of all, if authentic, in 1968 a piece of rock found in Utah was opened, revealing a fossilized imprint of what looked like a sandal some 10.5 inches (26 cm) long by 3.5 inches (8 cm) wide. The amazing thing is that in the heel (which was slightly more indented than the sole) was a crushed trilobite – a sea creature that became extinct some 280 million years ago – which seemed to have been trampled by the wearer of the sandal. It is said that the fossil may be 600 million years old!

These are only a few examples from a long list of discoveries that contradict the established view of human origins. See also http://www.paranormal.about.com/library/weekly/aa072098.htm.

3. van Andel, T. H., 'Late Quaternary sea-level changes and archaeology' in *Antiquity*, vol. 63, no. 241 (December 1989), pp.733–45

4. 'Red ochre or haematite/hematite: Oxide of iron, crystallizing in the trigonal system. Occurs in many forms: rhombohedral crystals from Elba, bedded ores of sedimentary origin from pre-Cambrian world. Also as a cement and pigment from sandstone.' *Dictionary of Science and Technology*, Peter M. B. Walker (ed.), Wordsworth Editions Ltd, 1995

5. In the outback of Australia, depictions of the anthropomorphic *wondjina*, or tribal ancestral spirits, which date back to 10,000 BC, show a distinct red band around their heads. Evidence from Australia shows that the early people were adept at utilizing and chemically altering the earth around them to produce the red ochre needed for their rites – a 'magical' process *kept secret* by the priesthood or medicine man – an early indication of 'keeping the power'. According to *The Paranormal* by Stuart Gordon (Headline, 1992), the Aborigines of Australia knew how to smelt the yellow hydrated iron oxide to produce this red ochre, which is a form of magnetite *(see Chapter 4)*. Is there some link here between the migratory ideas of early humans and their knowledge, in an almost alchemical way, of red ochre?

6. Plichta, Peter, *God's Secret Formula*, Element Books, Shaftesbury, 1997

7. See Gooch, Stan, *Cities of Dreams: The Rich Legacy of Neanderthal Man which Shaped our Civilisation*, Rider Books, 1991

8. E-mail from the author Michael Hayes to Gary Osborn, 8 May 2005.

Chapter 2: Kundalini and the Inner Sun

1. Krishna, Gopi, *Kundalini: The Evolutionary Energy in Man*, Shambhala, Boston, 1997

2. Ibid., p.12

3. Ibid., pp.13–14

4. Perhaps this explains why the word 'shaman' is also associated with fire and heat, since the shaman, familiar with this internal mechanism through his altered states, surely had this same experience: 'Translated, shaman means "to heat up; to burn; to work with heat and fire". The essential characteristics of shamans are mastery of energy and fire as a medium of transformation' *(see* http://www.kenaz.com/shaman/whatis.htm)*. On a physical level this could also be related to the fact that the traditional 'brother' of the shaman was the 'shaman smithy' – the blacksmith, who worked the furnace to produce metals, the foundation of alchemy also associated with transformation. However, on a higher level, this 'trial by fire' transformation is related to the 'serpent fire' of the kundalini – the internal processes associated with the 'inner sun' of enlightenment and rebirth.

5. Eliade, Mircea, *Shamanism: Archaic Techniques of Ecstasy*, trans. Willard

R. Trask, Princeton University Press, 2004

6. *Women's Health Information, Customs and Traditions* (Feminist Women's Health Centre), 1996–2003. *See* http://www.fwhc.org/health/moon.htm.

7. Ibid.

8. Ibid.

9. Ibid.

10. Ibid.

11. *See* our previous book, *The Serpent Grail*, Watkins, 2005

12. Harding, Esther, *Women's Mysteries*, Rider, 1971

Chapter 3: Three and Seven

1. Wilson, Colin, *Poltergeist: A Study in Destructive Haunting*, Llewellyn Publications, 1993, p.83

2. Miller, Crichton E.M., *The Golden Thread of Time*, Pendulum Publishing, 2000

3. Quoted in Ouspensky, P. D., *In Search of the Miraculous: Fragments of an Unknown Teaching*, Harcourt, 1949

4. Ibid.

5. It is well known that ancient shamans knew that the Earth was a sphere. See, for example: http://www.circlesanctuary.org/aboutpagan/sacred.htm; http://www.shamanelder.com/newsletterjuly.html.

6. The word 'dunce' derives from John Duns Scotus, 'the Subtle Doctor', born in 1266 in Duns, Scotland. He taught metaphysics and emphasized what he called the 'univocity of being'. Noting that wizards supposedly wore pointed conical hats, he believed in the wearing of conical hats to increase learning. The apex was 'considered a symbol of knowledge and the hats were thought to "funnel" knowledge to the wearer. Once humanism gained the upper hand, Duns Scotus's teachings were despised and the "dunce cap" became identified with ignorance rather than learning.' ('What's the Origin of the Dunce Cap?' from *The Straight Dope*, 2000, http://www.straightdope.com/mailbag/mduncecap.html.)

It is one of those strange synchronicities that Duns, where Duns Scotus was born, means 'hill' and is associated with the sacred mount or primordial mound of creation. The word 'dunn' also means 'twilight', the point between day and night which also corresponds to the neutral point in consciousness.

7. As we will see, it's possible that the seven deities or 'seven sages' associated with the Sumerian and Indian Shining Ones, and especially the nine deities of the ancient Egyptian Ennead, personify the different chakra layers or levels. The symbolism suggests that via his djed (spinal column or backbone) the god Osiris could descend from or ascend to Atum-Ra, the 'father god' who represents the source centre of creation. Atum-Ra, the centre of the sphere, represented the superconscious while the lowest god, Set, represented the unconscious. In this pantheon of gods and goddesses we see the transformation of one's consciousness from one frequency level to another. Looking at everything we have seen thus far, it is possible that this is the real meaning behind the djed column, a widespread Egyptian hieroglyphic symbol also referred to as 'the backbone of Osiris'.

8. The term 'wand', given to the traditional rod used in magic, has been said to mean to 'unite the two winds' (energies) and is associated with the central staff of the caduceus – which is also a rod or wand. It is a fact that shamans were known as 'walkers between winds', meaning that they were able to access the midpoint between realities and become a 'medium': 'To walk between the winds one has to look around the edge of reality to the paths between space' (*What is a Shaman?*, Kenaz Services/Four Feathers Bookstore, 430 Crape Myrtle Road , Laurens, SC 29360, USA, 1998–2004; see http://www.kenaz.com/shaman/whatis.htm).

The central staff symbolizes the neutral sushumna nerve channel in the spinal cord. The 'two winds' are the opposite nerve channels, the pingala (male) and ida (female). Shaman were also known as 'travellers of the air' or 'skywalkers' – an allusion to their supposed 'flying' abilities and no doubt a reference to their astral 'out of body' experiences.

9. Information Theory was introduced by Claude Shannon in 1948 to precisely characterize data flows in communications systems. It has been discovered that the same mathematics can also be productively applied to molecular-biological systems such as DNA.

Chapter 4: Light from Darkness

1. Hagger, Nicholas, *The Fire and the Stones*, Element Books, 1991, p.140

2. Ley lines are specifically Alfred Watkins' straight tracks, but today the term is also used for energy lines.

3. *The Journal of John Wesley*, Moody, Chicago, 1974, p.231, quoted in Payne, Franklin E., *Biblical/Medical Ethics: The Christian and the Practice of Medicine*, Mott Media, 1985

4. Gordon, Stuart, *The Paranormal*, Headline, 1992

5. Dunn, Mark, 'Sleipnir: Travelling without Moving', originally published in *Samhain*, 2002

6. *Dictionary of the Occult*, Geddes and Grosset Ltd, 1997

7. Quoted in 'Hinduism', *A Handbook of Living Religions*, John R. Hinnells (ed.), Viking, 1984

8. Lichfield Cathedral, Staffordshire, England, contains remarkable imagery relating to numerology, the cross, trees, mountains, Marian cults, Illuminati and much more.

9. 'The Toronto Blessing' – supposedly the spirit of the Lord coming down on massed Christians and blessing them so heavily that they fall over, speak 'in tongues' and generally appear as if they are intoxicated.

Chapter 5: The 'Source Civilization'?

1. See the last chapter of our previous book, *The Serpent Grail*, Watkins, 2005

2. Pinkham, Mark A., *The Return of the Serpents of Wisdom*, Adventures Unlimited Press, 1998, p.12

3. Ibid.

4. Ibid.

5. Rutherford, Ward, *Druids and their Heritage*, Gordon and Cremonesi, 1978

Chapter 6: The Tree and the Cross

1. Frazer, Sir James, *The Golden Bough*, Wordsworth, 1993

2. Wilson, Damon, citing evidence in Cyrus Gordon, *The Giant Book of Lost Worlds*, Paragon, 1998

3. In this depiction, note the seven 'nodules' or 'orbs' on the spine of the scales – the equivalent of the chakras? The snout of Ammut 'the Swallower' of sinful souls, intersects the point between the third and fourth 'chakra'. 'In terms of the kundalini, the message is clear: if the aims of the deceased in life were no higher than those of Chakra 3, the Swallower claims the soul; whereas, if love had been heeded in the lifetime (Chakra 4), Thoth will conduct the blessed soul …to Osiris's throne by the waters of eternal life.' (Chou, Peter Y., "Poetry, Power, and Cultural Definitions". Panel discussion at CPITS conference, August 26, 1995)

Chapter 7: The Myth of the Phoenix

1. Hall, Manly Palmer, *The Secret Teachings of All Ages: An Encyclopedic Outline of Masonic, Hermetic, Qabbalistic and Rosicrucian Symbolical Philosophy*, Philosophical Research Society, 1928, p.90

2. Others have made the same connections, as we see from a traveller who visited the pyramid of Kukulcan in Mexico:

'On one side there was also a fantastic totem pole, not joined but close to a corner of the pyramid. This was formed of three-dimensional stone glyphs and faces, notably one large caricature-like one which had a huge and bent-backwards nose, actually incredibly like an elephant trunk! I later saw other similar such faces on other temples which looked even more like elephants, with big round flat ears also. Strange, especially considering all the correspondences between Mayan and Hindu tantric traditions (e.g. chakras, kundalini/k'ulthanlinli).' http://www.crossroads.wild.net. au/mex2.htm

It has been suggested that the Mayan term *k'ulthanlinli,* has the same meaning as the Hindu term *kundalini.*

3. Galenorn, Yasmine, 'Dancing with the Sun: The Maypole', http://www.geocities.com/RainForest/Canopy/1956/maypole.htm

Chapter 8: The Eye of Ra

1. See also our previous book, *The Serpent Grail*, Watkins, 2005

2. The concept of the world mountain can be further explained in that an analogy was made with the 'liquid fire' (lava) that rises up from the depths or centre of the Earth and through a mountain volcano, exploding in all directions from the truncated summit (note that the

Great Pyramid is also truncated). The sexual imagery was not lost on those who noticed the correspondence between lava rising upward through the axis of the volcano, the kundalini prana energy – the mix of 'fire' and 'water' – rising up through the sushumna of the spine and semen rising up through the phallus at the climactic moment of sexual intercourse.

Chapter 9: The Anunnaki

1. O'Brien, Christian with Barbara Joy, *The Genius of the Few: The Story of Those Who Founded the Garden in Eden*, Dianthus Publishing, 1985, p.17

2. Ibid., p.24

3. Blavatsky, H. P., *Isis Unveiled*, Theosophical University, 1999

4. Higgins, Godfrey, *Anacalypsis – The Saitic Isis: Languages, Nations and Religions*, 1833, reprint A&A Book Distributors, 1992

5. Ibid.

6. Hall, Manly Palmer, *The Secret Teachings of All Ages: An Encyclopedic Outline of Masonic, Hermetic, Qabbalistic & Rosicrucian Symbolical Philosophy*, Philosophical Research Society, 1928, p.85

7. Ovason, David, *The Zelator: The Secret Journals of Mark Hedsel*, Arrow, 1999, p.420

8. Ibid., p.613

9. It was believed that like certain sounds, 'spoken words', create form. Mystics say that the vibrations of words – whether intoned in thought or spoken – resonate with similar associative energy/information, information that will then 'materialize' in the form of certain objects and events. The Logos was the divine word which brought the world into being.

10. Ovason, op. cit., p.400

11. Ibid., p.392

12. 'Inner Self Located', taken from the *Brhadaranyaka Upanishad* (4. 3. 18), Sri Ramakrishna Math, Madras, 1951; http://www.dreams-genes.info/inner_self_located.htm

13. Ibid.

14. Suckling, Nigel, *The Book of the Unicorn*, Paper Tiger, Limpsfield, 1996, p.128

Chapter 10: Neteru, Akhu, Shemsu Hor

1. Tomas, Andrew, *Atlantis: From Legend to Discovery*, Sphere, 1972, p.19

2. Plato, *Timaeus*, Focus Publishing, 2001

3. Rasmussen, Knud, *Intellectual Culture of the Igluik Eskimos: Report of the Fifth Thule Expedition, 1921–24*, vol. 7, no. 2, Gyldendalske Boghandel, Copenhagen, 1930; reprinted AMS Press, New York, 1976

4. The name 'Neter', translating as 'neuter', meaning 'neutral' or 'androgynous'. This would mean that these 'Neteru gods' were shamanic in origin, as we are told that: 'the concept and reality of mystical androgyny was central to the practice of the shaman and esoteric magicians.' Tsarion, Michael, *Astrotheology and Sidereal Mythology*, http://www.taroscopes.com/astro-theology/astrotheology.html

5. Rux, Bruce, *Architects of the Underworld: Unriddling Atlantis, Anomalies of Mars, and the Mystery of the Sphinx*, Frog Ltd, 1996, p.318

6. Diodorus Siculus, *Bibliotheca Historica*, c. 21 BC

7. Bauval, Robert, and Hancock, Graham, *Keeper of Genesis: A Quest for the Hidden Legacy of Mankind*, William Heinemann, 1996, p.221

8. Henry, William, 'Secrets of the Cathars: Why the Dark Age Church Was Out to Destroy Them', *Atlantis Rising* magazine, December 2002

9. Bridges, Vincent, 'The Gnostic Science of Alchemy, Part I: From its Origins in Alexandria to the Black Death', 1999, http://vincentbridges.com/highweirdness/gsa2.html

10. In the book *The Bible Code 2: The Countdown* by Michael Drosnin (Phoenix, 2003), special significance is given to the name 'obelisk'. We are told that the word 'obelisk' and the phrase 'mouth of obelisks' cross or are associated with the phrases 'an object of heaven', 'code key' and 'Lord of the Code'. It is tempting to think that this code could indeed be related to the themes that form the Grail code, especially the famous obelisk or pillar of Heliopolis, which we have now deciphered to some extent.

11. These connections between the bennu/heron hieroglyph and the Ichthys fish symbol have been made by American author William Henry in the brief commentary *Show Him the Door* (2003), in which he outlines some of his own interpretations of the 'numerous unexplained and enigmatic gateway episodes in the Bible as examples of ancient stargates and wormholes, i.e. doorways into other realms'. We came

across William Henry's commentary on the internet while in the final stages of preparing this book and much of what he has uncovered agrees with our own hypotheses. For instance, the main subject of his enquiry is the ancient Akkadian-Sumerian name 'Nibiru', which translates as 'star', 'gate' and 'crossing'. Henry says this is possibly a dimensional 'stargate' – a 'wormhole' to other worlds. The term has many different meanings. As Henry points out, the word is associated with 'crossing' or being some sort of 'crossing marker' or 'crossing point' and of course it contains the word *ru*, which means 'gateway'.

For more clues to the meaning of Nibiru, Henry quotes the Sumerian poem *The Epic of Gilgamesh*, in which it is said, 'Narrow is the way to it.' This all fits nicely with the zero-point node – the point which is crossed over twice in all periodic cycles and oscillating systems – and, more importantly, the hypnagogic state. Like the zero-node, the hypnagogic state is the fine and *narrow* 'borderline state' where waking crosses into sleeping and sleeping crosses into waking.

We would say that the Mesopotamian/Sumerian term NIBIRU is indeed a 'stargate' but it is the 'gateway' in consciousness – the hypnagogic third eye. Also, *nib* is another word for 'tip' or 'point' – the point of a pen is called the 'nib'. *Pen* means 'head', and so again, in a roundabout way (which is more synchronistic than coincidental) we have here a connection between the *ru* 'gateway' and a point within the head. However, Henry believes that a real 'nuts and bolts' stargate-wormhole technology existed in prehistoric times (possibly 'alien') and he does not connect this 'stargate' with the shamanic experiences and principles outlined in Chapter 2.

12. Bauval, Robert, and Hancock, Graham, *Keeper of Genesis: A Quest for the Hidden Legacy of Mankind*, William Heinemann, 1996, p.211

13. Ibid.

14. 'The Chaldean Legend', *Theosophy*, vol. 52, no. 6, April 1964, pp.175–82

15. 'Teachings on the Avatars', *Theosophy*, vol. 48, no. 12, October 1960, pp.561–6

16. Bauval and Hancock, op. cit., p.212, using as their source the book *Mythical Origins of the Egyptian Temple* by E. A. E. Reymond.

17. Fessenden, Reginald Aubrey, *The Deluged Civilisation of the Caucasus Isthmus*, Massachusetts Bible Library, 1927, Chapter XI

18. Sitchin, Zecharia, *The Wars of Gods and Men*, Avon Books, 1989, p.143

19. According to Gary A. David, in Hopi Native American cosmology, the Duat or Tuat is known as Tuuwanasavi – literally, 'centre of the earth' ('The Orion Zone: Ancient Star Cities of the American South West', Part Two, 2001, http://www.100megsfree4.com/farshores/amorion2.htm). He also tells us that 'Like the Giza pyramids, the Tuuwanasavi corresponds to the three stars in the Belt of Orion, which is the visual focus and spiritual heart of the constellation' ('The Great Pyramids of Arizona', 2002, http://azorion.tripod.com/azpyramids.htm).

This is highly interesting, and although people are still contesting Bauval's Orion correlation theory, we find these connections do fit the conclusions we have come to about the Great Pyramid and the other pyramids of Giza that are supposed to reflect these three belt stars. In view of everything we have seen already, it does make perfect sense.

20. Budge, E. A. Wallis, *Hieroglyphic Dictionary*, vol, 1, pp.22–3

21. Bauval and Hancock, op. cit., p.209

22. It is interesting that one of the most ancient forms of Horus was 'Horus of Behdet', represented as the hawk-winged sun-disc symbol that became pretty much universal throughout Egypt.

23. Strabo, lib xv. P.1022

24. Extract from the lecture 'Gateway to the Gods: A New Approach to the Mysteries of Ancient Egypt' by Lynn Picknett and Clive Prince at the Templar Lodge Hotel, Gullane, near Edinburgh, Scotland, 7 June 1999; http://www.pharo.com/intelligence/starcon_hypothesis/articles/ifsh_101_gateway_to_the_gods.asp

25. Bauval and Hancock, *Keeper of Genesis: A Quest for the Hidden Legacy of Mankind*, William Heinemann, 1996, p.212

26. Ibid., pp.212–13

27. Pliny the Elder, *Natural History*, vol. III, trans. H. Rackham, Harvard University Press, Cambridge, Mass., 1983, pp.293, 295

28. With regard to the Alpha-Omega, the A letter or symbol of the Greek alphabet 'Alpha', A, is associated with the head. The O letter or symbol of Omega, Ω, is associated with the feet, and as we can see this Omega symbol does look like two feet. The significance of these two symbols is that duality (symbolized by the two feet, Ω, the two sides of the body and the positive and negative phases of all cycles) becomes one at the

centre of the head and particularly at the bindu point above the head: A. A is symbolic of the triad in this regard and is also suggestive of the pointed magician hats, an ancient tradition also associated with this bindu centre.

29. To show this the Great Pyramid's location had to be just right. It is known that the exact date and time of the vernal equinox, when the sun moves into the astrological sign of Aries, does vary from year to year in a four-year cycle. Each year, the date and time of the equinox will move progressively later in March until the year before leap year is reached. During the leap year, it will return to its earlier date and time and so the four-year cycle is then repeated. However, despite this, the Great Pyramid would always mark the spring equinox, no matter what day the equinox falls on.

Chapter 11: Angels, Nephilim, Watchers, Dreamers

1. Rux, Bruce, *Architects of the Underworld: Unriddling Atlantis, Anomalies of Mars, and the Mystery of the Sphinx*, Frog Ltd, 1996, p.318

2. Ewald (trans.), *The Gentile and the Jew*, Gesch, d. Volk Israel, London, 1868

3. Hagger, Nicholas, *The Fire and the Stones*, Element Books, 1998

4. *The Book of Ceremonial Magic*, William Ryder and Son, 1911

5. *The Book of Enoch*, R. H. Charles, W. O. E. Oesterley (eds), Book Tree, 1998, Chapter 6

6. Ibid., Chapter 7

7. Ibid., Chapter 9

8. Ibid., Chapter 8

9. Ibid., Chapter 9

10. Ibid., Chapter 60

11. http://biphome.spray.se/d.scot/Necro/necro1.htm

12. Ibid.

Chapter 12: Giants

1. Deuteronomy 2:10–11

2. Numbers 13:28–33

3. Deuteronomy 2:20–21

4. Deuteronomy 3:11

5. Deuteronomy 3:13; *see also* Joshua 12:4, 13:12

6. Genesis 14:5; 15:20; *see also* 2 Samuel 5:18,22; 23:13

7. *The Book of Enoch*, R. H. Charles, W. O. E. Oesterley (eds), Book Tree, 1998, 15:8–10

8. Balfour, Michael, *Megalithic Mysteries*, Dragon's World, Limpsfield, 1992

9. Joshua 5

10. Hosea 12:11

11. Judges 2:1

12. Walker, B., *Gnosticism*, The Aquarian Press

Chapter 13: Israel in Egypt

1. Cantor. Norman, F., *The Sacred Chain: A History of the Jews*, HarperCollins, 1994

2. Hagger, Nicholas, *The Fire and the Stones*, Element Books, 1998

3. *See also* Judges 13:3, Luke 1:13, Samuel 14:21.

4. Gardner, Laurence, *Bloodline of the Holy Grail*, Element Books, 1996, p.68

5. Numbers 28:11

6. 2 Kings 21

7. Jeremiah 7:18

8. Other places to look into for sun, moon and star worship of the Hebrews: Gen. 1:14, 1:16, 37:9; Lev. 26:30; Deut. 4:19; 2 Kings 21:3, 21:5; 23:5; Ps. 104:19; Isa. 17:8; Ezek. 32:7; Job 31:26,27.

9. Deuteronomy 4:19

10. Wallis Budge, E. A., *From Fetish to God*, Dover Publications, 1989

11. Hanauer, J. E., *Folklore of the Holy Land*, The Sheldon Press, 1907

12. Acts 6:22

13. *Ancient Egypt, Myth and History*, Geddes and Grosset, 1997

14. Frazer, Sir James, *The Golden Bough*, Wordsworth, 1993

15. Schonfield, Hugh, *The Essene Odyssey*, Element Books, 1984

Chapter 14: Shining Ones of the East

1. Feder, Kenneth L., and Park, Michael Alan, *Human Antiquity*, Mayfield, 1992

2. *A Handbook of Living Religions*, Hinnells, John R. (ed), Viking, 1984

3. *Human Antiquity*, op. cit.

4. Apuleius, Lucius, *The Golden Ass*, Penguin, 1985

Chapter 15: Secret Societies

1. Von Hammer, quoted in Inquire Within, *The Trail of the Serpent*, 1936; reprinted R. A. Kessinger Publishing Co., 2003

2. Dargon, *Patriot*, September 14 1922

3. Shah, Idries, *The Sufis*, W. H. Allen, 1964

4. Pike, Albert, *Morals and Dogma*, R. A. Kessinger Publishing, 2004

5. Aristotle, *The Art of Rhetoric*, Penguin Books, 2005

6. Inquire Within, op. cit.

Chapter 16: The Present Day

1. On the influence of Freemasonry on world history, *see* Fisher, Paul A., *Behind the Lodge Door: Church, State and Freemasonry in America*, Shield Publishing Company, 1988

2. *See* Yallop, David, *In God's Name: An Investigation into the Murder of Pope John Paul I*, Jonathan Cape, 1984

3. Heindel, Max, *The Rosicrucian Cosmo-Conception*, The Rosicrucian Fellowship, 1910

4. Ibid.

5. Heindel, Max, *Christian Rosenkreuz and the Order of Rosicrucians*, Lightning Source UK, (no date)

6. Ibid.

7. Travis, John, 'Knights of Malta Fight New War', *Catholic News Service*

8. *Cronica* magazine, quoted by Henry McDonald in the *Observer* newspaper, 6 August, 2000

9. Rev. James Martin, *Controversy over Opus Dei: Some Criticize Group's Methods*, ABC News, 2001

10. See the ODAN (Opus Dei Awareness Network) website www.odan.org

11. Quoted in *Church Storm*, Melbourne, April 2001

12. Reproduced from an article by Richard J. Aldrich, Lecturer in Politics at Nottingham University, in *Diplomacy and Statecraft* (March, 1997). Dr Aldrich is the author of *The Hidden Hand: Britain, America and Cold War Secret Intelligence*, John Murray, 2001

13. Bilderberg Meetings, 1989

14. Trilateral Commission website

15. It is also no great stretch of the imagination to suggest that the 'Shining' Trinity of Christianity was instituted to attract as many pagan, or 'Gentile' – Greek, Roman and Celtic – converts as possible (*see* Appendix). However, it may also be true that in early times Christianity was led by a Shining One priesthood who developed the Trinity because it symbolized their own Shining beliefs

Appendix: Threes and Sevens in World Myth, Religion and Folklore

1. From *The Book of Dzyan*, quoted in *The Garden of the Golden Flower* by Longfield Beatty (Rider, 1938).

BIBLIOGRAPHY

Books on the Shining Ones

Bauval, Robert, and Graham Hancock, *Keeper of Genesis: A Quest for the Hidden Legacy of Mankind* , Arrow, 1996

Collins, Andrew, *From the Ashes of Angels: The Forbidden Legacy of a Fallen Race*, Bear & Company, 2001

Knight, Christopher, and Robert Lomas, *Uriel's Machine*. Arrow Books, 2000

O'Brien, Christian and Joy, *The Genius of the Few*, Dianthus Publishing, 1985

O'Brien, Christian and Joy, *The Shining Ones*, Dianthus Publishing, 1997

Sitchin, Zecharia, *Genesis Revisited*, Avon, 1990

Sitchin, Zecharia, *The 12th Planet (Book I of the Earth Chronicles)*, Avon, 1976

Sitchin, Zecharia, *The Stairway to Heaven. (Book II of the Earth Chronicles)*, Avon, 1980

Sitchin, Zecharia, *The Wars of Gods and Men (Book III of the Earth Chronicles)*, Avon, 1985

Sitchin, Zecharia, *The Lost Realms (Book IV of the Earth Chronicles)*, Avon, 1990

Sitchin, Zecharia, *When Time Began (Book V of the Earth Chronicles)*, Avon, 1993

Sitchin, Zecharia, *The Cosmic Code (Book VI of the Earth Chronicles)*, Avon, 1998

Twyman, Tracy R., *The Merovingian Mythos*, Dragon Key Press, 2004

Other publications:

Ableson, J., *Jewish Mysticism*, G. Bell and Sons Ltd, 2001

Ancient Egypt, Myth and History, Geddes and Grosset Ltd, 1997

Andrews, Richard, and Schellenberger, Paul, *The Tomb of God*, Little, Brown and Co., 1996

Apollodorus, *The Library of Greek Mythography*, trans. Robin Hard, Oxford Paperbacks, 1998

Apuleius, Lucius, *The Golden Ass*, Penguin Books, 1985

Aristotle, *The Art of Rhetoric*, Penguin Books, 2005

Ashe, Geoffrey, *The Quest for Arthur's Britain*, Pall Mall, 1968

Bacher, Wilhelm & Blau, Ludwig, *Shamir* (no date given)

Baigent, Michael, *Ancient Traces*, Viking, 1998

Baigent, Michael, and Richard Leigh, *The Elixir and the Stone*, Viking, 1997

Baigent, Michael, Richard Leigh and Henry Lincoln, *The Holy Blood and the Holy Grail*, Jonathan Cape, 1982

Balfour, Michael, *Megalithic Mysteries*, Collins and Brown, 1998

Balfour, Mark, *The Sign of the Serpent*, Prism Press, 1990

Barrett, David V., *Sects, Cults and Alternative Religions*, Cassell, 1996

Basham, A. L., *The Wonder that was India*, Sidgwick & Jackson, 1985

Bauval, Robert, and Adrian Gilbert, *The Orion Mystery*, William Heinemann, 1994

Bayley, Harold, *The Lost Language of Symbolism*, Bracken Books, 1912

Beatty, Longfield, *The Garden of the Golden Flower: The Journey to Spiritual Fulfilment*, Rider, 1938

Begg, Ean, *The Cult of the Black Virgin*, Arkana, 1985

Begg, Ean and Deike, *In Search of the Holy Grail and the Precious Blood*, Thorsons, 1995

Bible Explorer (Expert Software)

Blavatsky, Helena Petrovna, *Isis Unveiled*, reprinted Theosophical University Press, 1999

Blavatsky, Helena Petrovna, *Theosophical Glossary*, R. A. Kessinger Publishing Co. Ltd, 1918

The Book of Enoch, R. H. Charles, W. O. E. Oesterley (eds), Book Tree, 1998

Borchant, Bruno, *Mysticism: Its History and Challenge*, Samuel Weiser, 1994

Bord, Janet and Colin, *Earth Rites: Fertility Practices in Pre-Industrial Britain*, HarperCollins, 1982

Bouquet, A. C., *Comparative Religion*, Pelican, 1942

Brine, Lindsey, *The Ancient Earthworks and Temples of the American Indians*, Oracle, 1996

Bryant, Nigel, *The High Book of the Grail*, D. S. Brewer, 1996

Bryden, R., *Rosslyn: A History of the Guilds, the Masons and the Rosy Cross*, Rosslyn Chapel Trust, 1994

Bunker, Michael, *Homeland Security: The Jesuit Gestapo*, http://lazarusunbound.com/bunker_hsjesuitgestapo.shtml

Butler, E. M., *The Myth of the Magus*, Cambridge University Press, 1993

Cantor, Norman F., *The Sacred Chain: A History of the Jews*, HarperCollins, 1994

Carpenter, Edward, *The Origins of Pagan and Christian Belief*, Senate, 1920

Carpenter, Edward, *Pagan and Christian Creeds: Their Origin and Meaning*, R. A. Kessinger Publishing Co. Ltd, 1992

Carr-Gomm, Sarah, *Dictionary of Symbols in Art*, Duncan Baird Publishers, 2000

Cavendish, Richard, *Mythology*, Little, Brown and Co., 1999

Chadwick, N., *The Druids*, University of Wales Press, 2000

Cicero, *De Senectute*

Chiniquy, Charles, *Fifty Years in the Church of Rome*, Sovereign Grace Publishers, 2001

Clarke, Hyde, and C. Staniland Wake, *Serpent and Siva Worship*, R. A. Publishing Co. Ltd, 1996

Cole, Graham, and Lewis Higton, *What is the New Age?* Hodder and Stoughton, 1990

Cooper, J. C., *An Illustrated Encyclopaedia of Traditional Symbols*, Thames and Hudson, 1978

Croker, Thomas Crofton, *Legend of the Lakes*, Collins, 1829

Crooke, W., *The Popular Religion and Folk-lore of Northern India*, 1896; reprinted R. A. Kessinger Publishing Co. Ltd, 1996

Cumont, Franz, *The Mysteries of Mithra*, Dover Publications, 1956

Currer-Briggs, N., *The Shroud and the Grail: A Modern Quest for the True Grail*, St Martin's Press, 1988

Daraul, Arkon, *Secret Societies*, Müller, 1961

David-Neel, Alexandra, *Magic and Mystery in Tibet*, Dover Publications, 1971

Davidson, H. R. Ellis, *Myths and Symbols of Pagan Europe*, Syracuse University Press, 1988

De Martino, Ernesto, *Primitive Magic*, Prism Unity, 1988

de Santillana, Giorgio, and von Dechend, Hertha, *Hamlet's Mill: An Essay Investigating the Origins of Human Knowledge and its Transmission through Myth*, David R. Godine Publisher Inc., 1969

Deal, David Allen, *The Day Behemoth and Leviathan Died*, 1999

Devereux, Paul, *Secrets of Ancient and Sacred Places: The World's Mysterious Heritage*, Caxton Editions, 2001

Dictionary of Beliefs and Religions, Rosemary Goring (ed.), Wordsworth, 1997

Dictionary of the Bible, Collins, 1992

Dictionary of the Occult, Geddes and Grosset Ltd, 1997

Dictionary of Phrase and Fable, Ebenezer Cobham Brewer (ed.), Wordsworth, 1991

Dictionary of Science and Technology, Peter M. B. Walker (ed.), Wordsworth Editions Ltd, 1995

Dictionary of World Folklore, Alison Jones (ed.), Larousse, 1995

Dictionary of World Myth, Peter Bently (gen. ed.), Helicon (UK), Facts on File (US), 1995.

Didier, Charles, *Subterranean Rome*, New York, 1843

Diodorus Siculus, *Bibliotheca Historica, c.* 21 BC

Dodd, C. H., *Historical Tradition of the Fourth Gospel*, Cambridge University Press, 1976

Doel, Fran and Geoff, *Robin Hood: Outlaw of Greenwood Myth*, Tempus Publishing Ltd, 2000

Drosnin, Michael, *The Bible Code*, Weidenfeld and Nicolson, 1998

Drosnin, Michael, *The Bible Code 2: The Countdown*, Phoenix, 2003

Dunstan, V., *Did the Virgin Mary Live and Die in England?*, Megiddo Press, 1985

Eliade, Mircea, *Shamanism: Archaic Techniques of Ecstasy*, trans. Willard R. Trask, Princeton University Press, 2004

Encarta Encyclopaedia

Encyclopaedia of History, Dorling Kindersley

Ernst, Carl H., *Venomous Reptiles of North America*, Smithsonian Books, 1999

Evans, Lorraine, *Kingdom of the Ark*, Simon and Schuster, 2000

Faith in Every Footstep (CD-rom), The Church of Jesus Christ of Latter-Day Saints (Mormons)

Feather, Robert, *The Copper Scroll Decoded*, Thorsons, 1999

Feder, Kenneth L., and Park, Michael Alan, *Human Antiquity*, Mayfield, 1992

Fix, W. M., *Star Maps*, Octopus, 1979

Fontana, David, *The Secret Language of Symbols*, Chronicle Books, 2003

Ford, Patrick K, *The Mabinogi and other Medieval Welsh Tales*, University of California Press, 1977

Fortune, Dion, *The Mystical Qabalah*, Weiser Books, 2000

Foss, Michael, *People of the First Crusade*, Caxton Editons, 2000

Frazer, Sir James, *The Golden Bough*, Macmillan Press, 1922

Freke, Timothy, and Gandy, Peter, *Jesus and the Goddess*, Thorsons, 2001

Gardner, Laurence, *Bloodline of the Holy Grail*, Element Books, 1996

Gascoigne, Bamber, *The Christians*, Jonathan Cape, 1977

Gilbert, Adrian, *Magi*, Bloomsbury, 1996

Goldberg, Carl, *Speaking with the Devil*, Viking, 1996

Gooch, Stan, *Cities of Dreams: The Rich Legacy of Neanderthal Man which Shaped our Civilisation*, Rider Books, 1991

Gordon, Cyrus, *The Giant Book of Lost Worlds*, Paragon, 1998

Gordon, Stuart, *The Paranormal: An Illustrated Encyclopedia*, Headline, 1992

Gould, Charles, *Mythical Monsters*, W. H. Allen & Co., 1886

Gray Hulse, Tristan, *The Holy Shroud*, Weidenfeld and Nicolson, 1997

Guide to the Occult and Mysticism, Geddes and Grosset Ltd

Hagger, Nicholas, *The Fire and the Stones*, Element Books, 1991

Halifax, Joan, *Shaman: The Wounded Healer*, Thames and Hudson, 1982

Hall, Edward T., *The Dance of Life*, Doubleday, 1983

Hall, Manly Palmer, *The Secret Teachings of All Ages: An Encyclopedic Outline of Masonic, Hermetic, Qabbalistic and Rosicrucian Symbolical Philosophy*, Philosophical Research Society, 1928

Hanauer, J. E., *Folklore of the Holy Land*, The Sheldon Press, 1907

Hanauer, J. E., *The Holy Land*, reprinted Merchant Book Company, 1995

Hancock, Graham, *Fingerprints of the Gods*, William Heinemann, 1995

Hancock, Graham, *The Sign and the Seal*, William Heinemann, 1992

A Handbook of Living Religions, John R. Hinnells (ed.), Viking, 1984

Harding, Esther, *Women's Mysteries*, Rider, 1971

Harrington, Edward, *The Meaning of English Place Names*, The Black Staff Press, 1984

Heindel, Max, *Christian Rosenkreuz and the Order of Rosicrucians*, Lightning Source UK, n.d.

Heindel, Max, *The Rosicrucian Cosmo-Conception*, The Rosicrucian Fellowship, 1910

Henry, William, *Show Him the Door*, 2003, http://www.ancientwisdom.net/speakers/william/william.html

Higgins, Godfrey, *Anacalypsis – The Saitic Isis: Languages, Nations and Religions*, 1833, reprinted A&A Book Distributors, 1992

Hitler, Adolf, *Mein Kampf*, 1926

Hitler's Third Reich: A Documentary History, Louis L. Snyder (ed.), Nelson-Hall, 1981

The Holy Bible, New King James Version, Tyndale

Hooke, S. H., *Middle Eastern Mythology*, Penguin, 1991

Howard, Michael, *The Occult Conspiracy*, Rider & Co. Ltd, 1989

Jaurequi, A. B., *History of Central America*

Jennings, Hargrave, *Ophiolatreia*, R. A. Kessinger Publishing Co. Ltd, 1996

Jones, Steve, *In the Blood: God, Genes and Destiny*, HarperCollins, 1996

Josephus, *Antiquities of the Jews*, Indypublish.com

Krishna, Gopi, *Kundalini: The Evolutionary Energy in Man*, Shambhala, 1997

Laidler, Keith, *The Head of God*, Weidenfeld and Nicholson, 1998

Layton, Robert, *Australian Rock Art: A New Synthesis*, Cambridge University Press, 1992

Leakey, Richard, and Lewin, Roger, *Origins Reconsidered*, Abacus, 1993

Lemesurier, Peter, *The Great Pyramid*, Element Books, 1999

MacCana, Proinsias, *Celtic Mythology*, Hamlyn, 1970

Mack, Burton L., *The Lost Gospel*, HarperSanFrancisco, 1994

McFarlan, *Bible Reader's Reference Book*, Blackie, n.d.

Man, Myth and Magic: An Illustrated Encyclopedia of the Supernatural, Richard Cavendish (ed.), Marshall Cavendish Corporation, New York, 1983

Mann, A. T., *Sacred Architecture*, Element Books, 1993

Mason, Robert T., *The Divine Serpent in Myth and Legend*, http://www.geocities.com/Delphi/5789/serpent.htm, 27 January 2000

Matthews, John, *The Quest for the Green Man*, Godsfield Press, 2001

Matthews, John, *Sources of the Grail*, Floris Books, 1997

Matthews, John, *The World Atlas of Divination*, Tiger, 1992

Milgrom, Jacob, *The JPS Torah Commentary: Numbers*, The Jewish Publication Society, 1990

Monroe, Robert, *Journeys out of the Body*, Souvenir Press, 1972

Morison, Frank, *Who Moved the Stone?*, Faber and Faber, 1973

Muggeridge, Malcolm, *Jesus*, Fount, 1976

New Scientist of 21 March 1998 and 11 July 1998

Newton, Janet, 'Ancient Board Games', web article, 2001

O'Brien, Christian, *The Megalithic Odyssey*, Turnstone Press, 1983

O'Neill, John, *Nights of the Gods*, publisher unknown, 1893

Oliver, George, *Signs and Symbols*, R. A. Kessinger Publishing Co., 1999

Oppenheimer, Stephen, *Eden in the East*, Weidenfeld & Nicolson, 1998

Ouspensky, P. D., *In Search of the Miraculous: Fragments of an Unknown Teaching*, Harcourt, 1949

Ovason, David, *The Zelator: The Secret Journals of Mark Hedsel*, Arrow, 1999

Pagels, E., *The Gnostic Gospels*, Weidenfeld and Nicolson, 1980

Paris, Edmond, *The Secret History of the Jesuits*, Chick Publications, Inc., 1986

Paterson Smyth, J., *How We Got our Bible*, Sampson Low, Marson & Co. Ltd, 1856

Pennick, Nigel, *Sacred Geometry*, Turnstone Press, 1980

Pike, Albert, *Morals and Dogma*, R. A. Kessinger Publishing Co., 2004

Piggot, Stuart, *The Druids*, Thames and Hudson, 1985

Pinkham, Mark A., *The Return of the Serpents of Wisdom*, Adventures Unlimited Press, 1998

Plato, *Timaeus*, Focus Publishing, 2001

Plichta, Peter, *God's Secret Formula*, Element Books, Shaftesbury, 1997

Pliny the Elder, *Natural History*, vol. III, trans. H. Rackham, Harvard University Press, Cambridge, Mass., 1983

Porter, Prof. J. R, *The Lost Bible: Forgotten Scriptures Revealed*, Duncan Baird Publishers (UK) and Chicago University Press (US), 2001.

Powell, T. G. E., *The Celts*, Thames and Hudson, 1983

Randles, Jenny, and Hough, Peter, *Encyclopaedia of the Unexplained*, Brockhampton Press, 1995

Rees, Alwyn and Brynley, *Celtic Heritage*, Thames and Hudson, 1989

Reid, Howard, *Arthur: The Dragon King*, Headline, 2001

Religions of the World, Collins, 1991

Roberts, Alison, *Hathor Rising: The Serpent Power of Ancient Egypt*, Northgate, 1995

Roberts, J. M., *The Mythology of the Secret Societies*, Secker & Warburg, 1972

Roof, Wade Clark, *A Generation of Seekers*, HarperCollins, 1994

Rutherford, Ward, *Druids and their Heritage*, Gordon and Cremonesi, 1978

Rux, Bruce, *Architects of the Underworld: Unriddling Atlantis, Anomalies of Mars, and the Mystery of the Sphinx*, Frog Ltd, 1996

Sanella, Lee, *The Kundalini Experience*, Integral Publishing, 1987

Satinover, Jeffrey, *The Truth behind the Bible Code*, Sidgwick and Jackson, 1997

Schonfield, Hugh, *The Essene Odyssey*, Element Books, 1984

Schonfield, Hugh, *The Passover Plot*, Hutchinson, 1965

Seligmann, Kurt, *The History of Magic*, Gramercy Books, 1998

Shah, Idries, *The Sufis*, W. H. Allen, 1964

Sharper Knowlson, T., *The Origins of Popular Superstitions and Customs*, Merchant Book Company Ltd, 1994

Sherman, Edwin A. *The Engineer Corps of Hell*, no publisher, 1833

Shirer, William, *The Rise and Fall of the Third Reich*, Secker and Warburg, 1960

Signs, Symbols and Ciphers, New Horizons, 1989

Sinclair, Andrew, *The Secret Scroll*, Sinclair-Stevenson, 2001

Slemen, Thomas, *Strange but True*, London Bridge, 1998

Smith, Morton, *The Secret Gospel*, Victor Gollancz, 1974

Snyder, Louis L., *Encyclopaedia of the Third Reich*, McGraw-Hill, 1976

Spence, Lewis, *Introduction to Mythology*, R. A. Publishing Co. Ltd, 1997

Stone, Nathan, *Names of God*, Moody Press, 1944

Suckling, Nigel, *The Book of the Unicorn*, Paper Tiger, Limpsfield, 1996

Tenney and Cruden, *The Handy Bible Dictionary and Concordance*, Lamplighter Books, 1983

Thiering, Barbara, *Jesus the Man*, Corgi, 1993

Thomson, Ahmad, *Dajjal the Anti-Christ*, Ta-Ha Publishers Ltd, 1986

Thompson, William Irwin, *At the Edge of History*, 1989

Timelines of World History, Nigel Rogers (ed.), Bramley Books, 1989

Timms, Moira, *Prophecies to Take You into the Twenty-First Century*, Thorsons, 1996

Tolstoy, Nikolai, *The Quest for Merlin*, Little, Brown and Co., 1988

Tull, George F., *Traces of the Templars*, The King's England Press, 2000

von Däniken, Erich, *The Return of the Gods*, Element, 1989

von Däniken, Erich, *The Unexplained*, Focus

Waite, A. E., *The Book of Ceremonial Magic*, William Ryder and Son, 1911

Waite, A. E., *The Hidden Church of the Holy Grail*, Fredonia Books, Amsterdam, 2002

Wake, C. Staniland, *The Origin of Serpent Worship*, R. A. Kessinger Publishing Co. Ltd, 1996

Walker, Benjamin, *Gnosticism*, The Aquarian Press, 1983

Wallace-Murphy, Timothy, Hopkins, Marilyn, *Rosslyn*, Element Books, 1999

Wallis Budge, E. A., *Egyptian Magic*, 1901

Wallis Budge, E. A., *From Fetish to God,* Dover Publications, 1989

Waters, Frank, *The Book of the Hopi*, Viking, 1963

Watson, Lyall, *Dark Nature*, Hodder & Stoughton, 1996

Webb, James, *The Occult Underground*, Open Court Press, 1976

Webster's Encyclopaedia

Weisse, John, *The Obelisk and Freemasonry*, R. A. Kessinger Publishing Co. Ltd, 1996

Wilson, Colin, *The Atlas of Holy Places and Sacred Sites*, Dorling Kindersley, 1996

Wilson, Colin, *Poltergeist: A Study in Destructive Haunting*, Llewellyn Publications, 1993

Wilson, Damon, *Lost Worlds*, Paragon, 1989

Wilson, Hilary, *Understanding Hieroglyphs*, Caxton Editions, 2002

Wilson, Robert Anton, *Sex and Drugs*, Mayflower, 1975

Within, Inquire, *The Trail of the Serpent*, R. A. Kessinger Publishing Co., 2003

Wood, David, *Genesis*, The Baton Press, 1985

Zebrowski, Jr, *Perils of a Restless Planet*, Cambridge University Press, 1997

Zollschan, Dr G. K., Schumaker, Dr J. F., and Walsh, Dr G. F., *Exploring the Paranormal*, Prism Unity, 1989

Other Primary Sources

The Apocrypha, Qu'ran, Talmud.

The Dead Sea Scrolls: *The Damascus Document, The Community Rule, The War of the Sons of Light with the Sons of Darkness, The Messianic Rule of the Congregation, The Temple Scroll.*

Nag Hammadi Gnostic writings: *Gospel of Truth, Gospel of Mary, Gospel of the Egyptians, On Baptism.*

The I Ching (Richard Wilhelm Translation),

Other ancient sources: Ephraim the Syrian, Hippolytus of Rome, Pliny the Younger, Pythagoras,

Thanks also to the following for information or for documents used with their permission: Church of Scientology, Foundation for the Study of Cycles, Freemasons, Jehovah's Witnesses, Jewish Pentecostal Mission, Mormons (The Church of Jesus Christ of Latter-Day Saints), Rosicrucians, Inner Light; staff of Lichfield Cathedral. We will be glad to correct any omissions in future editions.

INDEX